Liberating Sojourn

Liberating Sojourn

Frederick Douglass
& Transatlantic Reform

EDITED BY ALAN J. RICE & MARTIN CRAWFORD

THE UNIVERSITY OF GEORGIA PRESS | ATHENS AND LONDON

© 1999 by the University of Georgia Press
Athens, Georgia 30602
All rights reserved
Designed by Kathi Dailey Morgan
Set in 10.3 on 14 Berthold Baskerville
by G & S Typesetters, Inc.
Printed and bound by Maple-Vail
The paper in this book meets the guidelines for
permanence and durability of the Committee on
Production Guidelines for Book Longevity of the
Council on Library Resources.

PRINTED IN THE UNITED STATES OF AMERICA

03 02 01 00 99   5 4 3 2 1

LIBRARY OF CONGRESS CATALOGING IN PUBLICATION DATA

Liberating sojourn : Frederick Douglass & transatlantic reform /
edited by Alan J. Rice & Martin Crawford.

    p.   cm.

Papers originally presented at a colloquium held under the auspices
of the David Bruce Centre for American Studies at Keele University in Sept.
1995. Includes bibliographical references.
ISBN 0-8203-2102-8 (alk. paper). – ISBN 0-8203-2129-X (pbk. : alk. paper)
1. Douglass, Frederick, 1817?–1895–Journeys–Great Britain.
2. Afro-American abolitionists–Biography. 3. Afro-American abolitionists–
Great Britain–Biography. 4. Douglass, Frederick, 1817?–1895–Relations
with the British. 5. Douglass, Frederick, 1817?–1895–Political and social views.
6. Great Britain–Race relations. 7. Social problems–Great Britain–History–
19th century. I. Rice, Alan J., 1960– . II. Crawford, Martin, 1948– .
E449.D75L53 1999   973.8'092–dc21   [B] 99-23997

BRITISH LIBRARY CATALOGING IN PUBLICATION DATA AVAILABLE

For Sam Shepperson

Contents

PART FIVE   *Douglass and Transatlantic Reform*

Acknowledgments

The essays in this volume were originally presented at a colloquium held under the auspices of the David Bruce Centre for American Studies at Keele University in September 1995. The occasion brought together scholars from both sides of the Atlantic in celebration of the 150th anniversary of Frederick Douglass's first visit to Britain. Many people contributed to organizing the meeting, but we would particularly wish to thank Professor David Adams, then director and now chair of the David Bruce Centre, and Anthony Mann, who took over as the colloquium secretary; both worked tirelessly to ensure its success. We also wish to acknowledge the contributions of all of the participants, who made the sessions, individually and collectively, such a stimulating and rewarding experience. A special mention also for Frank Faragasso and Douglas Stover, historian and curator, respectively, of the Frederick Douglass National Historic Site at Cedar Hill, whose presence and contributions greatly enhanced the colloquium.

The editors would like to thank their respective institutions, the University of Central Lancashire and Keele University, for granting research sabbaticals that facilitated progress on the project. We are also grateful to Malcolm Call and his colleagues at the University of Georgia Press for their faith and encouragement, to Stephen Barnett for his very helpful and keen-eyed copyediting, and to Christine Compton for the index. Finally, we would like to thank Louise Ryan and Stephen Mills for valuable comments on individual essays.

We are grateful to the University Press of Virginia for permission to reprint Anne Goodwyn Jones, "Engendered in the South: Blood and Irony in Douglass and Jacobs," which previously appeared in Jones and Susan V. Donaldson, eds., *Haunted Bodies: Gender and Southern Texts* (Charlottesville: University Press of Virginia, 1997), 201–19.

The opening presentation by William S. McFeely honored the work of Professor George Shepperson, who pioneered the study of Douglass's "liberating sojourn." This volume is dedicated to Professor Shepperson with our warmest regards.

Alan J. Rice
Martin Crawford

Liberating Sojourn

Triumphant Exile

Frederick Douglass in Britain, 1845–1847

ALAN J. RICE & MARTIN CRAWFORD

Y OU CANNOT WRITE THE BLOODY LAWS OF SLAVERY ON THOSE restless billows. The ocean, if not the land, is free."[1] Frederick Douglass, born a slave in Maryland in 1818, waxed so lyrically about the ocean because its traditions had provided him with his route to liberty when in 1838, dressed in sailor's clothes and with a free black sailor's papers, he escaped northward by ferry and train. More than this, though, Douglass's "maritime community" had equipped him for a life beyond slavery, providing him with an education and socialization that was a rare privilege for a slave youth. Reflecting later on the importance of his upbringing, he stated: "The shipyard was more to us than to many others. It was our schoolhouse, where we learned to write and to count. Its timber and boards were our first copy-books and the white carpenters writing 'larboard' and 'starboard' with chalk were our unconscious teachers."[2] This "schoolhouse" afforded him a grandstand view of the oceangoing vessels that, a decade later, were to be instrumental in his maturation.

In August 1845, by then a leading black abolitionist and veteran of North American speaking tours, Frederick Douglass boarded the Cunard liner *Cambria* on a visit to Britain. Although the most celebrated, Douglass was by no means the only black American to cross the Atlantic in the thirty years leading up to the Civil War. African Americans traveled to Britain for a variety of reasons, including education and fund raising, but they were invariably drawn there by what Richard Blackett calls the country's "moral prestige," a consequence of its decision in 1833 to abolish slavery in the West Indies. "Once the source of American civilization had ceased to endorse slavery and many of her citizens had committed themselves to its total extirpation, it was not unreasonable to hope, as many black Americans did, that America would follow Britain's lead and emancipate her slaves."[3]

Part of a rapidly expanding transatlantic abolition movement, Frederick Douglass's visit in 1845 was to serve the dual purpose of removing him from his own country at a point when the publication of his autobiography had threatened him with reenslavement and of giving the British public their first exposure to his commanding presence and fiery rhetoric on behalf of oppressed humanity. As Peter Ripley has noted, Douglass's "*Narrative* sent him into triumphant exile and made him the best known abolitionist on two continents."[4] Contemporary observers often remarked on the former slave's demeanor. "He was more than six feet in height," wrote one, "and his majestic form as he rose to speak, straight as an arrow, muscular, yet lithe and graceful, his flashing eye, and more than all, his voice, that rivaled Webster's in its richness, and in the depth and sonorousness of its cadences, made up such an ideal of an orator as the listeners never forgot."[5]

Such fine qualities were not universally admired, however. Prejudice dogged Douglass's passage across the Atlantic. Forced to accept a berth in steerage, he was to be the center of a controversial incident when, during a meeting organized in his honor, he contrasted his Atlantic crossing with that of the merchants who had used the route for centuries to transport a human cargo. The black abolitionist's indictment of the slave trade was too much for some American passengers who, fortified by drink, proposed to have him thrown overboard. In an ironic gesture of support that Douglass took particular delight in recounting, the ship's captain, the "gallant Judkins"–who only a year earlier, as Alasdair Pettinger's researches have discovered, had excluded a black passenger from cabin privileges aboard the *Acadia*–subdued the malcontents. As Pettinger's essay in this volume demonstrates, the *Cambria* incident exposed a complex legal, racial, and cultural dynamic that in many respects foretokened Frederick Douglass's life as a whole.

Douglass himself revelled in the propaganda that the incident afforded him. "Men in their senses, do not take bowie knives to kill mosquitoes, nor pistols to shoot flies," he recalled; "and the American passengers who thought proper to get up a mob to silence me, on board the *Cambria,* took the most effective method of telling the British public that I had something to say." [6] If nothing else, the incident on the *Cambria* ensured that the oxygen of publicity fueled his visit from the outset, awakening, in his own words, "something like a national interest in me." [7] His dramatization of the incident in speeches and in replies to newspaper reports revealed both the naked prejudice of the Americans involved in the confrontation and their ironic comeuppance—Judkins's threat to place "white slaveholders into irons." In a sense the incident thus stands as a dramatic reversal of a key moment in Douglass's earlier exposure to the violent extremes of proslavery agitation. At Pendleton, Indiana, in 1843, in company with other abolitionists, he had been set upon by a mob, barely escaping with his life. [8] There no law had come to his rescue. On the *Cambria* the racial world is turned upside down in a carnivalesque picture of enchained slaveholders and free-speaking African Americans that only becomes possible away from American mores in the liminal zone of the sea.

What Douglass achieved through the recounting of his triumph aboard the *Cambria* was a refiguring of the Atlantic crossing from a historically enslaving experience into a literally liberating one. The old Atlantic triangular trade had taken slaves to the Americas and brought back cotton and other raw materials that were turned into finished goods to be traded for slaves in Africa. Douglass's trip could be seen symbolically to mirror aspects of this trade. He came to Britain as raw material of a great black figure; he would leave in April 1847 the finished independent man, cut from a whole cloth and able to make his own decisions about the strategies and ideologies of the abolitionist movement. Yet surprisingly, the 1845 visit continues to arouse comparatively modest attention among Douglass scholars. William Andrews, for example, in the otherwise excellent new *Oxford Frederick Douglass Reader,* includes no passages culled from the visit. The effect is to present a lopsided and slightly insular view of the man and his accomplishments. A passage from *My Bondage and My Freedom* alludes tantalizingly to the visit, crediting it for Douglass's new-found independence, but this underplays the importance of the trans-atlantic environment in creating a new Frederick Douglass. In many ways the 1845 visit can be seen as one of the key events of Douglass's life, as pivotal to his educational and spiritual development as his victory over the "Negro Breaker," Edward Covey, or his conversion to Garri-sonian abolitionism.[9]

More materially, Douglass's eighteen-month visit provided him with the means to controversially purchase his own freedom (expedited by a collection organized by Miss Ellen Richardson of Newcastle) and to collect funds for the setting up of an independent African American newspaper edited by himself, the *North Star*. These projects brought him into conflict with the Garrisonian wing of the abolitionist movement, who were vehemently opposed to money being given to slaveholders and who saw little need for a new journal crowding the antislavery market-place of ideas. The two issues led to Douglass's split with those who had originally organized his British tour. Coming to Britain bound to a fun-damentally white-run abolitionist movement, he returned, buoyed by personal contacts with English, Irish, and Scottish abolitionists, with a more independent and radically changed agenda. As Paul Gilroy has written, Douglass's "consciousness of 'race,' self and society were pro-foundly changed by the experience of being outside America."[10]

Throughout his visit Douglass was prepared to speak at any forum against the scourge of slavery, even if this meant incurring the wrath of the Garrisonians. Unprepared to act as second fiddle in an ensemble orchestrated by others, his visit to Britain convinced him of the limita-tions of the Garrisonian mindset, which precluded alliances with certain other antislavery groups. William McFeely has described the relation-ship between white Bostonians and the black men in the abolitionist or-ganization as essentially that between theater director and fledgling, out-of-town actor: "black antislavery speakers were always treated as visiting artists in a production of which the white Bostonians never dreamed of losing the direction."[11] In Britain, far from these directing hands, Doug-lass developed his own strategies and alliances, much to the chagrin of the Garrisonians. Looking back on this period, Douglass characterized his visit as instrumental in gaining an independent voice as it gave him distance from his erstwhile allies and allowed him to see the limitations of their vision. "I am not sure that I was not under the influence of something like slavish adoration of my Boston friends," he noted in telling language.[12] Clearly, this "slavish adoration" was something the mature Douglass had now moved beyond.

Douglass's transatlantic progress was a source of great wonder to him, a "refuge from Republican slavery in monarchical England," as he described it in his 1855 autobiography.[13] Frederick Douglass was an "outlaw in the land of his birth."[14] However, the sense of personal security he discovered in Britain caused him to paint a utopian picture of race relations in the country that had banned slavery throughout its colonies only a decade earlier. In a letter to William Lloyd Garrison in January 1846, Douglass wrote that "the entire absence of anything that looked like racial prejudice against me, on account of the colour of my skin—contrasted so strongly with my long and bitter experience in the United States, that I look with wonder and amazement at the transition."[15] Douglass transformed such positive experiences into grist for his rhetorical mill, showing how the courtesy and civilization of the old country put the New Word to shame. By the end of his trip, in a playful series of rhetorical flourishes similar to those used about the *Cambria* incident, Douglass construes the experience as literally changing him in status from beast of burden to man of words: "Why, sir, the Americans do not know that I am a man. They talk of me as a box of goods; they speak of me in connexion with sheep, horses and cattle. But here, how different! Why, sir, the very dogs of old England know that I am a man!"[16] The world is truly made anew by his trip across the Atlantic.

This supposed absence of racial prejudice in Europe and its liberating effect on African American travelers was a theme echoed by others, from William Wells Brown later in the nineteenth century through James Weldon Johnson at the beginning of the twentieth to Paul Robeson in the interwar and immediate postwar years.[17] One of the few dissenters was Booker T. Washington, who typically used his 1899 trip to eulogize about the improvement in race relations in the United States. Washington contrasted Douglass's difficulties with American passengers on the *Cambria* with his own shipboard invitation to address a meeting, interpreting his treatment as proof of the efficacy of accommodation.[18] As James Olney has noted, Washington often adopted the strategy of "appropriating Douglass's life to his own and of incorporating and revising Douglass's text in the text of his own life."[19]

More fitted to travel in the firmament of Douglass's legacy was Paul Robeson, whose frequent journeys to Europe were often escapes from the realities of racism and political oppression at home. In introducing the celebrated black singer at an Edinburgh concert in 1949, Professor George Shepperson specifically compared his visit to that of Frederick Douglass a century before, noting how their leadership roles in the African American community were enhanced by their European sojourns.[20] Douglass and Robeson both helped to internationalize the African American struggle for full human rights; in the process they demonstrated how the struggle resonated far beyond the community itself in a relationship with other continents forged within what Paul Gilroy has more recently termed a "black Atlantic" discourse. Douglass's 1845 visit made a vital contribution to the transatlantic trade in reform ideas, and he was keenly aware of this, noting that "the denunciations against slavery, uttered in London this week may be heard in a fortnight in the streets of Boston."[21] Douglass's ideas were not confined to the antislavery message, and in Ireland particularly he spread the temperance message with equal fervor.

Like Robeson a hundred years later, Douglass found particular success in the Celtic regions. For instance, in Edinburgh, he took a leading role in the campaign to force the Free Church of Scotland to return monies collected by slaveholding clergy. "Send Back the Money" became a popular rallying cry, chanted on street corners and scribbled on walls throughout the Scottish capital. Douglass relates how street urchins shouted the phrase to him as he passed by, and it was not long before it was immortalized in a street ballad. Lionized by many ordinary Scots, Douglass the consummate rhetorician knew the value of entertainment in promoting the cause of human freedom.[22] On the other hand, as both Sarah Meer and Richard Blackett confirm in their discussions of blackface minstrelsy in this volume, not all popular entertainment projected images supportive of the racial ideals for which he fought.

Not all British people were so welcoming to Douglass and his writings.

His autobiography, though generally admired, was rather too indelicate for some tastes. In particular, the description of the whipping of his Aunt Hester found disfavor among some readers, even though, in deference to mid-nineteenth-century taste, Douglass had already elided a number of its more colorful oaths. John Estlin, a Bristol abolitionist, reported how a Quaker lady had written to him to thank him for "having erased the objectionable part in Douglass's Life, which she could not otherwise have put into the hands of her young people."[23] This passage from the *Narrative* still attracts controversy, as some feminist writers castigate Douglass for employing a male gaze that voyeuristically opens up a scene of black female mutilation to a public audience. As Deborah McDowell has written, black women's bodies "became the parchment on which Douglass narrates his progress from bondage to freedom."[24] Douglass himself had no such qualms about these passages in his autobiographies, arguing that the need to expose slavery's sadistic sexual exploitation and the debilitating effect of these practices on African American family structures overrode other considerations. Such brutality transformed into spectacle, as Cynthia Hamilton's essay in this volume suggests, left Douglass beholden to a domestic ideology that limited his effectiveness as a women's rights advocate. Rejecting the paternalism and property relations buttressing the slave system, Douglass, as Valerie Smith has also written, "appropriated those buttressing the structures and ideology of the family."[25]

The controversy over whether to censor negative images of the black body continues today, encompassing such cultural texts as the photographs of Robert Mapplethorpe and the films of Spike Lee. Douglass's reception thus presaged many of the debates which were to haunt African Americans throughout the next 150 years.

Despite the reservations of feminist and other critics, his role can yet be seen as that of a disturber of calm waters, his black presence undermining the easy certainties of middle-class reformers while always bringing home the physical and mental abuses of slavery. In fact, Douglass's visit exposed darker currents beneath the seemingly benign face of white abolitionists whose forced encounters with an actual black man revealed the boundaries of their racial vision. Writing to Samuel May in 1847, John Estlin observed of Douglass: "You can hardly imagine how he is noticed,–*petted* I may say by *ladies.* Some of them really exceed a little the bounds of propriety, or delicacy, as far as appearances are concerned; yet F. D's conduct is most guardedly correct, judicious and decorous. . . . My fear is that often associating so much with white women of education and refined taste and manners, he will feel a 'craving void' when he returns to his own family." [26] Such sentiments were not confined to England. In Ireland Richard Webb used very similar language to report to Mary Chapman his disquiet at Douglass's reception by female abolitionists. "I wonder how he will bear the sight of his wife, after all the petting he gets from beautiful, elegant and accomplished women," he noted.[27] Webb had already used the term "petting" with reference to Douglass in two earlier communications with American abolitionists. The word, which hints at the indulgence given to a domestic animal, uncomfortably resembles the language used by slaveholders about their favorite slaves.[28]

Estlin's depiction of an African American culture devoid of the nourishments of white civilization and a general unease with mixed-race relationships across the sexual divide exemplify a racist ideology that unfortunately transcended and continues to transcend differences between America and Europe, undermining Douglass's fond hope of a Britain "where no delicate nose grows deformed in my presence." [29] The delicate noses were just more discreet. His visit to Britain, therefore, should be seen as a liberating sojourn for him and also for those abolitionist women with whom he communicated especially well (perhaps because of their similarly degraded status to his own). As William McFeely contends, "something other than his sexual attractiveness drew these women to Douglass; in some way his quest for liberation urged them on in their repressed quest for their own." [30] Estlin's daughter Mary was one of many to fall under Douglass's spell and move from primary identification with a generalized commitment to abolitionism and reform to an overarching concern with "the poor blacks."

By contrast to the unequivocal support he received from white female abolitionists, Estlin and Webb's responses to Douglass's visit are emblematic of a troubled racialized discourse lurking beneath the surface in even the most philosophically liberal circles of nineteenth-century Britain. The repercussions of his visit expose this to a historian's gaze, even if it was often hidden from his own. Returning to America on the *Cambria* in early 1847, Douglass was again forced to travel steerage. As he said himself: "It was rather hard after having enjoyed nearly two years of equal social privileges in England, often dining with gentlemen of great literary, social political and religious eminence—never, during the whole time, having met with a single word, look, or gesture which gave me the slightest reason to think my color was an offense to anybody—now to be cooped up in the stern of the Cambria."[31] Frederick Douglass had expanded his horizons greatly through his visit to Britain only to encounter at its end the limitations of a worldview that could not see beyond the color of his skin. Luckily for Douglass his visit to Britain gave him strength for his journey home. As he himself said: "My heart could dwell on the many beloved friends whose homes and hearts opened to me when I sojourned among you."[32]

The nine essays in this collection offer no preconceived or uniform strategy for viewing Frederick Douglass and the transatlantic community. Rather, they take his visit to Britain in 1845 as a point of intellectual departure, an opportunity to reexamine aspects of a life, a culture, and a racialized world that has too often been analyzed in narrow, compartmentalized form. Two essays detail Douglass's links with Scottish and Unitarian religion, respectively. In his investigation of the "Send Back the Money" campaign, Alasdair Pettinger demonstrates that Douglass's crusade against the Free Church was far more complex in texture than previous accounts have allowed. Pettinger focuses on the moral rhetoric of the campaign and its associated effects; David Turley, by contrast, points to Douglass's importance as an "activist-intellectual" whose ideas on race broadly paralleled those of the Unitarian antislavery reformers with whom he engaged on his visit.

Essays by Cynthia Hamilton and Anne Goodwyn Jones provide complementary analyses of the strengths and frailties of Douglass's gender vision. Hamilton examines the transformations in the depiction of female relatives in Douglass's autobiographies as a function of his changing self-definition, which, following his return from Britain in 1847, was to lead him further and further from the experience of slavery. Anne Goodwyn Jones's starting point is a comparison of the abolitionist's reception in Britain with that of another, much less heralded African

American visitor in 1845, Harriet Jacobs, who like Douglass was a fugitive from servitude. Jones is keen to counter the view that "all gender possibilities were the same" in nineteenth-century America. The essential lives of both Douglass and Jacobs, she argues, were shaped by the realities of Southern slaveholding society, whereas it was the gender ideals of the industrializing North to which their public voices were increasingly directed.

If gender proved an inhibiting as well as a liberating element in Frederick Douglass's makeup, so more transparently did ethnicity. In his essay, Richard Hardack documents Douglass's ambivalent attitude toward the Irish, whose perilous condition in their home country was compromised, from the African American viewpoint, by their aggressive political and cultural stance in the United States. Sarah Meer's study of blackface minstrelsy, on the other hand, shows how important it was for Douglass to remain focused on African American aspirations, whose potentialities he powerfully embodied, notwithstanding the sympathy he manifestly felt and invariably expressed towards subjugated peoples everywhere.

One reform movement that Frederick Douglass necessarily engaged with was Chartism, which, as Richard Bradbury describes in his essay, was at an ideological and tactical crossroads at the time of his 1845 visit. Bradbury portrays Douglass as a man "influenced by, but not under the influence of, those around him," a distinction that allows us to appreciate how skillfully Douglass negotiated the often labyrinthine pathways of the transatlantic reform community. That these and other skills were patently needed is evident from Richard Blackett's essay, in which he examines Douglass's return visit to Britain on the eve of the Civil War. Although Douglass's popularity across the Atlantic continued unabated, there were disturbing signs that the international campaign against slavery—so vital to its success in America—was being undermined by new sources of racism. As the sectional crisis turned into sectional warfare, the consequences of a deteriorating racial climate in the transatlantic community were potentially profound.

It is fitting that this volume opens with an essay by Douglass's biographer, William McFeely, that takes its cue both from the anniversary of his first visit to Britain and from that of his death fifty years later in

1895. McFeely's preoccupations are contemporary: his purpose is to demonstrate that the struggles Douglass engaged in during his "liberating sojourn" and after have not lost their meaning. Frederick Douglass's achievement, he argues, was to find both critical and common ground with an America that had tried painfully to exclude him from its benefits. As in his time, so in ours, Douglass remains a figure of universal significance, his quest for inclusive justice as resonant at the end of the twentieth century as it was in the mid-nineteenth.

NOTES

1. Frederick Douglass, "The Heroic Slave," in *The Oxford Frederick Douglass,* ed. William L. Andrews (New York: Oxford University Press, 1996), 163.

2. Marifrances Trivelli, "'I Knew a Ship from Stem to Stern': The Maritime World of Frederick Douglass," *The Log of Mystic Seaport* 46 (spring 1995): 98–108.

3. R. J. M. Blackett, *Building an Antislavery Wall: Black Americans in the Atlantic Abolition Movement, 1830–1860.* (Baton Rouge: Louisiana State University Press, 1983), 4. Transatlantic antislavery cooperation can be pursued in detail in C. Peter Ripley, ed., *The Black Abolitionist Papers,* vol. 2, *The British Isles, 1830–1865* (Chapel Hill: University of North Carolina Press, 1985).

4. C. Peter Ripley, "The Autobiographical Writings of Frederick Douglass," in Frederick Douglass, *Narrative of the Life of Frederick Douglass, an American Slave, Written by Himself,* eds. William L. Andrews and William S. McFeely (New York: W. W. Norton, 1997), 143.

5. William S. McFeely, *Frederick Douglass* (New York: W. W. Norton, 1991), 124–25.

6. Frederick Douglass, *My Bondage and My Freedom,* ed. Philip S. Foner (1855; New York: Dover, 1969), 381.

7. Ibid., 368.

8. See McFeely, *Frederick Douglass,* 108–12.

9. See Waldo E. Martin, *The Mind of Frederick Douglass* (Chapel Hill: University of North Carolina Press, 1984), 3–25, for the centrality of these two events to his development. Notable exceptions to this neglect of the 1845 visit include McFeely, *Frederick Douglass;* and Blackett, *Building an Antislavery Wall.*

10. Paul Gilroy, *The Black Atlantic: Modernity and Double Consciousness* (London: Verso, 1993), 132.

11. McFeely, *Frederick Douglass,* 108.

12. Douglass, *Bondage,* 394.

13. Ibid., 365.

14. Ibid., 368.

15. Ibid., 370.

16. John W. Blassingame, ed., *The Frederick Douglass Papers. Series One: Speeches, Debates, and Interviews,* 5 vols. (New Haven: Yale University Press, 1979–), 2:50.

17. A new collection by Alasdair Pettinger, *Always Elsewhere: Travel Writings of the Black Atlantic* (London: Cassell, 1998), gathers together some of these disparate narratives.

18. Booker T. Washington, *Up From Slavery* (1901; Harmondsworth: Penguin, 1986), 288–89.

19. James Olney, "The Founding Fathers–Frederick Douglass and Booker T. Washington," in *Slavery and the Literary Imagination,* ed. Deborah E. McDowell and Arnold Rampersad (Baltimore: Johns Hopkins University Press, 1989), 17.

20. *Send Back the Money,* dir. Vicky Davidson, BBC Radio Scotland, 11 December 1996. On the singer's controversial 1949 visit to Europe, see Martin Duberman, *Paul Robeson: A Biography* (New York: Random House, 1989), 336–54.

21. Douglass, *Bondage,* 417.

22. See George Shepperson, "Frederick Douglass and Scotland," *Journal of Negro History* 38 (July 1953): 307–21.

23. John B. Estlin to [R. D. Webb?], 5 November 1845, in Clare Taylor, ed., *British and American Abolitionists: An Episode in Transatlantic Understanding* (Edinburgh: Edinburgh University Press, 1974), 240–41.

24. Deborah E. McDowell, "In the First Place: Making Frederick Douglass and the Afro-American Narrative Tradition," in *Critical Essays on Frederick Douglass,* ed. William L. Andrews (Boston: G. K. Hall, 1991), 201.

25. Valerie Smith, *Self-Discovery and Authority in Afro-American Narrative* (Cambridge, Mass.: Harvard University Press, 1987), 20.

26. John B. Estlin to Samuel May, 12 January 1847, in Taylor, *British and American Abolitionists,* 305.

27. Blackett, *Building an Antislavery Wall,* 112.

28. R. D. Webb to Maria Weston Chapman, 16 November 1845, 26 February, 1846, in Taylor, *British and American Abolitionists,* 243, 254. See also Nathan Irvin Huggins, *Slave and Citizen: The Life of Frederick Douglass* (Boston: Little, Brown, 1980), 31.

29. Douglass, *Bondage,* 371.

30. McFeely, *Frederick Douglass,* 142. These close relationships with white women in the reform movement were to continue. See Maria Diedrich, *Love Across Color Lines: Ottilie Assing and Frederick Douglass* (New York: Hill and Wang, 1999).

31. Douglass, *Bondage,* 391.

32. Letter of 29 April 1847, reprinted in *National Anti-Slavery Standard,* 8 July 1847, in Philip S. Foner, ed., *The Life and Writings of Frederick Douglass,* 5 vols. (New York: International Publishers, 1950–55), 1:52.

PART ONE

Douglass's Moral Legacy

Visible Man

Frederick Douglass for the 1990s

WILLIAM S. McFEELY

IT IS A PLEASURE TO BE IN BRITAIN TO CELEBRATE FREDERICK Douglass on the hundred and fiftieth anniversary of his first visit to Britain; it is an honor to be doing so with the Shepperson Lecture. Long ago, Professor Shepperson led the way in our study of Africans in Africa and of Africans in America and pioneered the field of African American history that engages the attention of all of us here. If I could add a personal note, I met Mr. Shepperson just once; I was beginning my work on Douglass and he was not only encouraging, but, proving his skill as a teacher, able to get through my secular American head at least the ecclesiastical polity of the Free Church of Scotland.

To describe Douglass's fight to end slavery and achieve full equality for African Americans or to recount his arrival in Liverpool in 1845 for his triumphal tour of Ireland, Scotland, and England would be a pleasant assignment, but given this audience's familiarity with the record of this giant of the nineteenth century an unnecessary one.

It would be equally easy to demonstrate how important Frederick Douglass's trip was in the development of his self-confidence. As he spoke in Cork, Belfast, Glasgow, Edinburgh, Birmingham, London, Bristol, and a remarkable number of other cities in between, he became

Originally presented as The George Shepperson Lecture, 1995, Keele University, Keele, Staffs.

triumphantly sure of himself. It was here in the British Isles, as Nathan Huggins observed, that he truly became "his own man." [1]

It was here too that Douglass confronted a good many issues that as historians concern us today. I am particularly happy that we will be exploring his contact with the Chartists and with a labor movement that identified itself with the antislavery movement in a way that none did in America. On this point I was reminded of another American tourist, General Ulysses S. Grant, who, in 1877, to his surprise, I'm sure, was greeted in Newcastle upon Tyne by eighty thousand members of marching workers' groups celebrating him as the Emancipator. The former slaves were, to them, fellow workers.

Frederick Douglass accomplished many things. But the history of which Douglass is so important a part has a way of not staying accomplished. Today much that Douglass hoped and worked for is in jeopardy. This fact leads me to focus not on still-unresolved historical questions of the nineteenth century but on Douglass's legacy as it affects us at the close of the twentieth. By looking back across the Atlantic toward America, I am in danger of totally neglecting the concerns of the rest of you here in Britain. But, as I do so, I will be in good company—that of Douglass himself. His subject here was America and American slavery. Perhaps my more tentative all-American concerns will have some transatlantic relevance.

Things are, in fact, in such a peculiar muddle that we have to ask ourselves whether Douglass has any relevance at all for the 1990s. Is Douglass just a majestic figure of a time gone by, or can we bring him into view in a way that might help us face the crises of our own decade? I want to argue that as we confront matters of race today there are two ways, one intensely personal, the other explicitly public, in which Douglass might if not come to our rescue, at least help us see our way forward.

Before we reach so comforting a posture, however, let's look at the record. It is true that Douglass's trip to Great Britain was wonderfully invigorating both for him and for the antislavery cause; it is also true that it was on this trip that he sowed the seeds of the criticism that has dogged his reputation ever since among militant members of the African American community and indeed among radicals in general.

Here is the indictment: Douglass liked Schubert better than slave music. The Sorrow Songs, about which Du Bois wrote so well, were distressing to him. (Douglass was even more unhappy about minstrelsy.) He read Goethe and Feuerbach with a free-thinking German woman rather than attend some local black Baptist church. Instead of to a prayer meeting, Douglass went to the opera. He was studiously careful in his dress and would never have pulled on jeans or khakis, let alone a dashiki. He lived the last sixteen years of his life in a handsome upper-middle-class house in Washington, D.C., that distanced him from both the urban and the rural poverty in which most of his fellow African Americans lived. And worst of all, he had many white female friends, one of whom, Ottilia Assing, was very probably a lover, and another, Helen Pitts, became his second wife.

How then can Douglass have remained a hero to his people in his own day? How, even more impossibly, can he make sense to those black Americans struggling today against the dual problems of racism, pernicious because often disguised, and terrible poverty with all of its attendant social ills? Wasn't Douglass hopelessly assimilated into a world inimical to his fellow African Americans?

Let's look at that forbidden term, assimilation. On the one hand, it is a subject that liberal historians of the African American experience, particularly those labeled white, have chosen largely to skirt. On the other, it has become an accusation that other historians, usually, but not exclusively, described as black, hurl at the likes of Frederick Douglass. It is also a word that deserves critical scrutiny.

In American English, *assimilate* can be understood to mean to consume and incorporate into the body; to absorb and incorporate into the mind; to make similar; or to cause to assume a resemblance.[2]

It is only the last meaning that suggests the accusation that one has given up on one's own values and been snookered into those of others. It is the second meaning – to absorb and incorporate into the mind – that accurately describes what Frederick Douglass did. It is assimilation thus understood that we all, black and white, might well adopt. Douglass made use of assimilate as an active verb – he absorbed and incorporated. He was not passively done to, not made similar.

Nor did he assume a resemblance. Yes, he was the quintessential high Victorian gentleman, always impeccably dressed and elegantly behaved. But he also was always himself. I can recall two summers ago sitting in a restaurant with Orlando Bagwell and Lisa Jones, two forthrightly black film makers who had embarked on the making of the now-acclaimed documentary film *Frederick Douglass: When the Lion Wrote History.* Since I had written about Douglass, they felt compelled to cope with me as what could be called an expert.

Politely, but on a fishing expedition, Orlando asked if Douglass hadn't completely blended into the white world. "If that was what he was up to," I replied, "why didn't he get a haircut?" Lisa almost choked on her french fries laughing at this irreverence. But she and Orlando got the point; Frederick Douglass, with his outrageous, unmistakable mane of wiry white African hair, could not step outside the door without being the most visible of Americans.

I would think only Mark Twain – another rebel – could have rivaled him in the matter of making a statement out of his appearance. Twain, with his white suits and *his* mane of hair – with his very person, with his body – said, "take note." And here Douglass had his rival beat; the ex-slave's rugged stevedore's body packed into those fine suits added power to the undeniably African head that topped it off.

It was not just in physical appearance that Douglass approached as-similation in the active voice. In his speeches, as in his three remarkable books, he demonstrated that he had absorbed and incorporated knowl-edge into his mind. And made himself the master of that knowledge.

Let's examine, briefly, the rhetoric of two speeches Douglass made on his trip to Scotland and England in 1846, one in Paisley, the other in Birmingham. Both were among his celebrated "Send Back the Money" speeches. Here I want to explore not the substance of his argument but his command of rhetoric, in order to show how he utilized his voice. Douglass made that instrument do two jobs: the telling of the personal story of a black man and the mastering of the immediate concern to his audience.

In Paisley, after a somewhat hurried and familiar litany of the general horrors of slavery – "driven like dumb cattle to the fields," and so on – Douglass told a story: "A husband and wife were brought to the auction mart. The wife was sold to one man and the husband to another, and the husband looked imploringly to the man who had bought his wife. But the wife was to go one way and he another. The husband asked to shake hands with the wife for the last time. He attempted to do it. He was struck on the head, and when he let go, he fell dead. His heart was broken."[3]

We can be certain that, away from his text, Douglass virtually acted out his tale, his voice dropping to a whisper as the man implores, rising to thunder as he is struck for having reached—and here Douglass's hand would have reached in emulation—to touch his wife. His audience would have been right there in that Baltimore slave market.

Then, having pulled the members of his audience into his world, Douglass abruptly leaped into theirs. Immediately after the sentence "His heart was broken!" and with no transition phrase, Douglass moved straight into the argument of the day among the antislavery people in his host city. "Who is responsible for slavery? The Free Church of Scotland has made itself responsible for slavery,"[4] he thundered. For accepting funds from slaveholding Presbyterians, the Free Church was much castigated in the British antislavery movement. Douglass had entered fully into its concerns. For the rest of his address, as more fully in others, Douglass demonstrated mastery of a world conventionally thought not to be his. But that world had not taken him in; rather, he was in full command of this second voice.

In Birmingham, once again Douglass began with a personal down-home story. It also happened to be a remarkably sophisticated analysis, straight out of what we would call developmental psychology, of how a person learns to read. Here is Douglass telling his story:

> the carpenter fit a piece of wood. . . . I observed, that on putting it aside, he took a piece of chalk from his pocket and made a mark on it, thus:—(drawing the letter S with his finger on the platform.) "What is that, Massa?" I asked, "That's the letter S, Nigger," said he. . . . "and what does the letter S stand for, Massa?" "It stands for starboard," said he.
>
> And while I was musing on the letter standing for starboard the carpenter chopped into shape another piece of wood, and tossing it aside made a chalk-mark on it thus (again imitating the act). "And what is that please, Massa?" "That is the letter L," said he, "which stands for larboard."[5]

And so on, until Douglass has told how, as a boy, he learned to turn a sign into a letter—learned to read. His literate audience would have been fascinated by the process and aware not only of Douglass's intellectual prowess but also, by implication, of how crippling it was for slaves not to be able to read. And, then, back at the lectern, without a pause, Douglass set about flogging the Free Church of Scotland.

Douglass had, as an orator, mastered two worlds: that of his own slave South and that of the transatlantic debate over American slavery. He had assimilated them into a single coherent narrative. Without yielding his sure sense of himself as an American out of Africa or forgetting how difficult it was to fit his own narrative into the official rendering of the composition of "We the People" of the American constitution, Douglass had gotten past a barrier that blocks the passage of so many of us.

We have, I would contend, overcategorized ourselves and been too insistent on proclaiming an exclusive identity. We have, for example, shouted from the rooftops that we are masculine, or feminine, only to have scholars like the critic Marjorie Garber and biologist Ann Fausto Sterling tug us back to earth. Garber, writing on bisexuality, and Sterling, discerning a plurality of sexualities, acknowledge – indeed welcome – the complexities of gender.

In matters racial, harking back to the Black Power movement and, before that, the New Negro consciousness of the Harlem Renaissance, African Americans have proudly said, "I'm black." There is a less militant note now; in some cases the statement is just plain comfortable, as in Henry Louis Gates Jr.'s *Colored People*. But the question that remains is whether such a statement of identity is made in the singular or the plural. American culture is richly complex, but it does have commonality. We are still one from many.

The common ground to which I refer is precisely not Newt Gingrich's "normal" America, by which he means a well-heeled, suburban, white, heterosexual, Christian swath of blandness. His is a commonality that excludes. Those of us whom this construct omits need to know ourselves in our particularities, but we also must find a common voice with which to protest, to claim our place.

In a beautifully written yet troubling book, Barack Obama, born in Hawaii the son of a white American mother and a black Kenyan father, tells of the racism that he encountered as he grew up struggling with his identity. After his father returns to Africa, he is raised by his mother and her parents, his grandparents. An able scholar, he attends good schools and becomes the first black editor of the *Harvard Law Review.* But, through it all, his father remains Obama's lodestone; finally, he travels to Kenya only to learn of his father's descent into failure – and death. But the power of this black legacy overwhelms the white. He pushes the latter into the margin and finds in his blackness his true center.

In a perceptive review in the *New York Times,* Paul Watkins, himself a memoirist, concludes: "Barack Obama has bravely tackled the complexities of his remarkable upbringing. But what would he have us learn? That people of mixed backgrounds must choose only one culture in which to make a spiritual home? That it is not possible to be both black and white, Old World and New? If this is indeed true, as Mr. Obama tells it, then the idea of America taking pride in itself as a nation derived of many different races seems strangely mocked."[6]

Obama, out of both Europe and Africa, has proclaimed his Africanness. Americans out of Europe, and as far as they know, not out of Africa, who are not racists, have been issued few proclamations of whiteness lately. When, in 1896, John Marshall Harlan, recognizing the total inequity of the separate but equal doctrine, dissented in *Plessy v Ferguson,* he felt comfortable stating that he did so pridefully aware that he was a white man. For the past several decades, even if they harbored racist thoughts, white Americans largely have refrained from claiming their whiteness as a badge of superiority.

Now, however, this is no longer true. Armed militia groups that, belatedly, we are learning about, speak openly of being white and despising those who are black. Equally dismaying is the call by Peter Brimelow, an immigrant from England, who is greatly alarmed by the result of the liberalization of immigration policy under presidents Kennedy and Johnson that has brought a great number of new nonwhite people into America. Brimelow, a *Wall Street Journal* columnist and author of *Alien Nation: Common Sense About America's Immigration Disaster* (New York: Random House, 1995), a book that is being taken seriously, flatly states that America began as a white society and must remain such.

The best refutation of such dangerous racism that I know of lies in the self-confidence that Frederick Douglass portrayed in his own person. He liked the concept of having been made of the clay of three continents – the legend of an Indian forebear was attractive to him. He knew, as I think we need to learn, how to read the meaning of assimilation. One present-day scholar who has done so is Priscilla Wald, a literary critic and cultural historian.

In *Constituting Americans,* she compares the narratives of five seemingly disparate writers: Frederick Douglass in *My Bondage and My Freedom,* Harriet Wilson in *Our Nig,* Herman Melville in *Pierre, or the Ambiguities,* W. E. B. Du Bois in *The Souls of Black Folk,* and Gertrude Stein in *The Making of Americans, Being the History of a Family's Progress.* Each of these writers was conscious of their otherness, racially, sexually, or artistically, and yet they sought "neither to reject, nor flee from their culture, but, on the contrary, to engage it."[7] Fully cognizant of the limitations placed on them by official narrative–Supreme Court decisions, presidential addresses–these memoirists, novelists, and essayists constructed a "We the People" both larger and more inclusive than the accepted definition.

Wald finds that Douglass not only acknowledges the difficulties of writing his way into the national story but also insists that the story is his. I would extend her idea by saying that in his oratory and also in his very deportment, Douglass underscored his ability to find both critical and common ground with his America. He has not been whitewashed into an America in which he does not fit; he staked his claim to the American story and has absorbed that story into his own. This was the personal legacy Douglass passed down to us.

I will return to Douglass and assimilation, but let me turn first to the realm of public policy and ask again if Douglass's stand on issues provides a legacy of worth to us as we face problems a century later. There are, it must be admitted, elements in Douglass's career that need to be confronted. Again, the indictment is strong. Douglass's vanity got the better of his judgement and he allowed himself to be elected president of the Freedman's Savings Bank. He got out without any personal financial loss when the bank went under, but thousands of black depositors, frugally putting away their earnings, lost everything. He was astonishingly callous in his response to the Exodusters left destitute on the levees of the Mississippi River as they tried to escape grinding poverty and gross exploitation in Mississippi and Louisiana.

As ambassador to Haiti, he helped keep American imperialism at bay and protect the sovereignty of one of the world's two black republics, but as he did so, he aided and abetted a dictator. He spoke out against lynching, but, until Ida B. Wells, the courageous editor who lost her newspaper to arsonists, set him straight, Douglass accepted the myth of uncontrolled black sexuality. He had argued only that it should be punished by law, not by outlaw lynchers. Wells taught him that lynching was a vicious form of social control that made use of a myth of black sexuality. In his final great 1894 speech, "Lessons of the Hour," he demonstrated that he had learned her lesson.

How can we be other than embarrassed at the thought of looking at such a man as we face the problems of the 1990s? The answer lies elsewhere in the Douglass story. All of the issues I have raised are post–Civil War matters. Let's, for a moment, go to the end of his story: "Picking up the papers to-day, the first word that caught my eye thrilled my very soul. Frederick Douglass is dead! What memories of the long years since he and I first met chased each other, thick and fast, through my mind and held me spellbound."[8]

That was Elizabeth Cady Stanton writing in her diary on 21 February 1895. She went on to recall Douglass's "burning eloquence" before a Boston antislavery meeting half a century earlier, when "with wit, satire, and indignation he graphically described the bitterness of slavery and humiliation of subjection to those who, in all human virtues and powers, were inferior to himself."[9]

Stanton, long-time foe of slavery and advocate of women's rights, was remembering the first time that she had seen and heard Douglass: "Around him sat the greatest orators of the day, earnestly watching the effect of his eloquence on that immense audience, that laughed and wept in turns, completely carried away by the wondrous gifts of his pathos and humor." For Stanton, "all other speakers seemed tame after Frederick Douglass." He "stood there like an African prince, majestic in his wrath."[10]

Douglass's subject on that occasion was, of course, slavery, and his voice was clear. To hear him as we need to, I would suggest that we make use, as, unconsciously, Stanton did, of selective memory and remember back to Douglass's earliest days as a protestor of injustice, to the days of speeches like those of 1846 and 1847, to his time as a powerful spokesman for reform. This is to say, to go back to the Douglass of the great antislavery speeches across the American North and here in Ireland, Scotland, and England. I would suggest that if we listen clearly, we will find that the Douglass voice is still dangerous. There are new targets for his wrath.

Douglass had his eye clearly on slavery as the greatest evil of his day, but abolition was but one of the many reforms that engaged his attention and that of those with whom he worked. To paraphrase the philosopher Alan Ryan, "If we are to think seriously about our fate at the end of the twentieth century, one thing we must do—infinitely far from the only thing, but one thing—is to recapture the intellectual, emotional, and political mood in which a certain kind of liberalism flourished in the first half of this century." [11] Ryan is writing about John Dewey; to his unfashionable but accurate formulation, I would urge a recapturing of the spirit of change that was alive both in the radical populist era of the 1890s and in the earlier decades of Douglass's antebellum America.

In our time, slavery is mercifully gone, but we are still cursed with some of its aftermath. What is more, several concerns of the reformers of Douglass's day bear a striking resemblance to issues that are troubling us today. Reformers in the 1840s, for example, pointed out the severely inhumane conditions in prisons. We might like to imagine that the horrors of the mistreatment of prisoners are far behind us. But where are we headed if our already-overcrowded prisons are to be jammed with men sentenced to mandatory long terms in technologically controlled facilities in which not even exercise machines are permitted? The United States, alone among the so-called civilized nations, has the death penalty, which it uses with increasing frequency and fervor. In the virulent talk of fighting crime, all concepts of rehabilitation are scoffed at. The ancient Christian tenet of redemption is ignored.

Behind the much-laughed-at temperance movement of Douglass's day, there was a genuine concern with the destructive force of alcoholism. That problem is scarcely conquered, and we could, I suspect, see in that concern a parallel to our own need to do something about the pervasiveness and destructiveness of drugs. But the prevailing response is to repress drug trafficking as a crime while draining away funds for the treatment of those addicted.

In the 1840s in Massachusetts, Horace Mann was constructing a public education system that was to be the model for the nation. Mann, like John Dewey generations later, argued that public schools are essential to the creation of a democratic society. Now many ignore the schools' communal worth. If public schools have never been perfect, some of us still regard them as an indispensable institution of American democracy. Those schools, now often in disarray, are in desperate need of rebuilding and more support.

Instead, we hear of converting public schools into for-profit schools; in the name of reform, we are told that there should be vouchers so that students can be sent to sectarian schools. And, of course, the flight of the well-off to the suburbs has left city schools neglected. "Bad" schools are those in which most of the students are black, especially poor and black. The response of those in power in Congress contains a poorly disguised component of racism as well as contempt for people, regardless of color, who struggle with poverty.

Implicit in all that is transpiring is an effort to build a wall of safety around the affluent. In the nineteenth century, Benjamin Disraeli warned the citizens of Great Britain that they were creating two nations, one rich, the other poor. And that is exactly what is happening in the United States today. Even paternalistic compassion is scoffed at, and those caught in poverty are viewed as a criminal class. Instead of the war on poverty, today we have what *New York Times* columnist Bob Herbert calls, flatly, "America's all-out war on the poor." [12]

How can we stand against this onslaught? A disproportionate percentage of those who are poor in America are, as they were in 1895, African Americans. We need people who can talk as Frederick Douglass did at Paisley and Birmingham, talk equally within the black experience and within the culture as a whole. We must widen that culture and yet keep it one. Fortunately, we have Americans who are doing so. Marian Wright Edelman of the Children's Defense Fund and Congressman John Lewis, both veterans of the toughest days of the civil rights movement, speak clearly, if in dissent, to our gravest problems.

Is there room for European Americans who feel connected to the

African American world to have a voice in this protest? It has seemed unseemly for white scholars to question any aspects of the African American search for identity or to speak for people who are as capable as Douglass was of speaking for themselves. Good liberals, we have kept our counsel while formerly liberal neoconservatives and the exponents of the radical right have preached.

I am willing to break the silence both because I feel no clear-cut sense of a one-dimensional identity and because I feel so strongly that only by standing as one can we stop the backward slide that is so powerfully in evidence on both the racial and the class fronts.

We are right to examine our several pasts, but we must keep our eye on the society that we would have those who follow us inhabit. Those with a very different view of the world, one driven by market competition, are only too eager to pounce on our examinations of diversity and make them excuses for dividing us rich from poor, black from white, immigrant with a long American past from those just off the boat—or the Concorde.

One credential for speaking out possessed by some white Americans is the same one that has validated our teaching of both black and white students. Those of us who have done our homework in the field have been able to make sense across the classroom racial line; it is incumbent on us to do so in whatever public realm we can muster a voice. For me, it can only be to give it my best try with my writing.

What should be our voice? Frederick Douglass's wrath was not the sputtering of one lost in frustration. Not for him was William Faulkner's image in *Absalom, Absalom!* of Miss Rosa Coldfield "sitting so bolt upright in the straight hard chair that was so tall for her that her legs hung straight and rigid as if she had iron shinbones and ankles, clear of the floor with . . . [an] air of impotent and static rage."[13] Instead, Douglass, against impossible odds, stood up to and protested a clearly defined wrong—slavery.

Today, the object of protest is far more amorphous, but not beyond our power to define. The voice that will articulate loudly and clearly a just society will be one that does not settle for glib universalities, but one able to command the history and the idiom of a culture and link that culture to the whole.

The antislavery Frederick Douglass–in his person, in public–linked his own story to that of the injustice he sought to rid his America of. Doing so, he made his country a better place; he made it his. To confront those who would despoil his land, we could do far worse than strive, however imperfectly, to find a voice as firm as his.

NOTES

1. Nathan Huggins, *Slave and Citizen: The Life of Frederick Douglass* (Boston: Little Brown, 1980), 38.

2. *The American Heritage Dictionary,* Second College ed. (Boston: Houghton Mifflin, 1985), 135.

3. Frederick Douglass, "Send Back the Blood-Stained Money," address at Paisley, Scotland, 25 April 1846, in John W. Blassingame, ed., *The Frederick Douglass Papers. Series One: Speeches, Debates, and Interviews,* 5 vols. (New Haven: Yale University Press, 1979–), 1:240–43, 240, 241.

4. Ibid., 1:241.

5. Frederick Douglass, "Slavery Attacks Humanity," address at Birmingham, England, 29 June 1846, in Blassingame, *Papers,* 1:308–16, 313.

6. Paul Watkins, "A Promise of Redemption," review of Barack Obama, *Dreams from My Father: A Story of Race and Inheritance,* in *New York Times Book Review,* 6 August 1995, 17.

7. Priscilla Wald, *Constituting America: Cultural Anxiety and Narrative Form* (Durham: Duke University Press, 1995), 3.

8. Theodore Stanton and Harriot Stanton Blatch, eds., *Elizabeth Cady Stanton, as Revealed in Her Letters, Diary and Reminiscences,* 2 vols. (1922; reprint, New York: Arno, 1969), 2:311.

9. Ibid.

10. Ibid.

11. Alan Ryan, *John Dewey and the High Tide of American Liberalism* (New York: W. W. Norton, 1995), 35.

12. Bob Herbert, "In America: Cruel Homeless Policy," Op-Ed page, *New York Times,* 15 February 1995.

13. William Faulkner, *Absalom, Absalom!* (1936; New York: Vintage, 1986), 3.

PART TWO

Douglass and Religion

Send Back the Money

Douglass and the Free Church of Scotland

ALASDAIR PETTINGER

T HE DISRUPTION OF THE CHURCH OF SCOTLAND, THOUGH somewhat neglected by historians today, was one of the most important events of the nineteenth century in Scotland. During the 1820s and '30s the evangelical wing replaced the moderates as the dominant force in the church. Their vision of a much more active and crusading future was disappointed, however, by the insufficiency of financial support from the state, coupled with a series of legal decisions in the House of Lords that seriously limited the church's control over its own internal affairs, most notably the appointment of ministers. Since the church was more central to social life in Scotland than in England, the resentment that arose was both antisecular and nationalist.

On 18 May 1843, Thomas Chalmers and his evangelical supporters walked out of the General Assembly to establish the Free Church of Scotland. Over a third of its ministers and perhaps half of its lay members declared allegiance to the new body, which, although not an established church, had high hopes of fulfilling the same role—a *national* church that would care for the spiritual and educational needs of the whole population. While the voluntary and dissenting churches could support themselves from the contributions of their congregations, they were only viable in the wealthier areas of the towns. In working-class districts and in the country, a church required additional sources of income. Not only that, of course, but the Free Church initially did not have any church or school buildings to call its own.[1]

A huge fund-raising program was set in motion, at home and abroad. Representatives were dispatched to England and Ireland the same summer, and, later in the year, a deputation set sail for the United States, where they reaped the benefit of long-standing links with the Presbyterians.[2] Reporting back on the visit to the Assembly of 1844, Dr. Cunningham estimated that £3,000 had been raised in America before the deputation left and £6,000 since, with a few thousand perhaps still to come.[3] He singled out the generosity of Mr. James Lenox of New York for special mention,[4] but it would appear that the bulk of the money was raised in the South, largely due, no doubt, to the efforts of Reverend George Lewis of Dundee, whose travels took him to Charleston, Mobile, New Orleans, and other cities. It was appropriate, then, that Lewis was the one member of the deputation who published a record of his experiences.[5]

News of the visit immediately set alarm bells ringing among the abolitionists in all sectors of the movement, which, at least since 1840, had been clear about the close links between the American churches and slavery.[6] In April 1844, the American and Foreign Anti-Slavery Society wrote an open letter to the Free Church condemning their actions.[7] The more radical Glasgow Emancipation Society was initially cautious — some of its members belonged to the Free Church. But spurred on by the Garrisonian activist Henry Clarke Wright (who had been in Scotland since early 1843), a campaign to "send back the money" was well under way the following year. In January 1846, Wright was joined by two more emissaries of the American Anti-Slavery Society, Frederick Douglass and James Buffum. Subsequently Garrison himself came over, and the four Americans worked closely with the English militant George Thompson, who had long been associated with the Glasgow society. The issue of the money dominated their speeches in Scotland in 1846.[8]

But without doubt it was Douglass's contribution that set the campaign alight. It was not just the sight of a former slave condemning the Free Church that lent the campaign's arguments greater authority. His ability to convey the human consequences of the deputation's visit was unequalled. Nowhere is this seen to better effect than in his address to a meeting at St. George's Chapel, Dundee, in March, that makes its point decisively by dramatizing a single imaginary episode, a speech in which Douglass expertly mimics the voices of four characters: George Lewis, Douglass's former master Thomas Auld, a slave auctioneer, and himself.

Sir, I see brother Lewis calling on the slaveholder. I can almost go down south, and see him, when I was a slave, calling on my old master, Mr Thomas Auld (who would be a very likely party to call on), with his subscription paper. When brother Lewis knocks at the door, I answer, and he asks, "Well, my lad, is your master in?" (Laughter.) "Yes, Sir." Well, he walks into the house, sees my master, and introduces himself thus (for my ear would be at the keyhole immediately on the door being shut)—"My object in making this call this morning is to see if you would do something for the cause of religious freedom in Scotland. We have been laboring some time back, and have undergone severe struggles, for Gospel freedom in Scotland, and we have thought it right to call upon you, as a benevolent man and as having means to bestow, to see what you can do for us." My master would reply, "Brother Lewis, I deeply sympathize with your efforts; and as I see the cause recommended by Deacon such-a-one, I would like to have my name down with his. I'll tell you what I will do. I have a fine young negro who is to be sold, and I will sell him to-morrow and give you a contribution to the cause of freedom. (Applause and laughter.) If you will call, brother Lewis, and take your breakfast with me, I will then see what I can do; and as the slave is to be sold at Easton, I will feel happy if you also take a ride so far with me, as you may not have seen the capital of the county. Come about nine o'clock, brother, and I will see what I can do for the cause of freedom in Scotland." (Laughter and cheering.)

The morning comes, and the breakfast hour, and brother Lewis also. (I have a son called Lewis, but I think I'll change his name.) (Applause.) The Bible is given to brother Lewis, and he reads, "Blessed are the poor in spirit—Blessed are they that give to the poor," and so on. All goes on delightfully. Brother L. prays, and after prayer sits down and partakes of the bounties produced by the blood of the slave, watered by the sweat and enriched by the blood of the half-famished negro. (Applause.) Brother Auld orders the carriage to be brought round to the door—I am tied behind the carriage and taken away, as I have seen often done: I am on the auction block, and the auctioneer is crying "Who bids for this comely stout young negro? He is accustomed to his work, and has an excellent trade on his hands." Well, 500 dollars are bid. Oh, how brother Lewis' eyes twinkle! (Laughter.) The auctioneer continues—"This is not half the value of the negro; he is not sold for any bad quality. His master has no desire to get rid of him, but only wants to get a little money to aid the cause of religious freedom in Scotland." Once, twice, thrice, is said by the auctioneer, and I am sold for 600 dollars.[9]

As the speech rises to its climax, its rhythms and repetitions draw the inevitable conclusion:

> When the Free Church says—Did not Abraham hold slaves? the reply should be, Send back that money! (Cheers.) When they ask did not Paul send back Onesimus? I answer, Send you back that money! (Great cheering.) That is the only answer which should be given to their sophistical arguments, and it is one which they cannot get over. (Great cheering.) In order to justify their conduct, they endeavor to forget that they are a Church, and speak as if they were a manufacturing corporation. They forget that a Church is not for making money, but for spreading the Gospel. We are guilty, say they, but these merchants are guilty, and some other parties are guilty also. I say, send back that money! (Cheering.) There is music in that sound. (Continued cheering.) There is poetry in it.[10]

The distinction Douglass makes here between moral principles and material self-interest is a common one. It still dominates discussions of abolitionism, where the debates continue to revolve around the relative historical weight given to ethics or economics in attempting to explain how Atlantic slavery—for so long unquestioned by church and state—quickly came to be the object of a concerted and eventually successful campaign to do away with it.

It is generally agreed that abolitionism could only emerge on the basis of a profound transformation of Western morality. Until the eighteenth century, the debates on the rights and wrongs of slavery focused on the treatment of slaves, the circumstances in which they were acquired and could be set free. The notion that slaveholding could be sinful in itself owes much to the development of a new mode of ethics rooted in independent general principles. Rather than demand that one obey rules and follow examples set by one's social superiors, this new mode required that one merely listen to the universal promptings of the human heart, the inner voice of conscience. Historians such as David Brion Davis have paid close attention to the impact of Enlightenment philosophers and Protestant religious reformers.[11] More recently, the existence of radical abolitionist thought among the slaves themselves has received more recognition, particularly in its utopian and apocalyptic dimension.[12]

But it is rarely claimed that the existence of the demand for the abolition of slavery can alone account for its attracting widespread support and translation into legislative action. Robert Fogel, for instance, has argued that abolitionism only became a formidable force in the Northern states when its leaders supplemented or diluted their religious appeals with secular arguments: they didn't just claim that slavery was wrong, but insisted that the South represented a growing political and economic threat.[13] Another approach, adopted by Davis in the sequel to his earlier book, suggests that abolitionism (in Britain, at any rate) became successful because of the ways in which it could serve—almost in spite of itself—as an ideological support for various domestic social interests, particularly those to do with the new forms of wage-labor emerging in the industrial towns.[14]

But the dispute between Douglass and the Free Church is not easily accommodated in such a framework. The main issues are neither humanitarian principles nor sectarian advantage. To understand the encounter, we must highlight a third dimension, one often overlooked in studies of abolitionism. More mundane and practical than the former, yet broader and aspiring higher than the latter, this dimension might be called "ethical culture."

Modern ethics is not reducible to general principles. Older forms of governing conduct have survived because the categorical imperative is a poor guide to everyday behavior. It cannot help resolve difficult choices, cannot provide skills that would enable one to be, say, a good judge of character, or to appreciate other people's feelings. Nor will it offer much in the way of an inducement to virtue. So it should not be thought surprising that, although customs such as casuistry, duelling, public humiliation, and elaborate codes of social etiquette were discredited, new techniques took their place.

If the seventeenth and eighteenth centuries witnessed an obsessive interest in the minutiae of daily life on the part of the absolutist state (of which the Slave Codes are an example), the liberal regimes that followed were no less concerned with individual behavior, although responsibility was dispersed across a wide range of agencies, many of them "private." Concern over such things as diet, child rearing, household management, sexuality, and work discipline is in evidence everywhere through the nineteenth century on the plantations as elsewhere, from the design of buildings and the organization of the manufacturing process to the pastoral attentions of doctors, ministers, schoolteachers, and social philanthropists.

Such practices are the stuff of ethical culture. Indeed, it may be more illuminating to think of humanitarianism less as a philosophy than as an ensemble of techniques developed to help people "govern themselves." But these techniques are not simply a series of measures to secure an efficient labor force or docile citizenry—tools of a particular economic or political elite. They are moral technologies that encourage people to act in altruistic and conscientious ways, that promote self-discipline and collective identities. Enabling and empowering, they deserve to be taken seriously in their own right.[15]

DESPITE THE ARGUMENTS of the abolitionists, the Free Church had persisted in keeping up links with churches that admitted slaveholders as members. In a notorious letter he wrote to the *Witness* newspaper, Dr. Thomas Chalmers insisted that a "distinction ought to be made between the character of a system and the character of the persons whom circumstances have implicated therewith."[16] He admits that slavery is a fertile breeding ground of vice (fornication, covetousness, idolatry, intemperance, and so on) and that therefore "there will . . . be a more frequent call for ecclesiastical discipline in the slave-holding congregations"[17]—but only if the individuals concerned *do* succumb to such vices. Being a slaveholder in itself is no sin, and so no one should be excluded from church membership on that ground alone.

Douglass refers to this letter several times in his speeches. Here he is in Arbroath in February 1846, in a response which uses Chalmers's words as an ironic refrain:

> "DISTINCTION *ought to be made between the character of the system and the character of the person whom* CIRCUMSTANCES *have implicated therewith.*" The Doctor

would denounce slaveholding, robbery, and murder as sin, but would not denounce the slaveholder, robber, and murderer as a sinner: he would make a DISTINCTION between sins and the persons whom CIRCUMSTANCES have implicated therewith; he would denounce the dice, but spare the sharper; he would denounce the adultery, but spare the adulterer; for, says the Doctor, "distinction ought to be made between the character of the system and the character of the person whom circumstances have implicated therewith." "Oh! The artful Dodger."

This earns appreciative laughter each time Douglass makes the comparison, but as if comparing the great man to a fictional pickpocket is not enough, he goes on to make another parallel:

He says that distinction should be made between the character of a system, and the character of the persons whom circumstances have implicated therewith. Yes, circumstances – the doctrine of circumstances. Who proclaims it? Dr. Chalmers. Yes, this doctrine, which has justly brought down upon the head of infidel, Robert Owen, the execrations of Christendom, is now proclaimed by the eloquent Scotch divine. The Doctor has been driven to this hateful dilemma by taking a false step, in fellowshipping slaveholders as Christians. This doctrine carried out does away with moral responsibility. All that a thief has to do in justification of his theft is to plead that circumstances have implied him in theft, and he has Dr. Chalmers to apologise for him, and recognize him as a Christian.[18]

At the General Assembly of the Free Church in May, however, Chalmers's younger colleagues showed that the distinction was more complex. Robert Candlish and William Cunningham made it clear that they believed that there were definite shortcomings in the attitude of the American Presbyterian churches. They were not so serious as to warrant the Free Church severing any connection with them: this should only be considered as a last resort. But it was important that the Assembly made it clear that their willingness to admit slaveholders was problematic to say the least. Although, like Chalmers, Candlish and Cunningham did not go so far as to make slaveholding as a practice sinful, they insisted that it carries with it a whole range of moral obligations. Even if the law places restrictions on emancipation, on slave marriages, and on teaching slaves to read and write, the slaveholder must convince the church he is doing all he can despite such restrictions – treating the slaves humanely, looking after their moral and religious improvement. The American Presbyterians, they argue, are too easily convinced and must be persuaded to take a more forceful stand—including a vigorous attempt to repeal the relevant laws. At the same time, it was recognized that the particular circumstances in which the churches found themselves meant that it was not always a good idea that they "should expel every slaveholder from communion, or should carry on a constant and open war against slavery, when the effect would, to all appearances, be that of losing their existing opportunities of Christian usefulness, and of increasing rather than diminishing the oppression." [19]

Douglass—who attended the Assembly—was characteristically sarcastic about Cunningham's refusal to say that slavery was sinful and that slaveholders were necessarily guilty. Cunningham's attempts to justify himself by means of hypothetical legal scenarios and scriptural authority are certainly confused.[20] But his position did not proceed from an abstract consideration of the nature of slavery, but rather from a weighing up of the various consequences of excluding slaveholders from church membership. Douglass chooses to ignore this and explains it in the simplest terms: "I tell you why he does it. He's got the bawbees. (Loud and long-continued cheering.)" [21]

Modern accounts of the debate tend to agree with Douglass that the distinction between the system of slavery and the actions of slaveholders is a wholly discreditable one.[22] But I think it deserves a more sympathetic consideration. It may well be true that it is not sufficient to justify the policy of the Free Church in accepting the donations from its American brethren, and it is certainly clouded by a poor grasp of some of the facts. Yet the idea that abstract principles are not the *only* criteria in assessing an individual's conduct does not require one to abandon any notion of moral responsibility and endorse the free pursuit of immediate self-interest.

In practice the mundane issues of social administration (from country medicine to the sentencing of courts, from marriage guidance to the design of classrooms) all work on the basis not of measuring behavior against a universal perfectionist standard but of attending to—and changing—the circumstances that encourage people to act in some ways rather than others. The "doctrine of circumstances," as Douglass calls it, is little more than a summary of what these moral technologies have in common. Cunningham is thus merely rehearsing a commonplace of liberal governance when he states:

> there is somehow or other a class of cases intermediate between those, on the one hand, which are characterised by eternal and immutable morality, and those, on the other, which are merely expedient, proper, and becoming, or the reverse – a class of cases in regard to which there are some moral considerations bearing on their general character and affecting the general duty of men regarding them, but respecting which you are not at liberty to look upon them as involving in every instance direct and immediate obligation.[23]

Consider Thomas Chalmers's own rather notorious experiments in poor-relief. On three occasions over some thirty years, he placed his faith in a series of "model" schemes in some of the worst areas of Glasgow and Edinburgh that aimed to show that a cheaper and more efficient alternative to the Poor Laws was possible. Rather than statutory handouts from the public authorities, the church would set up an intensive program of door-to-door visiting, closely acquainting its officers with detailed knowledge of the circumstances of each household. Its primary focus would be to conduct religious and moral education and provide assistance in finding work for the unemployed; financial aid would be dispensed only in certain cases, and even then, from voluntary contributions from the wealthy.

In general, Chalmers paid little attention to the need to improve working conditions, housing, and so on, and the schemes foundered from a lack of central government support. And yet for all their faults, the experiments at St. John's, Water of Leith, and West Port were intended to promote certain ways of thinking and modes of conduct (thrift, temperance, piety) whose desirability few would question today, objectives that continue to elude contemporary welfare states. Chalmers has been credited as one of the pioneers of techniques subsequently developed in social work – techniques that were in many ways heavy-handed and patronizing by present-day standards but by no means reducible to methods of "social control." These techniques intend to give a sense of dignity and purpose to individual lives and provide the basis for collective action.[24]

What, then, about slavery? Chalmers surely saw the parallel between his internal missionary efforts and those of Southern churches in the United States. His colleague, George Lewis, reported on those efforts in some detail, although the Presbyterians were shown to be rather less impressive in this area than the Baptists and Methodists.[25] The Free Church clearly believed that much more could be done but fell short of recommending that these churches should automatically expel slaveholders. "We are prepared," argued Candlish, "to consider the circumstances in which they are placed, and to make allowances for the difficulties of their position."[26] It appears that the Free Church believed that the Southern churches' work among the "coloured population" could only continue if the churches remained circumspect on the matter of slavery as an institution. Perhaps that was as much as they could realistically hope for. Lewis himself, after attending the disappointing General Assembly of the Presbyterian Church in Louisville in 1844, was confident that the "destruction of slavery in the South will not be gradually accomplished, and that the dissolution of the Union must, in all probability, precede it. The hand of violence will alone accomplish the ejection of this great national evil."[27]

Recent studies of religion in the antebellum South have recognized the value of this missionary work. It was not reducible to securing docile, obedient servants nor restricted to moderating the cruel hand of certain masters. The result was the formation of a distinctively black Christianity and a sense of slave community in which characteristic patterns of conduct and self-identification could flourish.[28] In the light of this research, it would seem that Douglass's radical rhetoric prevented him from recognizing what Chalmers and his colleagues appreciated only too well: if Southern churches agreed to deny literacy to the slaves, they nevertheless could impart other skills and capacities that were just as important.

IF CHALMERS and the Free Church have rather more noble intentions than is commonly allowed, Douglass and his comrades are less enthralled by utopian, romantic ideals than their critics sometimes assume. They too operate on the terrain of practical ethical culture.

In practice, even Garrisonian abolitionists were never content to issue condemnations of slavery and slaveholders in the abstract. A purely "moral" position can admit only an appeal to conscience: its aim is to awaken a universal sentiment. A more workaday ethic involves a rhetoric of persuasion, education, and training: to win support for the cause, its task is not so much to unveil an innate compassion but rather to inculcate a disposition.

Humanitarian reformers commonly expressed reservations about moral rhetoric; they were worried that it might exceed its subordinate role as an aid to reflection and influence behavior more surreptitiously. People may end up doing the right thing, but out of habit or community pressure rather than on the basis of conscious rational decision. Such actions would be inauthentic and not really virtuous at all.

And yet rhetoric is central to abolitionism, and the "Send Back the Money" campaign was no exception. Let us consider some examples. There is rhetoric in the narrow sense: the brilliant oratory of Douglass that adopts the wide range of voices (slaveholders, Southern preachers, Free Church leaders) that weave in and out of his speeches; and the powerful shifts of tone, the subtle changes of rhythm, and the prodigious range of direct quotations from newspapers, pamphlets, literature and social philosophy.

Alongside the speeches themselves, one finds their message conveyed in many other ways: the display of instruments of bondage on the stages of the halls and theaters he spoke in—and the appearance of messages of support daubed on the walls of Scottish towns (even cut out of the turf of the slopes of Arthur's Seat in Edinburgh) and the rewordings of popular songs that warned that there will be no "peace till that siller's sent hame." [29]

One can see the effect of all this in an anonymous letter sent by a woman to Chalmers:

Dear Dr C. These strangers were not sent to teach you alone. To me also were there words reproofs. I was shewing a little of the slaveholder my own conscience telling me so. I was also beginning to murmur for more liberty I thought that I could not well get alone. But it was the Grand *Intruder* that was ever following me with his suggestions. God in Mercy sent these men to shew me my transgressions, by telling me what my sisters are suffering pent up in chains, bloodhounds their guardians *Iron Collars their* necklaces, *Whips* instead of the strong arm of Man to lean on or ward off ill. And are we content to leave it *so* . . .

I heard the strangers they told the wrongs of the oppressed. They also quoted some of your and Rev. L's words at this no friend of the oppressed could find fault. When the Collar and whip were produced it was remarked would the applications of these to *you* or your daughters make you *change* your views on slavery. This caused *laughter*. . . . Oh it is too serious a matter to make sport of–Fre. Douglass did make me laugh when he preached the boys in Dundee send *back* the money–[30]

This text is revealing in many ways, not least because it shows how Douglass departs from abstract moral argument and instead–adopting a classic joke format–invites his audience to imagine the instruments of torture being applied not to themselves but an absent third party.

As well as trying to create a climate in which Southern slavery was unacceptable to Scottish audiences, Douglass sought to challenge an image of Scotland that prevailed in the South. In fact, "Scotland" figured large in the proslavery culture there: not merely as an image to be deployed by way of justification (in defensive response to the attacks from the North) but at a more basic level.

Several historians have observed that while the casuistical practices of the church fell from favor as a cornerstone of ethical culture by the early eighteenth century, they reappeared elsewhere in another guise. For a detailed discussion of how to conduct oneself in particular circumstances, one was less likely to follow the instruction of priests than to listen to the cacophony of advice found in journalism and popular fiction. The literature of Fielding, Defoe, and their successors marks the birth of a form that–through the elaboration of imaginary "cases"–provided more valuable practical guidance than the abstract treatments of moral philosophy ever could.[31]

The importance of Sir Walter Scott to the Old South has been well documented. Mark Twain famously held him responsible for the Civil War.[32] Others have not gone quite so far but have acknowledged that his novels helped to create and sustain what some have called the "patriarchal" regime that was at its height in the first half of the nineteenth century. Plantations were named after places in Scott's novels, and many of his leading characters were role models for Southern gentlemen who aspired to the chivalric ideal.[33] Small wonder, then, that the Grimké sisters figuratively broke with their upbringing by destroying his books.[34] But if the fictional world of *Waverley* or *Rob Roy* served as a kind of moral blueprint for slave society, it was historical Scotland itself that figured in its racial fantasies. Scotland lies at the heart of the South's most emotive symbols: the Confederate battle flag, which incorporates the St. Andrew's Cross, and the "fiery cross," a Highland tradition appropriated by the Ku Klux Klan. The same network of associations made it possible for Henry James, expressing revulsion at what we would today call "multicultural" New York City, to yearn for "the luxury of some such close and sweet and *whole* national consciousness as that of the Switzer and the Scot."[35]

Judging by his speeches and letters during his visit, it is clear that Douglass was keen to challenge this monopoly on Scotland that the proslavery forces seemed to enjoy. In changing his own name from Bailey to Douglass (after the hero in *The Lady of the Lake*), he "signifies" on a characteristically Southern gesture. If a wealthy slaveholder may have identified with the tolerant and generous Douglas rather than his impetuous and harsh nephew Roderick Dhu, this may have something to do with shifting notions of Southern honor among the influential and powerful in the early part of the nineteenth century.[36] When a former slave presumes to lay claim to the same lineage, the effect is somewhat different, especially when one considers that in choosing his new name he may also have had in mind the fact that the literary Douglas is an outlaw and exile. At one point in the poem Scott compares him to a "hunted stag," an image that must be understood in conjunction with the famous opening in which the King hunts a real stag.[37] Significantly, the "antler'd monarch" gets away. This must have had some resonance to the author of the 1845 *Narrative* as he recounted his escape from "the hunters of men."[38]

His new name also allows him the pleasure of invoking "the ancient 'black Douglass,'"[39] another historical figure who also appears in Scott.[40] Again it is the qualities not of genteel nobility that are celebrated but a fierce rebellious spirit, the chance epithet helping him to complete an ideological realignment of the "free hills of old Scotland,"[41] no longer set against the abolitionist North but now firmly in opposition to the slave South.[42]

> I am now as you will perceive by the date of this letter in Scotland, almost every hill, river, mountain and lake of which has been made classic by the heroic deeds of her noble sons. Scarcely a stream but has been poured into song, or a hill that is not associated with some fierce and bloody conflict between liberty and slavery. I had a view the other day of what are called the Grampion [sic] mountains that divide eastern Scotland from the West. I was told that here the ancient crowned heads used to meet, contend and struggle in deadly conflict for supremacy, causing these grand old hills to run blood-warming cold steel in the others heart. My soul sickens at the thought, yet I see in myself all those elements of character which were I to yield to their promptings might lead me to deeds as bloody as those at which my soul now sickens and from which I now turn with disgust and shame.[43]

Perhaps the most interesting aspect of Douglass's creation of an anti-slavery Scotland are his references to Robert Burns, whose work he clearly knew well. Quoting *Tam o' Shanter* in a speech in Dundee—to laughter and cheers—he says of the defenders of the Free Church "that, to use the language of one of your own poets, 'the De'il has business on his hands.'"[44] A visit to London yields the following remark in a letter to Garrison: "There is no distinction on account of color. The white man gains nothing by being white, and the black man losing nothing by being black. 'A man's a man for a' that.'"[45]

But it is in the county of the poet's birth that Douglass dwells more at length on the man and his work. A speech in Ayr on 24 March 1846—a long one recounting the story of his life as a slave, his learning to read and write, his escape, his work in New Bedford, and then his new career as an abolitionist orator and author with his subsequent voyage to Britain—concluded with an apostrophe to Burns.[46] Both men rose to literary fame from lowly origins, and yet, while Douglass crossed the Atlantic to escape the long arm of slavery, Burns nearly sailed in the other direction to become one of its agents.[47]

> The day before his speech at Cathcart St. Chapel he wrote a letter in which he described at length a visit to Burns' Monument and to the cottage of

Burns's surviving sister and her two daughters. The text dwells on inanimate memorials of the poet's life: a marble bust, two statues, letters in his own hand, and an original portrait, but what moves him most is a Bible, given by Burns to his "sweet Highland Mary"—there is also in the same case a lock of hair he so dearly loved, and who by death was snatched from his bosom, and up to his bust glowing with expression, I received a vivid impression, and shared with him the deep melancholy portrayed in the following lines.[48]

Douglass also quotes in full the poet's song *The Banks o' Doon,* in which the river serves as an unwelcome reminder of "joys,/departed, never to return." But what is most interesting is his assessment of the poet and the man:

> Burns lived in the midst of a bigoted and besotted clergy—a pious, but corrupt generation—a proud, ambitious, and contemptuous aristocracy, who, esteemed a little more than a man, and looked upon the plowman, such as was the noble Burns, as being little better than a brute. He became disgusted with the pious frauds, indignant at the bigotry, filled with contempt for the hollow pretensions set up by the shallow-brained aristocracy. He broke loose from the moorings which society had thrown around him. Spurning all restraint, he sought a path for his feet, and, like all bold pioneers, he made crooked paths. We may lament it, we may weep over it, but in the language of another, we shall lament and weep with him. The elements of character which urged him on are in us all, and influencing our conduct every day of our lives. We may pity him, but we can't despise him. We may condemn his faults, but only as we condemn our own. His very weakness was an index of his strength. Full of faults of a grievous nature, yet far more faultless than many who have come down to us in the pages of history as saints. He was a brilliant genius, and like all of his class, did much good and much evil. Let us take the good and leave the evil—let us adopt his virtues but avoid his vices—let us pursue his wisdom but shun his folly; and as death has separated his noble spirit from the corrupt and contemptible lust with which it was encumbered, so let us separate his good from his evil deeds—thus may we make him a blessing than a curse to the world.[49]

Douglass poured scorn on Chalmers's distinction between character and system as tending to undermine moral responsibility. Individuals ought to be accountable for their own actions. And yet his speeches were meant to influence people. Antislavery rhetoric was not just an appeal to reason but was intended to create a social climate in which certain choices were acceptable and others not. Burns had his faults but he is not blamed for them: the forces that made him what he was are acknowledged. But Burns himself can be made a force in his turn. In this letter, which was published in the *New York Tribune,* Douglass invokes him as a role model, a man whose example is in some respects worth following. And as a political radical, the poet suggests a different Scotland from the one that prevailed among the "contemptuous aristocracy" of the South.

THE ENCOUNTER between Douglass and the Free Church cannot readily be understood in terms of a conflict between high principles and material self-interest. Such an understanding would only make sense if the disagreement were solely over the general question of slavery as a system. In fact, as we have seen, both parties were also deeply concerned about the trickier and more complex issues of conduct. Does this mean, then, that the two adversaries were in essential agreement and that the whole episode was a big misunderstanding? Certainly there is more in common between them than has usually been acknowledged. One instance in particular shows this quite clearly.

On his outward voyage, Douglass was invited by Captain Judkins of the *Cambria* to address his fellow passengers on the subject of slavery. A few of them, bold enough to give voice to their prejudices, took exception to the suggestion and tried to prevent him from speaking, even threatening to throw him overboard.

> A little man from Philadelphia here stepped up and said I should not speak. The captain put him aside, when he put his hand under his coat, and he looked for him drawing out a dagger, but it was a card with a request to meet the captain in Liverpool. "Very well," replied the captain, "I will be there." (Cheers and laughter.) However, these gentlemen continued to show up their democratic injustice till the captain brought them to silence, by first threatening them then ordering the boatswain to produce the necessary implements to put them into irons. That was a new thing under the sun to put white slaveholders into irons! (Cheers.) They had been accustomed to put irons upon black people, but the idea of putting irons upon democratic republicans they could not understand; but seeing the captain was in earnest

the creatures began to drop down, and in about ten minutes they had all disappeared. (Loud and continued cheering.)[50]

On learning of the incident, the Glasgow Emancipation Society passed a resolution "signifying their high approbation of the magnanimous conduct of Captain Judkins," which was conveyed to him by letter.[51] What Douglass may not have realized, however, was that he was reaping the benefit of an earlier episode in which the same Judkins was not quite so magnanimous.

The previous year, a man traveling back from the United States on the *Acadia* noted in his journal that

> the only disagreeable circumstance that occurred in the home-ward voyage was the exclusion of a young gentleman, a passenger from Hayti, who had paid a cabin passage, and yet was not permitted to enter the saloon and dine at the common table. About one-third of the passengers joined in a request to the captain that he should be invited to join us in the saloon. The remonstrance was unheeded. The Captain at one moment saying that it was contrary to orders, and at another time declaring that he had no authority on the subject, but that the American passengers would not tolerate it. Finding no redress from Captain Judkins, we drew up a remonstrance to the owners at Glasgow and Liverpool, against this ungenerous outrage on the feelings of a coloured gentleman in a British vessel carrying her Majesty's mail.[52]

The author of this account—and one of the signatories of the remonstrance, which was later published (to the evident displeasure of the company directors) in the *Glasgow Argus*—was none other than the Rev. George Lewis, returning from his fund-raising mission among the slaveholding churches of the South. It is perhaps not unreasonable to suppose that Judkins, following the outcry, may have reconsidered—or been encouraged to reconsider—his earlier attitude.[53]

This anecdote shows some of the common ground shared by Douglass and the Free Church. But considerable differences between them remain. The Free Church's refusal to break fellowship with the American Presbyterians was not a cynical move to justify accepting their money. It was born of an assessment of the likelihood of the Southern churches embracing radical abolitionism and a recognition of the valuable work they were – or rather could be – doing to contribute to the physical, moral, and religious improvement of slaves, including working for the repeal of laws that made this task particularly difficult. Cordial criticism rather than sanctimonious denunciation was felt to have a better chance of success in persuading them to take a more active approach.

But Chalmers and his colleagues were quite wrong to think that the Southern churches were simply victims of laws made by others. While Candlish and Cunningham were critical of the inadequate response of the churches to those laws (though the criticism, once spelled out at the Assembly of 1846, evaporates[54]), they seriously underestimated the complicity of church members and some of its ministers in the formulation of those laws.[55] And, furthermore, the Free Church seriously misjudged the propaganda coup of their close public and financial links with their American brethren to the proslavery cause. Douglass illustrates this very well by quoting from the *New Orleans Picayune* of July 1845:

> "Dr Chalmers, the eloquent Scotch divine, having been appealed to by the members of the Free Church of Scotland, on the subject of receiving contributions from churches in the slave states of America, to say whether religious fellowship could consistently be extended to slaveholding churches, the Doctor repudiates the spirit that would narrow the sphere of Christian union, and says that the refusal of such fellowship would be 'most unjustifiable.'"[56]

And then comments:

> Do you think Dr Chalmers would ever have said this, if, like me, he had four sisters and one brother in bondage? (Cheers, and cries of "No.") Would this paper have eulogised George Thompson or William Lloyd Garrison, or any other eminent abolitionist? (No, no!) Well, the slaves run away – the bloodhound has not been able to follow their tracks, and the paper which eulogises Dr Chalmers thus advertises the fugitives:–
>
> "Forty Dollars Reward will be given for the delivery or detention of the following Negroes, who ran away from my plantation, near Fort Pikes, La, on the 3d instant, or Twenty Dollars for either of them:–viz. Phil, aged about 40 years, dark complexion; has a deep scar on (perhaps) his left hand, and a piece off one ear. Sam, aged about 20 years; has a scar on his chin, several lumps on his neck and back and walks rather lame."[57]

But the abolitionists made strategic errors of their own. Certainly they misjudged the extent to which their campaign could be turned into a vehicle for domestic sectarianism: many of those who gleefully took up the slogans were venting their hostility to the Free Church for entirely different reasons.[58] The tone of the campaign was perhaps ill-chosen too: such an uncompromising burst of self-righteous anger did not make it easy for the Free Church leadership to make a dignified U-turn[59]—although the more diplomatic overtures from more neutral sources did not appear to have had any effect either.[60] It is probably true, though, that this is less a fault of Douglass than of some of the more radical campaigners such as Henry C. Wright and others.[61]

In a sense, the "failure" to persuade the Free Church to return the money it had raised in the United States is almost irrelevant. The campaign doubtless had its effects at the time: in 1846 the British section of the Evangelical Alliance stood their ground and refused membership to slaveholders.[62] And the campaign surely had some impact in the States in "shattering Southerners' hopes that they might share their communion with their Scottish brethren in quiet confidence-restoring comfort."[63]

If the campaign was not simply a plea to send back the money but also an important rhetorical struggle over "Scotland" and the South, then perhaps it is still too early to judge the outcome. If it is true that Scottish roots are being rediscovered by Southern nationalists today—in a context that leaves little room for Southerners of African descent[64]—then it may be appropriate to end with words from a speech Douglass made in Rochester, New York, nearly two years after his departure from Liverpool in April 1847. Invited to address a Burns Supper, he reflects on his travels in Scotland and his meeting with the poet's sister, and clearly he could have gone on at length:

> But, ladies and gentlemen, this is not a time for long speeches. I do not wish to detain you from the social pleasures that await you. I repeat again, that though I am not a Scotchman, and have a colored skin, I am proud to be among you this evening. And if any think me out of my place on this occasion (pointing at the picture of Burns), I beg that the blame may be laid at the door of him who taught me that "a man's a man for a' that."[65]

NOTES

1. See Stewart J. Brown, "The Ten Years' Conflict and the Disruption of 1843," in *Scotland in the Age of Disruption,* ed. Stewart J. Brown and Michael Fry (Edinburgh: Edinburgh University Press, 1993); and Stewart J. Brown, *Thomas Chalmers and the Godly Commonwealth in Scotland* (Oxford: Oxford University Press, 1982).

2. See *Proceedings of the General Assembly of the Free Church of Scotland held at Glasgow, October 17–24, 1843* (Edinburgh: W. P. Kennedy, 1843), 69–82, 39–45 and 170.

3. *Proceedings of the General Assembly of the Free Church of Scotland held in Edinburgh May 1844* (Edinburgh: W. P. Kennedy, 1844), 71. For further discussion of the amount raised, see George Shepperson, "Thomas Chalmers, the Free Church of Scotland, and the South," *Journal of Southern History* 17 (November 1951): 519–20. But note that the amount raised represented a very small proportion of the total raised for the sustenation fund, which was, in the financial year 1844–45, £334,000 (Brown, *Thomas Chalmers,* 344).

4. *Proceedings of the General Assembly of the Free Church of Scotland,* 72.

5. George Lewis, *Impressions of America and the American Churches* (Edinburgh: W. P. Kennedy, 1845).

6. This was one of the main topics of discussion at the annual meeting of the British and Foreign Anti-Slavery Society in 1840, at which Thomas Clarkson made his last public appearance. His address, later published as *A Letter to the Clergy of Various Denominations, and to the Slave-Holding Planters, in the Southern Parts of the United States of America* (London, 1841), and James Gillespie Birney's pamphlet *American Churches the Bulwarks of American Slavery* (London, 1840) were to be influential texts in the movement during the following decade. See, for example, Betty Fladeland, *Men and Brothers: Anglo-American Anti-Slavery Co-Operation* (Urbana: University of Illinois Press, 1972), 270–72.

7. *Letter from the Executive Committee of the American and Foreign Anti-Slavery Society to the Commissioners of the Free Church of Scotland* (Edinburgh, n.d.).

8. The most detailed accounts of the campaign are George Shepperson, "The Free Church and American Slavery," *Scottish Historical Review* 30 (October 1951): 126–43; "Thomas Chalmers, the Free Church of Scotland, and the South," and "Frederick Douglass and Scotland," *Journal of Negro History* 38 (July 1953): 307–21; and C. Duncan Rice, *The Scots Abolitionists, 1833–1861* (Baton Rouge: Louisiana State University Press, 1981), 124–46.

9. John W. Blassingame, ed., *The Frederick Douglass Papers. Series One: Speeches, Debates, and Interviews,* 5 vols. (New Haven: Yale University Press, 1979–) 1:179–80. See also 193–94.

10. Ibid., 181–82.

11. See, for example, David Brion Davis, *The Problem of Slavery in Western Culture* (Ithaca: Cornell University Press, 1966).

12. See, for example, Cedric Robinson, *Black Marxism: The Making of the Black Radical Tradition* (London: Zed, 1983), and Paul Gilroy, *The Black Atlantic: Modernity and Double Consciousness* (London: Verso, 1993).

13. Robert William Fogel, *Without Consent or Contract: The Rise and Fall of American Slavery* (New York: W. W. Norton, 1989), esp. 324–454.

14. David Brion Davis, *The Problem of Slavery in the Age of Revolution, 1770–1823* (Ithaca: Cornell University Press, 1975), esp. 346–73. See also the discussion of this in Thomas Bender, ed., *The Antislavery Debate: Capitalism and Abolitionism as a Problem in Historical Interpretation* (Berkeley: University of California Press, 1992).

15. For a general history of abolitionism that pays attention to some of these issues, see David Turley, *The Culture of English Anti-Slavery, 1780–1869* (London: Routledge, 1991). My general approach in this section owes much to Jeffrey Minson, *Questions of Conduct: Sexual Harassment, Citizenship, Government* (Basingstoke: Macmillan, 1993), esp. part one, "Introducing Ethical Culture."

16. Thomas Chalmers to *The Witness* (12 May 1845), in William Hanna, *Memoirs of the Life and Writings of Thomas Chalmers,* 4 vols. (Edinburgh: Sutherland and Knox, 1852), 4 : 583.

17. Ibid., 4 : 584.

18. Blassingame, *Papers,* 1 : 162–64; see also 192–93 and 236–37. Several other contemporaries compared Chalmers's ideas to those of Robert Owen, and the two men corresponded. See Brown, *Thomas Chalmers,* 122, 149–51, 247.

19. Free Church of Scotland, *Report of the Proceedings of the General Assembly on Saturday, May 30, and Monday, June 1, 1846, regarding the Relations of the Free Church of Scotland and the Presbyterian Churches of America* (Edinburgh, 1846) (hereafter *Presbyterian Churches*), 42.

20. Ibid., 38–40.

21. Blassingame, *Papers,* 1 : 430.

22. See, for example, R. J. M. Blackett, *Building an Antislavery Wall: Black Americans in the Atlantic Abolitionist Movement, 1830–1860* (Baton Rouge: Louisiana State University Press, 1983), 91.

23. *Presbyterian Churches,* 40.

24. Brown, *Thomas Chalmers,* 122–44, 239–41, 355–63; and on social work, see 376 and 416 n. 68. See also Rice, *Scots Abolitionists,* 125. For an important reappraisal of nineteenth-century philanthropy see Frank Prochaska, *The Voluntary Impulse: Philanthropy in Modern Britain* (London: Faber and Faber, 1988).

25. Lewis, *Impressions of America,* 85–87, 97–99, 120, 127–31, 143–44, 167–70, 174–78, 194, 207–17, 412–14.

26. *Presbyterian Churches,* 18.

27. Lewis, *Impressions of America,* 298.

28. See, for instance, Milton C. Sernett, *Black Religion and American Evangelism: White Protestants, Plantations Missions, and the Flowering of Negro Christianity* (Metuchen, N.J.: Scare-

crow Press, 1975); Donald G. Mathews, *Religion in the Old South* (Chicago: University of Chicago Press, 1977); A. J. Raboteau, *Slave Religion: The "Invisible Institution" in the Antebellum South* (New York: Oxford University Press, 1980); and many of the essays collected in John B. Boles, ed., *Masters and Slaves in the House of the Lord: Race and Religion in the American South, 1740–1870* (Lexington: University Press of Kentucky, 1988).

29. See George Shepperson, "The Free Church and American Slavery," 128; George Shepperson, "Frederick Douglass and Scotland," 314–17; and Rice, *Scots Abolitionists,* 144–46.

30. Anon. to Chalmers, 2 April 1846, Thomas Chalmers Papers, New College Library, Edinburgh.

31. See Edmund Leites, "Casuistry and Character," in *Conscience and Casuistry in Early Modern Europe,* ed. Edmund Leites (Cambridge: Cambridge University Press, 1988), 132–33; Albert R. Jonsen and Stephen Toulmin, *The Abuse of Casuistry: A History of Moral Reasoning* (Berkeley: University of California, 1988), 163–64.

32. Mark Twain, *Life on the Mississippi* (London: Chatto and Windus, 1883), 420.

33. G. Rollin Osterweis, *Romanticism and Nationalism in the Old South* (New Haven: Yale University Press, 1949), 41–53; Robert C. Gordon, "Scott, Racine, and the Future of Honor" in *Scott and His Influence: The Papers of the Aberdeen Scott Conference, 1982,* ed. J. H. Alexander and David Hewitt (Aberdeen: Association for Scottish Literary Studies, 1983), 255–265.

34. Willie Lee Rose, *Slavery and Freedom,* ed. William W. Freehling (New York: Oxford University Press, 1982), 147.

35. Henry James, *The American Scene* (1907; reprint, New York: Charles Scribner's Sons, 1946), 86.

36. See Bertram Wyatt-Brown, *Southern Honor: Ethics and Behavior in the Old South* (New York: Oxford University Press, 1982), esp. part 1; and also his "Modernizing Southern Slavery: The Proslavery Argument Reconsidered," in *Region, Race, and Reconstruction: Essays in Honor of C. Vann Woodward,* ed. J. Morgan Kousser and James M. McPherson (New York: Oxford University Press, 1982), 27–49.

37. Walter Scott, *The Lady of the Lake,* 2.xxxvii; 1.i–ix. See J. Logie Robertson, ed., *The Poetical Works of Sir Walter Scott* (London: Oxford University Press, 1904), 229, 208–209.

38. Frederick Douglass, *Narrative of the Life of Frederick Douglass, An American Slave* (1845; Harmondsworth: Penguin, 1982), 149.

39. *The Life and Writings of Frederick Douglass,* 5 vols. Philip S. Foner (New York: International Publishers, 1950–55), 1:133.

40. The original "Black Douglas" was the Good Sir James Douglas (ca. 1286–1330), who earned the nickname due to his swarthy complexion. As Robert Bruce's greatest captain in the war of independence, he presumably fought alongside him at Bannockburn (1314). But the whole line of the Douglasses, the Earls of Douglas, were known as the

"Black Douglasses," starting with James' son, William, the first Earl (?1327–1384). It is the third Earl who appears in Scott's *Fair Maid of Perth.* The Black Douglasses must be distinguished from the illegitimate descendants of William, the Earls of Angus, who became known as the "Red Douglasses" at a time when they supported the Crown against the Black Douglasses who were in rebellion during the late fifteenth century. But a few decades later it was Archibald Douglas, Sixth Earl of Angus (ca. 1489–1557) who threatened King James V and imprisoned him in 1525. James escaped in 1528 and won back his authority, and subsequently passed sentence of forfeiture against Douglas and his kinsmen. This is the Douglas (and the King) who figures in *The Lady of the Lake.* See Rosemary Goring, ed., *Scottish Biographical Dictionary* (Edinburgh: Chambers, 1992), 121–22.

41. Blassingame, *Papers,* 1 : 185; Foner, *Life and Writings,* 1:133.

42. In his account of his change of name, Douglass gives all the credit to Nathan Johnson, his abolitionist protector in New Bedford, who "had just been reading *The Lady of the Lake*" (*Narrative,* 147; *My Bondage and My Freedom,* ed. Philip S. Foner [1855; New York: Dover, 1969], 342–33). False modesty perhaps. But even if his own reading of Scottish history and literature only followed later, it is clear that it retrospectively confirmed the choice as a happy one that he fully exploited in 1846. Douglass's adoption of the Scottish name is a perfect example of what William McFeely refers to as active assimilation: the way he actively "absorbed and incorporated" both Southern and Scottish cultural traditions to his own ends. See McFeely's essay in this volume.

43. Foner, *Life and Writings,* 1:135–36.

44. Blassingame, *Papers,* 1 : 173–74.

45. Foner, *Life and Writings,* 1:170.

46. Blassingame, *Papers,* 1 : 195–204.

47. In 1786 Burns made plans to emigrate to Jamaica. It was probably only the success of his first volume of poetry that enabled him to exchange a future as a "poor Negro-driver" in the Caribbean for one in which he would head for the "new world" of literary Edinburgh. See G. Ross Roy, ed., *The Letters of Robert Burns,* vol. 1, *1780–1789* (Oxford: Clarendon Press, 1985), 144–45.

48. Douglass, *Bondage,* 151.

49. Ibid., 153.

50. Blassingame, *Papers,* 1 : 142. Text amended slightly to be consistently in first person direct speech. In a subsequent speech, Douglass calls for protests against steamship companies who practice discrimination (see 215).

51. Glasgow Emancipation Society, *Twelfth Annual Report* (Glasgow 1847), 5–6.

52. Lewis, *Impressions of America,* 390–91.

53. The incident is discussed in Glasgow Emancipation Society, *Tenth Annual Report* (Glasgow, 1844), Appendix 1, 21–22. The letter, dated 3 August 1844 and published in the *Glasgow Argus* on the 5th, is reproduced in Appendix 2, 40–41, and reads as follows:

SIR,– The following Memorial from passengers on board the steam-ship *Acadia,* during her last trip from Boston and Halifax to Liverpool, was presented to the Directors and Managers of the British and North American Royal Mail Steam-Packet Company on the 23d ultimo, and still lies before them for their consideration. By giving this a place in your columns you will oblige yours, &c. ALEX ARTHUR.

STEAM-SHIP ACADIA, *July,* 1844.

GENTLEMEN,– The undersigned cabin passengers on board the British and North American Royal Mail Steam-Packet Company's ship *Acadia,* on her passage from Boston to Liverpool, having observed that a gentleman of Colour from St Domingo has been excluded from the use of the saloon and common table during the voyage, notwithstanding application to Captain Judkins for his admission; and learning that this exclusion is made on account of Colour, from instructions issued by the agents of the Company, hereby request the Directors to give the matter their most serious consideration, for the following reasons:–

1st. Because, according to natural and revealed religion, all men are of one blood, and should, in a general passenger-ship, be accorded equal rights, so long as their conduct is such as becomes gentlemen.

2d. Because it is at variance with the Royal Mail Steam-Packet Company's advertisements for passengers generally, when a gentleman of Colour presents himself to subject him to the degradation of being denied the common privileges of a passenger.

3d. Because the British nation having granted equal privilege to persons of every Colour throughout her dominions, it is derogatory to her honour that such distinctions should exist in ships bearing the British flag, and more especially in those carrying her Majesty's mail.

4th. Because, independent of such injustice towards the Coloured race, it makes the conduct of persons of the United Kingdom, who may be passengers, appear inconsistent in countenancing such invidious distinctions.

JOHN HODGE, of London. ALEX C. LOGAN, Jamaica. THOMAS Wm. HILL, Bristol. GEORGE LEWIS, Dundee. WILLIAM ROY, Montreal. JOHN ARMOUR, Montreal. JOSEPH MACKAY, Montreal. BONAVENTURE ARMENGOT, P. of New Orleans. W. D. MACLAGAN, Leeds. ALEX. ARTHUR, Quebec. F. MEDICE, New York. ALLAN ARTHUR, Glasgow. ERAS. P. COLLEY, Quebec. Wm. TARISH, Hamilton, C. W. DUNCAN MACFARLANE, Glasgow. FELIX DICHARRY, Native of Louisiana. R. S. D. VEBER, St John's, N. B. JOHN J. RYAN, London. S. A. SCHUMACHER, New York. D. S. MACPHERSON, Canada. Wm. WAKEFIELD, Canada.

To the Directors of the British and North American Royal Mail Steam-Packet Comp.

54. See the reply to the Americans drafted following the debate: no sooner is the debate over than the criticisms of the Presbyterians become less earnest, and persistent criticism gives way to a lackluster ticking-off: "It is not with a view to a prolonged discussion . . ." *Presbyterian Churches,* 50

55. They also erroneously believed that the Presbyterian Church was a *national* one: see ibid., 21. In fact it had split—on roughly sectional lines—in 1837–38. See H. Shelton Smith, *In His Image, But . . . . : Racism in Southern Religion, 1780–1910* (Durham: Duke University Press, 1972), chapter 2, for a brief account.

56. Blassingame, *Papers,* 1 : 154.

57. Ibid., 155. Text changed to preserve consistency of first person.

58. See Rice, *Scots Abolitionists,* 137–39; Blackett, *Building an Antislavery Wall,* 94–95; and William S. McFeely, *Frederick Douglass* (New York: W. W. Norton, 1991), 135.

59. See Blackett, *Building an Antislavery Wall,* 94.

60. See, for example, letters to Chalmers from Adam Black, 15 May 1846, and Chalmers's reply, 23 May 1846; and from A. Ross, 10 November 1846, Chalmers Papers, New College Library, Edinburgh.

61. See Rice, *Scots Abolitionists,* 130–32.

62. See Blackett, *Building an Antislavery Wall,* 208.

63. McFeely, *Frederick Douglass,* 135. However, we do need more research on the impact in the South of Douglass's visit before we can assert this more confidently.

64. See, for instance, Grady McWhiney, *Cracker Culture: Celtic Ways in the Old South* (Tuscaloosa: University of Alabama Press, 1988).

65. Blassingame, *Papers,* 2 : 148.

British Unitarian Abolitionists, Frederick Douglass, and Racial Equality

DAVID TURLEY

I T MAY SEEM CURIOUS TO SELECT UNITARIAN ABOLITIONISTS
for special attention in relation to Frederick Douglass. Unitarians were a small body at the time of Douglass's visit in
1845. In 1830 there were about two hundred congregations in England,
and about fifty thousand attendees were recorded in the 1851 religious
census, though there were probably rather fewer active members. Even
if one adds evidence of activity elsewhere in the British Isles, mainly in
Northern Ireland, Unitarians were numerically far inferior to the evangelical wing of the Church of England and the evangelical nonconform-
ist denominations that had provided many of the generals and most of
the foot soldiers of the campaign for West Indian emancipation in the
1820s and 1830s.[1]

Yet, as a group, Unitarians possessed characteristics that, when some
of them adopted antislavery, made them peculiarly useful to Douglass.
They had chapels in the major towns and smaller centers of substantial
wealth and local influence. Disproportionately they drew together landed
and mercantile wealth, leading local members of the professions, and, in
some cases, manufacturers. Material substance and high educational levels were united in city chapels, and both there and in smaller centers, the

ordinary members of the congregations could give Douglass on his tour of 1845–47 an entrée to the class of retailers, small businessmen, and schoolmasters.

Nor were Unitarians constrained by strong denominational discipline. The British and Foreign Unitarian Association was founded in May 1825 but did not undercut the deep attachment to congregational autonomy or the willingness of district and regional associations to debate their own resolutions and pursue their own courses of action. There was thus considerable institutional latitude within Unitarianism for the adoption of positions that could be deemed by others, including fellow Unitarians, unorthodox, radical, or extreme.[2]

These were necessary conditions for the usefulness of Unitarians to Douglass but they do not sufficiently explain why a network of Unitarian abolitionists, in company with such unorthodox Quakers as the Webb family in Dublin and one branch of the Pease family in Darlington, emerged as the most reliable supporters of the Garrisonians in England and Ireland after British reformers become aware of American abolitionist divisions in 1840. The central paradox of the Unitarian minority was that, despite their often substantial economic and professional success and frequently high educational attainments, many of them nurtured a consciousness of having suffered discrimination for their beliefs. This not only encouraged sympathy for the victims of the oppression of slavery but led Unitarians to describe themselves as "theological Negroes." In part they perceived themselves as outsiders, despite local influence, because they had come under open rhetorical and legal attack in the years preceding Douglass's visit from militant evangelicals whose distrust of the religious liberals had forced Unitarians out of the Dissenting Deputies and compelled them to fight for control of their chapel property. What the Unitarians saw as evangelical intolerance in Britain, American Garrisonians of the "old organization" American Anti-Slavery Society experienced as the charges of "infidelity" and "fanaticism" in the United States, charges relayed to British evangelicals by American colleagues from the time of the London World Anti-Slavery Convention of 1840 onwards. The British Unitarians who became Garrisonians did so in considerable part because they sympathized with American reformers subject, like themselves, to evangelical animus. Such solidarity was confirmed through the influence of the pro-Garrison writing of Harriet Martineau on the denomination in which she had been brought up, as well as the visit of the American Unitarian Garrisonian, Samuel May Jr., in 1843[3] and was strong enough to overcome the doubts some of the Unitarian abolitionists entertained about Garrisonian radicalism.

Coming to Britain as a prominent member of the American Anti-Slavery Society in 1845, Douglass was welcomed into the Unitarian antislavery network. On occasion, in his speeches, he explicitly or indirectly paid tribute to Unitarian abolitionists for standing out against the evangelical mainstream, even at the cost of being charged with infidelity. His meetings received extensive coverage in the weekly *Inquirer,* edited by William Hincks, an acquaintance of Garrison, and he later elicited regular favorable comment in the younger Aspland's monthly magazine, the *Christian Reformer.* These were the two main Unitarian publications in the 1840s and 1850s. In practical arrangements Douglass often received assistance from the Unitarians, through hospitality, hiring of halls or meeting places, and in publicity for his meetings with and without Garrison. Unitarian abolitionists were prominent during his visits to Dublin, London, Bristol, Exeter, Bridgwater, Taunton, and Leeds and by no means absent elsewhere. They formed the core of the British reformers who prepared for, and then took part in, the meeting in August 1846 with Garrison, Douglass, and Henry C. Wright to launch the Anti-Slavery League as a British Garrisonian alternative to the British and Foreign Anti-Slavery Society. The only serious attempts to establish local auxiliaries of the League were undertaken by Unitarian reformers in Bristol and Exeter; Douglass and Garrison were called upon to speak on both occasions.[4] The Unitarian abolitionists' network linked London, Dublin, the North of England, and the West Country. It associated Douglass and other American reformers with a range of people, from metropolitan reformers like John Bowring, M.P., W.J. Fox (the Unitarian minister, journalist, and later politician), and the lawyer W. H. Ashurst to provincial chapel ministers and prominent lay Unitarians such as the Estlins and the Carpenters in Bristol, the Luptons in Leeds, and the Haughtons in Dublin. There is much testimony to the admiration Douglass elicited from women reformers; some of the most active of them who, for example, worked hard for the Garrisonian Boston Anti-Slavery

Bazaar, were the Bristol Unitarians Mary Estlin, Mary and Anna Carpenter, and Frances Armstrong. Garrison had no doubt, and Douglass would probably have agreed with him, that the Unitarians were "much better than their revilers and persecutors" and had been "the foremost" in aiding the American antislavery mission.[5]

There is, however, another layer of meaning to Douglass's links with Unitarian abolitionists during his visit of 1845–47. In his speech at the farewell soirée held for him in London, Douglass expressed his conviction that, while in Britain, he had changed and grown through being able to live his life without fear of threat to his freedom. He was conscious of having pursued a course in the British Isles that was manifestly his own, while he still expressed his full admiration for Garrison. He had stood up to Mrs. Chapman and the Dublin Quaker Richard Webb when they had shown lack of confidence in him. Because he believed that Henry C. Wright had "created against himself prejudices which I as an abolitionist do not feel called upon to withstand," he had deliberately held himself somewhat apart from Wright. And there is evidence that the "peculiar opinions" associated with some of the Garrisonians did cause disquiet among other abolitionists in addition to Anti-Slavery Society loyalists. Firmly but politely, Douglass had explained, but had refused to apologize for, temporarily collaborating with the committee of the Society in the Free Church controversy. He pointedly told Mrs. Chapman: "I will speak in any meeting when freedom of speech is allowed and where I may do anything towards exposing the bloody system of slavery." Similarly, in controversy with Dr. Samuel Cox, an American clerical delegate to the World Temperance Convention in London in the summer of 1846, he justified bringing the question of American slavery into the proceedings by defining an "abolition agitator" as "one who dares to think for himself." He was fulfilling his God-approved duty in using his "health and strength and intellectual ability" in "promoting the cause of righteousness."[6]

Douglass's conscious expression of his autonomy in terms of freedom of speech and thought, his pursuit of the truth through the confident use of his intellectual ability is the key to the especially warm admiration Unitarian abolitionists had for him. A consistent theme of his speeches in the British Isles involved the presentation of himself as an intellectual being, for it was "the intellectual coloured man" who most challenged white American racial theories, he told a Coventry audience. Just as when he had begun his speaking career in the United States, much of Douglass's content in his speeches on the early Irish leg of his tour was autobiographical. But, even before the end of 1845, though he continued to make reference to his personal experience, he offered historical context and political analysis in discoursing on the annexation of Texas and moral disquisition in linking temperance to the problem of slavery. Recurrently he took up white assumptions about black inferiority and offered analysis and persuasion that did not depend merely upon anecdote or reminiscence from his own experience. Much of his rhetoric in 1846 showed Douglass seizing effectively on the issues of the day – the Free Church of Scotland's link with the South and the Evangelical Alliance's troubles over slavery. At a few meetings he was pressed by his chairman or the audience to tell them his own story and then did so, but only after he had already dealt with other topics. Overall, on his British tour Douglass extended his intellectual range and moved well beyond personal testimony and victimhood to set his own terms as a spokesman for his people. The project for his return to the United States he announced at his farewell soirée was thus implicitly constructed on what he had achieved in Britain. "I prefer to live a life of activity . . . I go back for the sake of my brethren. I go back to suffer with them, to toil with them, to endure insult with them, to speak for them, to write for them, to struggle in the ranks with them, for that emancipation which is yet to be achieved by the power of truth over the basest selfishness." Logically the soirée was also an occasion for inviting contributions to a fund to set up Douglass's own newspaper.[7]

The kinds of response to Douglass to be found among British abolitionists were usually common to reformers of different religious traditions. Yet Unitarians do seem to have responded discernibly to Douglass's intellectual qualities. Some abolitionists continued to react to him as a remarkable man for an ex-slave and were won over to greater activity on American slavery when they encountered "a person who had himself suffered." He was "a walking, a talking and a personal refutation of all the evil sayings which have been used against his race." He was no mere chattel "formed for herculean labour." More positively, what struck the Unitarian Mary Estlin most strongly was that he exceeded in person anticipations of him derived from his *Narrative,* which she had read largely as an account of oppression. She was impressed by his "intellectual power and culture and eloquence." A report in the *Inquirer* from Cork acknowledged him as a man of "knowledge, power and a sound mind" whose "mental and physical powers are both harmoniously developed." From evidence of his campaigning on the Free Church issue the *Christian Reformer* anticipated a "powerful influence upon the thinking population of the kingdom" while by January 1847 its editor confessed that the power of the *Narrative* had opened his eyes to the true sinfulness of an institution that he had previously believed might be operated "with kindness and humanity." The *Inquirer* gave a report of Douglass's Leeds meeting at the end of 1846 that asserted that "none can look upon him but to feel that he is a man possessed of all the faculties and powers which make men noble."[8]

Unitarians' especial appreciation of Douglass's intellectual distinction arose from their own particular and cherished approach to reform. Late-eighteenth-century Rational Dissenters, main progenitors of nineteenth-century Unitarian reformers, had been devoted to individual pursuit of the truth and rational inquiry to understand the nature of God's order. This led many of them to be critical and active in reform of political and religious establishments that justified themselves by appeals to prescriptive authority rather than through their harmony with the providential order. Educated Unitarian reformers continued this rational and critical spirit and saw Douglass as sharing it in his powerful intellectual and moral dissection of slavery as a sinful distortion of the true moral order.

The intellectual liberalism to which Unitarian abolitionists were attached indicated considerable optimism about the ability of individuals to follow enlightened and civilized ways without the imposition of substantial restrictions. Devising opportunities for self-improvement to achieve self-dependence constituted a continuous thread in Unitarian projects of reform. When, however, they confronted West Indian and American racial slavery, unavoidable questions arose for the most intellectually alert of them, both because of the requirements of internal coherence within their outlook and because of the surrounding cultural discourse on race. Part of that discourse on race was particularly provoking to British antislavery Unitarians since it came from prominent coreligionists in the United States. Most notably was Dr. Orville Dewey, whose 1844 pamphlet *On American Morals and Manners* committed him to the view that there were "impassable physical, if not mental barriers" between the races. There is evidence of rising concern over the intensification of racial prejudice in the 1840s and early 1850s in Britain. Some of the best Unitarian minds, with their belief in open intellectual debate and persuasion, could not but pose these issues and try to deal with them. Were there limits set by racial character to individual improvement and the achievement of civilized self-dependence? How far was it possible to generalize from Frederick Douglass and other prominent individuals to the equality of races? The form these questions took in the minds of abolitionists was, of course, culturally determined and implicitly Eurocentric. But they were particularly acute for Unitarians, given their rather pure philosophy of liberal individualism suffused with the spirit of benevolence, the seemingly fixed category of race with which they had to deal, and their belief in rational investigation.[9]

Thus in the 1840s and early 1850s there was published, or republished, an interesting body of writing on race by antislavery Unitarian intellectuals and close associates. It exhibited a limited range of answers to the questions reformers seem to have posed for themselves but suggests that Douglass was familiar with at least some of the more egalitarian of these writings at the time of his own most intellectually formal treatment of race in these years: his address at Western Reserve College in July 1854.

All of the Unitarian writers seem to have agreed, by implication if not explicitly (in the terms employed by the Leeds minister Charles Wicksteed), that all men possessed a soul and a conscience capable of moving them to religious faith and a sense of duty. All men manifested a "mental and social nature" capable of improvement, and all were influenced by the environment (such as slavery or other forms of social oppression) that denied some of them the improvement of which they were capable.[10]

Such common ground, however, did not indicate general agreement on the equality of races. Dewey's position came in for widespread criticism from British Unitarians, in part because it was a justification for his support of the American Colonization Society, which was in bad odor amongst abolitionists on both sides of the Atlantic. But some reformers, such as John Bowring and the young minister Charles Beard, had doubts about how much improvement was possible among African Americans while confessing the need for more educational opportunities for them. Russell Carpenter, writing of his American stay in 1849 and of his re-acquaintance with Douglass, expressed the same doubt equally conde-scendingly, though slightly differently. Carpenter had met a local black minister in Worcester, Massachusetts, who had known Douglass as a young man. This prompted him to remark: "I felt that it was much eas-ier to feel on terms of equality with such men as Douglass, than with coarser, commonplace specimens of the race. This worthy man went out as waiter or coachman, I believe, to increase his means of living, for which he is of course to be commended."[11]

Unitarian antislavery intellectuals did, however, advance substantial arguments intended to sustain pretty unambiguously, if not completely, equality of the races. The first form they took was that of "moral his-tories," narratives of individuals of African origin or descent whose achievements were used as the basis for racially egalitarian generaliza-tions. This style of argument was by no means unique to Unitarians in the 1840s and 1850s but one may detect in their contributions a charac-teristic stress on civilized and intellectual qualities. This is apparent in two accounts of Toussaint L'Ouverture, both openly written to advance the cause of black freedom: Harriet Martineau's *The Hour and The Man* (1841) and John Relly Beard's *The Life of Toussaint L' Ouverture, The Negro Patriot of Hayti* (1853). Martineau's selective and partly fictionalized nar-rative emphasized Toussaint's capacities as both a political and military leader but denied as hostile charges emanating from European sources that he behaved savagely as a ruler or was hypocritical in religion. On the contrary, she portrayed him as merciful, intent on curbing ferocity in revolutionary warfare, and seeking social and racial reconciliation, which he briefly achieved before being removed through French treachery.

Beard specifically intended to vindicate the capacity of blacks for free-dom through revising recent denigratory accounts of Haiti that he at-tributed to "a mulatto pen." In underlining that Toussaint was "wholly without white blood" Beard also implicitly countered the view that achievements by people of African descent were disproportionately by people of mixed race. In characterizing Toussaint's outlook Beard him-self advanced an argument for the unity of mankind: he suggested that Toussaint "could in no way understand how the hue of the skin should put so great a social and personal distance between men whom God, he saw, had made essentially the same, and whom he knew to be useful if not indispensable to each other."

Neither writer doubted the larger significance of Toussaint's career. While there might only be one Toussaint, "history sets forth many black men who were possessed of great faculties and accomplished great deeds," and the narrative even of Haitian history demonstrated that "in the ordinary powers and virtues which form the texture and ornament of civilized life an African origin and negro blood involve no essential disqualification." Significantly Douglass's name is more than once in these years associated with that of Toussaint.[12]

As Robert Stepto and Eric Sundquist have both argued, Douglass himself also deployed the "moral history" of the heroic African American. He did so briefly in accounts of Madison Washington and his leadership of the revolt of the slaves on the *Creole* in speeches at Cork in October 1845, Paisley in April 1846, and Edinburgh in May 1846; in speeches on his return to the United States; and, above all, in his story based on Washington and the *Creole* revolt, "The Heroic Slave" (1853). Stepto suggests the broadly parallel character of Washington's and Douglass's lives, and perhaps this allows us to see his recurrent interest in Washington as an implicit claim by Douglass for his own inclusion in such "moral histories." As has been indicated, by the 1850s others were beginning to oblige. At the very least, in this form of argument for equality of the races Douglass, Unitarian writers, and a number of other British reformers were at one.[13]

The second kind of egalitarian argument—quasi-scientific and ethnological, but presented as reconcilable with the religious view of the unity of mankind—was more particularly the product of Unitarian intellectual circles. Its main exponents in the 1840s were the physiologist William Benjamin Carpenter, the ophthalmologist John Bishop Estlin and, most authoritatively, the ethnologist James Cowles Prichard. The latter, raised in the Society of Friends but having spent many years doing scientific work in Bristol, became Carpenter's brother-in-law and a friend of Estlin; he was essentially a part of Unitarian intellectual circles in the West of England.

Prichard in his *The Natural History of Man* (1845) made sympathetic acknowledgement of the scriptural notion of the unity of mankind but proposed to stamp the authority of scientific evidence and argument on the question of race. He exploded the "impassable barrier" argument by pointing not only to the existence of mixed-race people but to their prolific character "when the most dissimilar varieties are blended together." From this he concluded "unless there be in the instance of human races an exception of the universally prevalent law of organized nature, that all the tribes of men are of one family." Human variety was to be accounted for not by different species with separate origins but as paralleling well-authenticated diversification within other animal species. Physical variety and change within humankind, including skin color and head shape, "have taken place in nations who have changed their manner of life." In developing such arguments Prichard presented himself as a friend and disciple of the earlier German physiologist Blumenbach, whose scientific authority was quite frequently called upon by racial egalitarians in this period.[14]

Carpenter, whose scientific work brought him a professorship at the Royal Institution and a fellowship of the Royal Society at a comparatively early age, sought to harmonize religious and scientific arguments more closely than Prichard but confessed himself intellectually indebted to him, as did Estlin. In his writings Carpenter passed on Prichard's main scientific arguments but in the *Inquirer* in the summer of 1845 particularly took up the harmonization of religious and scientific views. He presented God as having created both the moral and scientific laws by which the world and human life were governed. The more investigation and understanding of them progressed, the more they would be seen to converge in their implications. Thus the moral and the scientific both demanded acceptance of divine guidance. Yet Carpenter also inserted a principle of active human responsibility; although moral and scientific laws were part of God's plan, human beings experienced themselves as "perfectly free" and thus had to acknowledge accountability for their actions. He considered the implications for relations between the races clear; action to create circumstances in which the black race could attain the equality with the white to which both religious and scientific authority pointed.[15]

Estlin's distinctive contribution to the scientific egalitarian argument was an onslaught on the pretensions of phrenology, with its stress on the characteristic sizes and physical contours of the heads of different races to demonstrate the inferiority of Africans and African Americans. He took a rigorously scientific attitude in criticizing phrenology's lack of concern with anatomy and its hasty claims based on observation of far too few human beings over far too short a time.[16] He was essentially concerned to refute a species of biological determinism by undermining the scientific credibility of its procedures while leaving room intellectually for the possibilities of physical change of the kind that Prichard had advanced.

On the second type of argument for racial equality the parallels between Douglass and the Unitarian intellectuals were stricter than with the "moral histories." As Douglass revealed in a number of his British speeches, he shared the common conviction that environment had held African Americans back, and initially this was the ground of his criticism of Dewey. Equally he was sure that opportunity for enlightenment would mark the path to equality. But it was in his address at Western Reserve College during commencement week in July 1854 that he demonstrated the most familiarity with both the Unitarian intellectuals' general perspective and their scientific and ethnological arguments as well as with their attempts to harmonize religious and scientific positions. Like Carpenter he made plain that the positions intellectuals adopted in this "moral battlefield" had to be committed to a just solution to the race question within the context of freedom of thought. Men, including African Americans, possessed "certain definite faculties and powers" distinguishing them from the lower animals. These were evident both in physical and mental organization but also in moral and emotional characteristics. Douglass followed this general argument for the unity of mankind by explicit use of Prichard and reference to Blumenbach, both of whose views on human unity and physical change in adaptation to environment he considered harmonized with contemporary developments in seeing the world as an integrated whole. The argument of the American School of ethnologists—Nott, Gliddon, and Morton—for separate race origins was not merely "scientifical moonshine" but anachronistic. Both they and the phrenologists lacked a proper scientific approach. In Douglass's words, it is somewhat remarkable that, at a time when knowledge is so generally diffused, when the geography of the world is so well understood—when time and space, in the intercourse of nations, are almost annihilated—when oceans have become bridges—the earth a magnificent ball—the hollow sky a dome—under which a common humanity can meet in friendly conclave—when nationalities are being swallowed up—and the ends of the earth are being brought together—I say it is remarkable—nay, it is strange that there should arise a phalanx of learned men—speaking in the name of science—to forbid the magnificent reunion of mankind in one brotherhood. A mortifying proof is here given, that the moral growth of a nation, or an age, does not always keep pace with the increase of knowledge, and suggests the necessity of means to increase human love with human learning.[17]

The parallels are clear; at least in the debate on race, Douglass and antislavery Unitarian intellectuals shared a mental world. But the point is not to argue that Douglass took his arguments from the Unitarians. He had no need of Carpenter or anyone else to tell him there was a religious justification for racial equality; he knew that in producing his brilliant denunciation of "false religion" in the appendix to his *Narrative*. He had some independent knowledge of the "moral histories" of people of African descent. He *did* rely on British scientific and ethnological writings in 1854, but he discussed the issues with president M. B. Anderson and ethnologist Henry Wayland of the newly established University of Rochester while reading the material they suggested to him as helpful preparation for his lecture. Little American work was available to refute the pro-Southern American School. Thus it was Douglass who brought in the Old World to redress the balance of the New. Yet, quite as important as the source of the arguments, is the fact that it was Douglass who combined them and conducted himself as an intellectual on the same level as any potential opponent on the occasion of the formal academic ritual of commencement week at a leading western college of the day. In doing so, he achieved in the United States, at least symbolically, the kind of intellectual recognition for himself and the egalitarian argument to which he had aspired, and had achieved in the eyes of Unitarian abolitionists, on his British tour seven years earlier.[18]

Yet Douglass's sense of his own role in the United States, his primary political function, pointed to a significant element of divergence in the understanding of race between Douglass and some positions implied in Unitarian writing. The differences arose from ambiguities in some Unitarian discussions of racial equality. The ambiguities expressed a tension between a typical Unitarian focus on the individual and the notion of race as a fixed category so that members of a particular racial group were deemed to have settled characteristics. One example, juxtaposing Beard and Douglass, will illustrate this. Despite his belief in the possibility of racial equality Beard's book on Toussaint exhibited some intellectual confusion. He seemed clear that the proper terms for equality were those of white European civilization and that Toussaint had demonstrated the possibility that blacks could reach that level. But in his determination to defend *black* achievements against claims of mulatto superiority, and aware of the low esteem in which Haitian civilization was held by most outside observers in the mid-nineteenth century, he also revealed hints of a relativist approach. He admitted that Haitians might have different concerns from members of European societies, with the implication that they should therefore be judged by different criteria. His desire to revise mulatto claims about black capacities did, at moments, push him towards recognizing that skin color could not be a fixed marker of race and that meanings were constructed around color, but he was not intellectually consistent about it. At the same time he attributed stereotyped, if largely favorable, characteristics to Africans and their descendants – dancing ability, strong family affections, emotionalism – that he clearly thought of as racial.[19]

Douglass, by contrast, had a somewhat more consistent sense that aspects of the idea of race were socially and culturally constructed. The 1854 lecture located the diversity of races on physical and historical bases within the fundamental unity of mankind. However, he argued that supposedly "natural" attributes of races were often the product of particular social arrangements and varied with circumstances, a conclusion he tried to illustrate by linking his own experience of being called "nigger" by children in New England with an incident from the career of the explorer Mungo Park, who was termed a "devil" by Africans because of his appearance. It followed that if different racial characteristics used to justify oppression were partly constructed, then, with effort, they could be deconstructed. On occasion, Douglass argued, they had been, as when segregated facilities were eliminated on several Massachusetts railroads and the law against intermarriage had been repealed in the same state. Douglass's ideas about race thus reflected the results of activism and justified his continuing role at the center of the struggle to end slavery and bring legal and political equality to the United States. He was the supreme activist-intellectual for whom ideas had to be true and weapon-sharp.[20]

NOTES

1. Alan D. Gilbert, *Religion and Society in Industrial England: Church, Chapel and Social Change, 1740–1914* (London: Longman, 1976), 40–41.

2. David Turley, *The Culture of English Antislavery, 1780–1860* (London: Routledge, 1991), 10–11, 202–3.

3. Ibid., 95, 203; Douglas Charles Stange, *British Unitarians against American Slavery, 1833–1865* (Toronto: University of Toronto Press, 1984), 13, 56–57, 61–63. Stange's work has provided a number of valuable leads without which this essay would have been much impoverished.

4. John W. Blassingame, ed., *The Frederick Douglass Papers. Series One: Speeches, Debates, and Interviews,* 5 vols. (New Haven, Yale University Press, 1979–), 1:29, 34, 342, 353, 372, 475; W. L. Garrison to R. D. Webb, 5 September 1846, in Walter M. Merrill, ed., *The Letters of William Lloyd Garrison,* 6 vols. (Cambridge, Mass.: Belknap Press of Harvard University Press, 1971–81), 3:397.

5. Garrison to Edmund Quincy, 14 August 1846; Garrison to Helen E. Garrison, 18 August 1846; Garrison to Henry C. Wright, 26 August 1846; Garrison to Quincy, 29 August 1846; Garrison to J. B. Estlin, 8 Sept. 1846; Garrison to Webb, 12 September 1846; Garrison to Samuel J. May, 19 December 1846 in Merrill, *Letters,* 3:371–72, 377–79, 387–89, 391, 400–401, 409–10, 462–63; Stange, *British Unitarians,* 146–50; Frances Armstrong to Garrison in Clare Taylor, ed., *British and American Abolitionists: An Episode in Transatlantic Understanding* (Edinburgh: Edinburgh University Press, 1974), 284.

6. *Report of Proceedings at the Soiree given to Frederick Douglass, London Tavern, March 30, 1847* (London, 1847), 28–29, 22; Frederick Douglass to Maria Weston Chapman, 29 March 1846; Webb to Chapman, 16 November 1845; Douglass to Webb, 10 November 1845; Catherine Clarkson to Estlin, 19 May and 2 June 1846; Estlin to May, 1 October 1846; Douglass to Chapman, 18 August 1846 in Taylor, *British and American Abolitionists,* 258–59, 243, 241, 262–64, 290–91, 277; *Correspondence between the Rev. Samuel H. Cox, D. D. of Brooklyn, L. I. and Frederick Douglass a fugitive slave* (New York, 1846), 10–11.

7. Meeting at Coventry, 2 February 1847, in Blassingame, *Papers,* 2:5; 1:vii–x; 1:7; 2:52 55; *Soiree,* 29–30ff.

8. Isabel Jennings to Maria Weston Chapman [autumn, 1845]; Maria Webb to secre-

tary of Massachusetts Female Anti-Slavery Society, 17 June 1846; Sarah Hilditch to Chapman, 31 October 1846, Mary Estlin to Chapman, [?] September 1846 in Taylor, *British and American Abolitionists,* 243–44, 270, 282; *Soiree,* 14; *Inquirer* (London), 15 November 1845; *Christian Reformer* (London), 23 November 1846, pp. 650–51, 25 January 1847, p. 31; *Inquirer,* 2 January 1847.

9. Turley, *The Culture of English Antislavery,* 20–21, 113–15; Blassingame, *Papers,* 1:66 n. 16; Russell Lant Carpenter, *A Fast Day Sermon preached in Christ Church Chapel, Bridgwater* (London, 1847), preface; Stange, *British Unitarians,* 171.

10. Charles Wicksteed, *The Englishman's Duty to the Free and Enslaved American* (London and Leeds, 1853), 4–5; *Inquirer,* 19 July 1845.

11. *Christian Reformer,* 4 April 1845, p. 213, 22 October 1846, pp. 597–98; Russell Lant Carpenter, *Observations on American Slavery after a Year's Tour in the United States* (London, 1852), 58, 59–60.

12. Harriet Martineau, *The Hour and The Man* (1841; reprint, London, 1904), 344–47; John R. Beard, *The Life of Toussaint L' Ouverture, The Negro Patriot of Hayti* (London, 1853), v–vi, 23–25, 29–36, 278–80. For an example of the fear of pro-slavery use of the "mixed race" argument, see Catherine Clarkson to Maria Weston Chapman, 2 August 1846 (in relation to Douglass), in Taylor, *British and American Abolitionists,* 275; Blassingame, *Papers,* 1:26 (N. P. Rogers on Douglass and Toussaint); Henry G. Adams, ed., *God's Image in Ebony* (London, 1854).

13. Eric J. Sundquist, "Introduction," in *Frederick Douglass: New Literary and Historical Essays,* ed. Eric J. Sundquist (Cambridge: Cambridge University Press, 1990), 11–12; Frederick Douglass, "The Heroic Slave," in *Autographs for Freedom,* ed. Julia W. Griffiths (London, 1853); Adams, *God's Image;* Wilson Armistead, *A Tribute for the Negro* (London, 1848), for recurrent mentions of Douglass.

14. James Cowles Prichard, *The Natural of Man,* 2d ed. (London, 1845), 5–8, 26, 76–95, 108.

15. *Inquirer,* 19 July 1845.

16. *Christian Reformer,* 22 October 1846, p. 599.

17. Blassingame, *Papers,* 1:97–98, 98–99, 345–46, 2:52–55; 499–525 (Western Reserve College), esp. 503–504.

18. Ibid., 2:498–99.

19. Beard, *Life of Toussaint L'Ouverture,* 138, 233–34.

20. Speech in Boston, 31 May 1849, in Blassingame, *Papers,* 2:212–14.

PART THREE

Douglass and Gender

Frederick Douglass and the
Gender Politics of Reform

CYNTHIA S. HAMILTON

FREDERICK DOUGLASS DECLARED HIMSELF A "WOMAN'S rights man." Nonetheless, he gave very slight attention to the subject of woman's rights in any of his three autobiographies. He also failed, in his autobiographies, to chronicle his involvement in the campaign to secure women's property and voting rights. One would have expected, at the very least, that his role at the Seneca Falls Convention (1848) warranted discussion, but that convention does not receive a mention. His strangely defensive contention in the *Life and Times* that he is glad to say that he has "never been ashamed" to be designated a woman's rights man is also puzzling.[1] When one adds to such paradoxical indicators the transformations in the depiction of particular women in Douglass's first two autobiographies, one is left with much food for thought, especially as the process of transformation is not uniform, leaving some women frozen in the postures in which Douglass had first drawn them. What, then, is Douglass playing at, or, more to the point, what is Douglass playing with?

Douglass's depiction of women can be seen as a necessary correlative of his evolving presentation of himself. When Douglass published his second autobiography in 1855 after his triumphal tour of the British Isles (1845–47) and the launch of the *North Star* (1847), his self-image was much more that of a bourgeois gentleman than that of a runaway slave, and by the time Douglass revised the final account of his life in 1892, he could legitimately condescend to provide his public with the reminiscences of an elder statesman. The social positions to which Douglass progressively lays claim require his female adjuncts to take on changing roles defined both by the domestic ideology of the period and by a gender politics of reform heavily reliant on an ethos of sentimentality. Douglass has not merely written three autobiographies, he has written them within three distinct autobiographical traditions, each with its own conventions of character. As Douglass switches from slave narrative to exemplary autobiography in *My Bondage and My Freedom* and finally to memoir in the *Life and Times,* he must supply himself with foils appropriate to his changing self-image. This essay concentrates on the first such transformation, from slave narrative to exemplary autobiography.

The slave narrative of the antebellum period was, as both William L. Andrews and John Sekora have noted, fraught with tension as the black voice sang variations on a tune given structural shape by white abolitionists.[2] These slave narratives articulate the slave's desire for freedom and celebrate his courage and resourcefulness in achieving self-liberation. But the polemical agenda of the slave narrative required a demonstration of victimization sufficient to document the abuses of slavery and to discredit Southern claims that slavery was an essentially benevolent institution that civilized, Christianized, and looked after its wards. To this end, the slave narratives sought to shock and offend the sensibilities of their audience, sensibilities shaped by the domestic ideology.

The slave's victimization was therefore conceived in terms of domestic ideology. For the male, the debilitating effects of slavery were defined in terms of the attenuation or nullification of traits identified as masculine: aggression, ambition, daring, industry, rationality, and practicality. In *The Narrative of Lunsford Lane* (1842), Lane explains that as a slave he had felt it necessary to present himself in a guise acceptable to the whites who held him in their power. Despite his business acumen, he was careful to conceal both his intellectual powers and his material accumulations.[3] In addition to such deprecations, the male slave's inability to fulfil his patriarchal duties, to protect and provide for those under his care, was seen as further evidence of his degraded condition. "If a man have a wife in the same field with himself," Moses Grandy explains in his *Narrative* of

1844, "he chooses a row by the side of hers, that, with extreme labor, he may, if possible, help her. But he will not be in the same field if he can help it; for, with his hardest labor, he often cannot save her from being flogged, and he is obliged to stand by and see it, he is always liable to see her taken home at night, stripped naked, and whipped before all the men."[4] The female slave was also depicted in terms of the domestic ideology. The violation of her chastity, the offences to her modesty, the defilement of her spiritual and moral powers, and the usurpation of her role as nurturer were all seen as evidence of the corrupting power of slavery. In *A Narrative of the Adventures and Escape of Moses Roper* (1837), Roper, who had been separated from his mother at the age of five or six, runs away and searches for her. They are reunited after a long separation, and Roper's narration of the scene is used to comment on the human costs of slavery: "At last, I got to my mother's house!! my mother was at home, I asked her, if she knew me? she said no."[5] Roper's mother mistakes her son for one of the workmen digging a well. He tells her that he knows her well and suggests that she look at him more closely. This has no effect, and he has to work to convince his mother that he is truly her son. In the slave narratives published after Douglass's *Narrative,* the gendered images of victimization would become even more striking.

The importance and pervasiveness of the domestic ideology even within the Garrisonian faction of the antislavery movement, a faction committed to the struggle for women's rights, can be seen in the pages of *The Liberator,* particularly during the 1830s when Garrison appears to have needed extra material to fill his column inches. In an article on "How to Choose a Good Husband," *The Liberator* counselled: "When you see a young man who is attentive and kind to his sisters, or aged mother . . . and who will attend to all her wants with filial love, affection and tenderness, take him girls, if you can get him."[6] To make a good husband, a man should be of "frugal, industrious habits," and should use "his best endeavors to raise himself from obscurity to credit." *The Liberator* also printed "Maxims for Husbands and Wives" informing husbands of their duty to keep their wives "properly supplied with money for furnishing his table in a style proportioned to his means, and for the purchase of dress suitable to her station in life."[7] The good wife, the reader is told, complies "in everything reasonable" with her husband's wishes and "as far as possible, anticipates them," a domestic angel as florid as that depicted in "The Ladies," published in *The Liberator* of 31 March 1837:

> A good wife will soften the asperity of thy temper, and smooth the brow, clouded with sadness. She will kindly watch over thy bed of sickness, and whisper in softest accents the language of consolation to thy drooping heart. She will form thy mind to generous exertions, and make thee nobly emulous of greatness; and when the last faint flashes of life's expiring lamp have quivered out their little moment, her tears will moisten the clay-cold form; and her prayers, ascending for thy final happiness, will gently waft the disembodied spirit to the garden of the paradise of God.[8]

This image of domesticity is used in a rhetoric of victimization to give power to abolitionist writings. "Those for whose emancipation we are striving," states the "Declaration of Sentiments" (1833) of the American Anti-Slavery Society, "are plundered daily of the fruits of their toil without redress; really enjoy no constitutional nor legal protection from licentious and murderous outrages upon their persons; are ruthlessly torn asunder—the tender babe from the arms of its frantic mother—the heartbroken wife from her weeping husband—at the caprice or pleasure of irresponsible tyrants."[9] Domestic deprivation is articulated with particular clarity in the first two stanzas of "Blood Upon the South," a hymn included in *Freedom's Lyre* (1840), a compilation for the American Anti-Slavery Society by Edwin Hatfield:

> Unshelter'd from the burning rays,
> The panting bondman lies,
> Toil and the scourge cut short his days,
> He sinks—he faints—he dies!
>
> No Wife's—no Mother's hand is there,
> To close his failing eyes;
> Unsooth'd by Friendship's tender care,
> The wretched bondman dies![10]

Although these stanzas focus on the man deprived of his domestic comforts, they also imply the wife's and mother's loss. A reversal of this situation is more usual, however, for within the gender politics of reform, the shame of the abused female is shared by her protector. "I have seen women, with their frantic children surrounding them," Douglass told his audience in Sheffield on 11 September 1846, "tied to a post and lashed by an overseer until their blood covered their garments. The children were screaming for the release of their mother, while the husband was standing by with his hands tied, and after his wife was castigated, he received the same punishment." [11]

Douglass used his cousin Henny to supply the role of the female victim in his antislavery speeches, echoing Garrisonian abolitionist rhetoric. "I have seen this pious class leader cross and tie the hands of one of his young female slaves, and lash her on the bare skin and justify the deed by the quotation from the Bible," Douglass said in his speech at Lynn, Massachusetts, in October 1841. [12] Holding up a blood-stained whip for his listeners in Limerick in his speech of 10 November 1845, he again invoked the whipping of his cousin. [13] The image is again used in his speech in Sheffield on 11 September 1846. [14] In his speech at Leeds on 23 December 1846, Douglass recounts the same incident, though here Henny is referred to as his sister. [15] In Rochester, New York, on 13 March 1848, the incident is mentioned again, but here Douglass does not claim the victim as a relative. [16] Such images stand behind the evocative epithets of abolitionist rhetoric that Douglass and the Garrisonian abolitionists used for slave owners: they were "man stealing, cradle robbing, woman beating," or "Slave holding, woman-stripping, cradle plundering Americans." [17]

In Douglass's speeches, as in his autobiographies, we see a progressive distancing of himself from his experiences as a slave, a distance that allows him to manipulate the "material" provided by his experiences during slavery more effectively. In his early speeches he refers graphically to his own abuse as a slave. In a very early speech in Lynn, Massachusetts, Douglass praises the knowledge that the abolitionists have of slavery but comments, "though they can depict its horrors, they cannot speak as I can from experience; they cannot refer you to a back covered with scars, as I can; for I have felt those wounds; I have suffered under the lash without the power of resisting. Yes, my blood has sprung out as the lash embedded itself in my flesh." [18] But Douglass shifts the burden of his argument very early in his lecturing career from the cruelties he has experienced to the cruelties he has witnessed. In this transition, the whipping of his cousin Henny plays an important role, for by foregrounding Henny's mistreatment rather than his own, Douglass is able to protect his own masculinity from the depredations of acknowledged helplessness while using the specter of the abused female to raise an outcry against the abuses of slavery.

The significance of the suffering female in the domestic ideology was augmented by her significance in the sentimental ethos of the antebellum period. With its roots in the Scottish Common Sense philosophy of David Hume and Adam Smith, the sentimental ethos assumes that empathy provides the stimulus for moral action and that literature as well as life can engage sympathy and prompt action.[19] Sentimental appeals asked an audience to consider particular groups as objects for sentimental regard. "Is slavery, as a condition for human beings, good, bad, or indifferent?" Theodore Weld asks in the introduction to *American Slavery As It Is* (1839): "You have common sense, a conscience, and a human heart;–pronounce upon it. You have a wife, or a husband, a child, a father, a mother, a brother or a sister–make the case your own, make it theirs, and bring in your verdict."[20] The audience so addressed was asked to display a sentimental regard for the suffering brought before them. The helpless victim excited solicitude and allowed the audience to validate their sentimental regard by displaying the expected conventional responses in keeping with their roles in the domestic ideology. Because of her acknowledged weakness and vulnerability, the suffering female–provided that her modesty was under threat and that her chastity had not been violated–invited both male chivalry and sisterly compassion. The appeal of the suffering male was more problematic, for insofar as he was seen as responsible for his own protection, his victimization involved a diminution of his masculinity.

The problematic nature of images of male victimization can be seen in the work of white abolitionists, where the male slave's emasculation prompts a corresponding aggrandizement of the abolitionist, whose active agency on the part of the immobilized slave takes on heroic proportions. William Lloyd Garrison's poem "The Triumph of Freedom," published in *The Liberator* on 10 January 1845, provides a compact example. In the first stanza we see the slave's degraded masculinity:

God speed the year of jubilee,
The wide world o'er!
When from their galling chains set free,
Th' oppressed shall vilely bend the knee,
And wear the yoke of tyranny,
Like brutes, no more:–
That year will come, and Freedom's reign
To man his plundered rights again
Restore.[21]

With the slave in chains, Garrison takes on the role of heroic liberator:

Until that year, day, hour arrive,–
If life be given,–
With head and heart and hand I'll strive
To break the rod, and rend the gyve,
The spoiler of his prey deprive,–
So witness heaven!
And never from my chosen post,
Whate'er the peril or the cost,
Be driven.

Although such extreme portrayals of black immobilization and white heroism are the stuff of white abolitionist writing, in slave narratives, one finds hints of such role-playing primarily in the prefaces of the white abolitionists, not in the slave's narratives, where the subject's self-expression and efforts toward self-liberation deny such immobility. Typically, in the slave narrative, images of personal victimization are associated with the slave's youth or with his acts of rebellion. This, together with the strategy of including episodes of extreme cruelty that have been witnessed rather than experienced, allows the ex-slave to provide evidence of victimization without compromising his masculine integrity.

If Frederick Douglass's *Narrative* is read within the gendered rhetoric of abolition, his description of his lost mother resonates with the abolitionist rhetoric of domestic deprivation: "I never saw my mother, to know her as such, more than four or five times in my life; and each of these times was very short in duration, and at night."[22] By evoking the lost mother of his childhood, Douglass can gain sympathetic regard for his deprivation without losing masculine integrity. Douglass's description of his grandmother's fate provides another image of domestic deprivation. Left in the hands of strangers despite her long and faithful service to her master's family, she is turned out to die, "her frame already racked with the pains of old age, and complete helplessness fast stealing over her once active limbs."[23] Here, Douglass's indignation invites emulation; his grandmother becomes an object of sentimental regard and is used to critique the "peculiar institution" that has deprived her of the rewards of her nurturing domesticity.

Douglass's presentation of his grandmother's plight is remarkably similar to Moses Grandy's description of his mother's declining years:

> When my mother became old, she was sent to live in a little lonely log-hut in the woods. Aged and worn-out slaves, whether men or women, are commonly so treated. No care is taken of them, except, perhaps, that a little ground is cleared about the hut, on which the old slave, if able, may raise a little corn. As far as the owner is concerned, they live or die, as it happens: it is just the same thing as turning out an old horse. Their children, or other near relations, if living in the neighborhood, take it by turns to go at night with a supply saved out of their own scanty allowance of food, as well as to cut wood and fetch water for them: this is done entirely through the good feelings of the slaves, and not through the masters' taking care that it is done. On these night-visits, the aged inmate of the hut is often found crying on account of sufferings from disease or extreme weakness, or from want of food or water in the course of the day: many a time, when I have drawn near to my mother's hut, I have heard her grieving and crying on these accounts: she was old and blind too, and so unable to help herself. She was not treated worse than others: it is the general practice. Some few good masters do not treat their old slaves so: they employ them in doing light jobs about the house and garden.[24]

Although Grandy's narrative had been published in London in 1843, it was issued in 1844 by the Massachusetts Anti-Slavery Society, the same office that first issued Douglass's *Narrative*. Thompson, a close associate of Garrison and a leading figure in the British campaign for abolition, had written the introduction for Grandy's narrative. The suspicion that Grandy's description of his mother's old age affected Douglass's account of his grandmother's declining years is fuelled by the fact that

Douglass did not have concrete knowledge of his grandmother's fate at the time he wrote his *Narrative.*

Both Douglass and Grandy may well have been consciously working to discredit the sentimental scenes of homely comfort and mutual regard employed by Southern writers in their plantation novels. The visit to the slave quarters to see an aging retainer is a recurring feature of the plantation novel. Typically, the elderly slave has been allowed to retire in relative comfort, with time to relish his or her memories of more active days. The warm bonds of affection and gratitude that exist between the master's family and the old slave are emphasized. George Tucker's *The Valley of the Shenandoah* (1824) gives a typically reassuring picture. Edward and a friend from New York pay a visit to Granny Mott in her humble but well-maintained log cabin, with its earth floor "made hard by long use, and clean by sweeping, which a tidy mulatto girl of fourteen, her granddaughter, regularly performed every morning." The appearance of the old woman measures the care and compassion with which she is treated as she sits by the door winding cotton thread, "dressed in a yellow and white striped homespun wrapper, and petticoat," with "a cap tied under her chin that partly discovered her grisly locks, and round her neck a handkerchief, which (as well as the cap,) from its whiteness and fineness, had probably once the honor of belonging to some more dignified member of the family." When Edward appears, she turns to face him and says, "God bless my young master—how has he been this long time? I thought you would come to see Granny. . . . And how did you leave them all at Williamsburg?"[25] Granny Mott goes on to question Edward about various family members. Both the master's kindness in visiting his elderly slave and the tenor of his conversation with Granny Mott, which recognizes deep bonds, work to portray slavery as benign paternalism.

Douglass invokes such scenes when he describes the shameful treatment of his own grandmother, who "had served my old master faithfully from youth to old age." Where Tucker portrays Granny Mott as "servant," Douglass is careful to point out his grandmother's property value: "She had been the source of all his wealth; she had peopled his plantation with slaves; she had become a great grandmother in his service." Where Tucker dwells on the bonds of sentiment, Douglass points out the master's failure to acknowledge, let alone meet, the obligations such bonds imply: "She had rocked him in infancy, attended him in childhood, served him through life, and at his death wiped from his icy brow the cold death-sweat, and closed his eyes forever," says Douglass, as he measures the debt of obligation. "She was nevertheless left a slave—a slave for life," he tells us, and adds "a slave in the hands of strangers; and in their hands she saw her children, her grandchildren, and her great-grandchildren, divided, like so many sheep, without being gratified with the small privilege of a single word, as to their or her own destiny."[26] Where Tucker depicts an idyllic "retirement," Douglass speaks of the slaveholder's "base ingratitude and fiendish barbarity" in renouncing responsibility for his grandmother in her helpless old age; "they took her to the woods, built her a little hut, put up a little mud chimney, and then made her welcome to the privilege of supporting herself there in perfect loneliness; thus virtually turning her out to die!"[27] The contrasts between Tucker's portrayal and Douglass's can be seen almost point by point. What is equally striking is the extent to which both Douglass's *Narrative* and Tucker's novel employ sentimental appeals based on domestic ideology. "The hearth is desolate," Douglass says of his grandmother's cottage, "the children, the unconscious children, who once sang and danced in her presence, are gone. She gropes her way, in the darkness of age, for a drink of water. Instead of the voices of her children, she hears by day the moans of the dove, and by night the screams of the hideous owl. All is gloom. The grave is at the door."[28] Douglass depicts his grandmother as the ultimate victim of domestic deprivation. "Will not a righteous God visit for these things," Douglass asks.[29]

It is not insignificant that by the time he wrote *My Bondage and My Freedom,* Douglass sought to distance himself from such deprivation by quoting from his earlier *Narrative* rather than claiming direct, contemporary ownership of the scene described. "Ten years ago, while speaking of the state of things in our family, after the events just named, I used this language," Douglass explains before describing his grandmother's fate.[30] Later still, Douglass would be forced to admit that he had based his sentimental portrayal on conjecture rather than on personal knowledge. In the *Life and Times,* during a scene of reconciliation with his old master, Captain Auld, Douglass admits that he "had made a mistake in my narrative . . . in attributing to him ungrateful and cruel treatment of my grandmother." Douglass's grandmother had not, in fact, been Captain Auld's property; but she had been purchased by him after reading Douglass's *Narrative* in order to care for her during her declining years. In the *Life and Times,* Douglass brings the episode to a close by commenting that "I had at no time any wish to do him injustice – that I regarded both of us as victims of a system."[31] By the time Douglass wrote these words, slavery had been abolished, and Douglass could relish the hospitality of his former master, giving due acknowledgement to the civilities expected of a gentleman in such a situation.

In Douglass's *Narrative,* Henny and Esther document brutality of another kind. Henny, the cousin whose abused body would take on representative significance in Douglass's antislavery lectures, is described in virtually the same language in his *Narrative,* where her later symbolic significance is belied by her relatively insignificant role in Douglass's personal history. More significant in this regard is his witnessing, as a young boy, of the whipping of his aunt Hester. This Douglass calls "the blood-stained gate, the entrance to the hell of slavery, through which I was about to pass."[32] Douglass follows his emotive introduction with a starkly objective description of the whipping itself. Observed as a series of movements, the reader is forced to follow the progress of the whipping step by deliberate step:

> Before he commenced whipping Aunt Hester, he took her into the kitchen, and stripped her from neck to waist, leaving her neck, shoulders, and back entirely naked. He then told her to cross her hands, calling her at the same time a d---d b---h. After crossing her hands, he tied them with a strong rope, and led her to a stool under a large hook in the joist, put in for the purpose. He made her get upon the stool, and tied her hands to the hook. She now stood fair for his infernal purpose. Her arms were stretched up at their full length, so that she stood upon the ends of her toes. He then said to her, "Now, you d---d b---h, I'll learn you how to disobey my orders!" and after rolling up his sleeves, he commenced to lay on the heavy cowskin . . .[33]

Douglass only provides one interpretative comment in the whole passage. For the rest, the reader must digest unaided young Douglass's reconstructed vision. It is for the reader, as for Douglass, an initiation into the hell of slavery.

Jenny Franchot's assessment of this scene's significance is compelling, but her assessment does not explain the transformation the scene undergoes in *My Bondage and My Freedom*.[34] No longer depicted – through the eyes of a naive observer – as Douglass's traumatic initiation into the meaning of slavery, in Douglass's second autobiography Esther's whipping prompts deliberation and questioning. In Douglass's extended commentary, Esther becomes representative.[35] Like Henny, she is converted into symbolic coinage for antislavery propaganda.

Douglass's depiction of the victimization of women, like his treatment of domestic deprivation, finds a precedent in Moses Grandy's *Narrative,* where brutality is transformed into spectacle:

> I have seen the overseer beat them with raw hide, so that blood and milk flew mingled from their breasts. A woman who gives offence in the field, and is large in the family way, is compelled to lie down over a hole made to receive her corpulency, and is flogged with the whip, or beat with a paddle, which has holes in it; at every hole comes a blister. One of my sisters was so severely punished in this way, that labor was brought on, and the child was born in the field. This very overseer, Mr. Brooks, killed in this manner a girl named Mary; her father and mother were in the field at the time.[36]

Such spectacles of victimization were effective indictments of the barbarity of slavery, but they did so by shocking an audience through the display and mistreatment of the naked female body. Display alone, particularly when presented through a male gaze, would render such images shocking to an audience for whom such display was a violation of female chastity and sanctity as defined by the domestic ideal. Mistreatment was a further violation of accepted notions of propriety. Indeed, in her article on "Wife Beating: The Darker Side of Victorian Domesticity," Myra C. Glenn asks why, with the "outcry against corporal punishment, especially when inflicted on women . . . did the problem of wife-beating receive little public attention in the antebellum United States?"[37] While part of her argument implicates a failure to agree on a working definition of culpable domestic violence, a more interesting strand of her argument, for the purposes of this essay, looks at the ideology of domesticity itself. Ultimately, Glenn argues, the writers of popular manuals on marriage and the family chose to ignore the problem of domestic violence because exposure threatened to undermine the basic assumptions of the cult of domesticity:

> By its very nature the problem of wife-beating threatened to explode the myths cultivated by the canon of domesticity. It dramatically contradicted this cult's cherished idealized views of marriage and the family. Violent husbands and their suffering wives were a far cry from the loving, gentle and happy spouses depicted in popular domestic works. Instead of strengthening this idyllic image of domesticity, wife-beating graphically illustrated how an allegedly sacred, natural and benevolent bond – that between husband and wife – could degenerate into a blatantly cruel power relationship.[38]

The fears that enforced this conspiracy of silence lent added power to the trope of the suffering female in the slave narrative, where such display was more acceptable because forces external to the home itself could be implicated in the destruction.

Douglass's appropriation of the trope of the suffering female for his presentation of Aunt Hester, later Aunt Esther, is explicable, even predictable, within the gender politics of abolitionist rhetoric, but the transformations of his mother and grandmother in *My Bondage and My Freedom* are not so easily accounted for. The grandmother held up as a symbol of base ingratitude and neglect in the *Narrative* becomes in *My Bondage and My Freedom* a figure of some prestige in the community, her isolated cabin transformed into a symbol of privilege during Douglass's stay with her:

> My grandmother – whether because too old for field service, or because she had so faithfully discharged the duties of her station in early life, I know not – enjoyed the high privilege of living in a cabin separate from the quarter, with no other burden than her own support, and the necessary care of the little children, imposed. She evidently esteemed it a great fortune to live so. The children were not her own, but her grandchildren – the children of her daughters. She took delight in having them around her, and in attending to their few wants.[39]

In *My Bondage and My Freedom*, Douglass enjoys an early childhood nurtured by his grandmother's care and surrounded by the relative plenty that her privileged position in the community conferred. "This high reputation was full of advantage to her, and to the children around her,"

Douglass recalls. "Though Tuckahoe had but few of the good things of life, yet of such as it did possess grandmother got a full share in the way of presents."[40] Through this thorough reconstruction of his grandmother, Douglass created for himself a family more in line with his aspirations. It is little wonder, therefore, that Douglass felt the need to distance himself from his earlier accounts of his grandmother's victimization.

The transformation of Douglass's mother is equally striking. Although she remains a tragic figure, lost to her children in *My Bondage and My Freedom,* Douglass conjures up a heroic portrait for this woman of whom he had claimed to know so little that he "received the tidings of her death with much the same emotions I should have probably felt at the death of a stranger."[41] Later portraits of his mother claim for her the striking visage of a pharaoh, an image borrowed from page 157 of Prichard's *Natural History of Man.*[42] In *My Bondage and My Freedom,* Douglass's mother also becomes something of a savior who appears in young Frederick's hour of need bearing comfort for him, reproof for his tormentor, and a tasty sweet cake as compensation for ill usage "in the shape of a heart, with a rich, dark ring glazed upon the edge of it."[43] She is also credited with the ability to read and was, according to Douglass, "the *only* one of all the slaves and colored people in Tuckahoe who enjoyed that advantage."[44] It is to her that Douglass attributes "any love of letters I possess . . . *not* to my admitted Anglo-Saxon paternity."[45] In *My Bondage and My Freedom,* Douglass's mother becomes an object of sentimental regard. Writing with the deathbed scene of many a sentimental novel no doubt in mind, including *Uncle Tom's Cabin,* Douglass comments on his mother's deprivation:

> The mother, at the verge of the grave, may not gather her children, to impart to them her holy admonitions, and invoke for them her dying benediction. The bondwoman lives as a slave, and is left to die as a beast; often with fewer attentions than are paid to a favorite horse. Scenes of sacred tenderness, around the deathbed, never forgotten, and which often arrest the vicious and confirm the virtuous during life, must be looked for among the free, though they sometimes occur among the slaves.[46]

Nonetheless, Douglass seeks to minimize the impact of this deprivation on himself. While he concedes that it has "been a life-long, standing grief to me, that I knew so little of my mother," he claims that "the side view of her face is imaged on my memory, and I take few steps in life, without feeling her presence." Nonetheless, "the image is mute, and I have no striking words of hers treasured up," Douglass admits.[47]

Such transformations should alert us to Douglass's changing agenda and to his willingness to cut his life and the lives of those around him to fit new generic templates. In *My Bondage and My Freedom,* the new template is that of exemplary autobiography. In using this tradition, Douglass was doing for himself what Mason L. Weems had done for Franklin and Washington.[48] Douglass's letter to his publisher, included in the preface, hints at this shift to exemplary autobiography, for it discounts the relevance of his personal experience of slavery to the antislavery position he has adopted after mature reflection. "In my letters and speeches, I have generally aimed to discuss the question of Slavery in the light of fundamental principles, and upon facts, notorious and open to all; making, I trust, no more of the fact of my own former enslavement, than circumstances seemed absolutely to require," he says.[49] Douglass's stated first intention, to expose slavery "by letting the light of truth in upon [the] system," seems unlikely to have been his primary motivation.[50] Douglass had other forms and forums for such an exercise: his antislavery lectures and his weekly *Frederick Douglass's Paper.* Furthermore, his conventional, modest disclaimers of his appropriateness as a subject for public interest and his stated second reason for complying with his publisher's wishes point elsewhere. "I see, too, that there are special reasons why I should write my own biography, in preference to employing another to do it," he says. "Not only is slavery on trial, but unfortunately, the enslaved people are also on trial. It is alleged, that they are, naturally, inferior."[51] To such charges Douglass's exemplary autobiography supplies a fitting rejoinder, and James McCune Smith's introduction sets up Douglass's enterprise when he introduces the man with these words:

> When a man raises himself from the lowest condition in society to the highest, mankind pay him the tribute of their admiration; when he accomplishes this elevation by native energy, guided by prudence and wisdom, their admiration is increased; but when his course, onward and upward, excellent in itself, furthermore proves a possible, what had hitherto been regarded as an impossible, reform, then he becomes a burning and a shining light, on

which the aged may look with gladness, the young with hope, and the down-
trodden, as a representative of what they may themselves become. To such
a man, dear reader, it is my privilege to introduce you.[52]

The rebellious slave of Douglass's *Narrative* becomes in *My Bondage and
My Freedom* a representative figure in the Emersonian sense of embody-
ing human potential. Both William S. McFeely and David Leverenz have
noted the shifts in Douglass's portrayal of himself that credit him, in his
second autobiography, with increased agency and self-consciousness in
his progression toward freedom and recognition.[53] But Douglass's extraordinary commentary on his early youth also deserves comment. For
those familiar with the stark portrayal of his boyhood in the *Narrative,*
Douglass's reappearance in his second autobiography as a good bad boy,
a kind of Huck Finn figure, is bound to produce a certain shock.

> The slave boy escapes many of troubles which befall and vex his white
> brother. He seldom has to listen to lectures on propriety of behaviour, or
> on anything else. He is never chided for handling his little knife and fork
> improperly or awkwardly, for he uses none. He is never reprimanded for
> soiling the table-cloth, for he takes his meals on the clay floor. He never has
> the misfortune, in his games or sports, of soiling or tearing his clothes, for he
> has almost none to soil or tear. He is never expected to act like a nice little
> gentleman, for he is only a rude little slave. Thus, freed from all restraint, the
> slave-boy can be, in his life and conduct, a genuine boy, doing whatever his
> boyish nature suggests; enacting, by turns, all the strange antics and freaks of
> horses, dogs, pigs, and barn-door fowls, without in any manner compromis-
> ing his dignity, or incurring reproach of any sort.[54]

Douglass is certainly using irony in this depiction. Deprivation is indicated as well as untrammelled freedom, and his commentary on socialization for middle-class respectability is also an exercise in one-
upmanship. But Douglass is also distancing himself from his youthful
experiences in a way that downplays the importance of the physical and
emotional deprivation of his youth, an importance that the slave narrative, in contrast, had sought to emphasize. The passage echoes with
middle-class platitudes and clichés, and his closing wry comment that
the slave boy can be "as happy as any little heathen under the palm trees
of Africa" would sound racist coming from the pen of another.[55]

While Douglass preens his own image, he totally reconstructs his mother and grandmother. Both are refashioned to furnish him with African American antecedents capable of supporting the greatness of their progeny without reference to his white blood. And both are refashioned to provide an image of domestic relations more in keeping with the conventional image of domesticity. Clearly, too, the naive eye that had witnessed the whipping of his aunt was not the eye of a representative man; this too required refashioning. Through it all, however, Douglass is consistent in one important respect: in his portrait of rebellious slave and representative man he pays tribute to the American ideology of success and to the masculine virtues of competitiveness, ambition, industry, perseverance, self-improvement, and self-reliance. And in his portraits of suffering females and domestic paragons one sees the same domestic ideology in its cautionary and exemplary modes. With the best of intentions, Douglass has been true to the domestic ideology to which he has sacrificed the integrity of his mother, grandmother, Henny, and Esther in the name of reform.

NOTES

1. Frederick Douglass, *Life and Times of Frederick Douglass* (1893; New York: Collier-Macmillan, 1971), 472. The text of this edition is based on the revised edition of 1892.

2. See John Sekora, "Black Message / White Envelope: Genre, Authenticity, and Authority in the Antebellum Slave Narrative," *Callaloo* 10 (summer 1987): 482–515; John Sekora, "Is the Slave Narrative a Species of Autobiography?," in *Studies in Autobiography,* ed. James Olney (New York: Oxford University Press, 1988), 99–111; and William L. Andrews, *To Tell a Free Story: The First Century of Afro-American Autobiography, 1760–1865* (Urbana: University of Illinois Press, 1988), especially chapter 1.

3. Lunsford Lane, *The Narrative of Lunsford Lane, Formerly of Raleigh, N.C. (Embracing an Account of His Early Life, The Redemption, By Purchase of Himself and Family From Slavery, And His Banishment From the Place of His Birth For the Crime of Wearing a Coloured Skin) Published By Himself,* 4th ed., (Boston, 1848), 31.

4. Moses Grandy, *Narrative of the Life of Moses Grandy, Late a Slave in the United States of America* (Boston, 1844), 17–18.

5. Moses Roper, *A Narrative of the Adventures and Escape of Moses Roper From American Slavery; With a Preface by the Rev'd T Price, D.D.* (London, 1837), 32.

6. *The Liberator,* 16 May 1835, p. 80.

7. *The Liberator,* 7 February 1835, p. 24.

8. *The Liberator,* 31 March 1837, p. 56.

9. Reprinted in the *Proceedings of the American Anti-slavery society, at its Third Decade: held in the city of Philadelphia, December 3 – 4, 1863,* (New York, 1864), 18.

10. Edwin A Hatfield, *Freedom's Lyre: Or, Psalms, Hymns, and Sacred Songs for the Slave and his Friends,* (New York, 1840; reprint, Mnemosyne, 1969), hymn number 78. The hymn has four stanzas.

11. "A Simple Tale of American Slavery: An Address Delivered in Sheffield, England, On 11 September 1846," in John W. Blassingame, ed., *The Frederick Douglass Papers. Series One: Speeches, Debates, and Interviews,* 5 vols. (New Haven: Yale University Press, 1979 –), 1 : 401 – 402.

12. "I Have Come to Tell You Something About Slavery: An Address Delivered in Lynn, Massachusetts, in October 1841," Blassingame, *Papers,* 1 : 3.

13. "Slavery and America's Bastard Republicanism: An Address Delivered in Limerick, Ireland, on 10 November 1845," Blassingame, *Papers,* 1 : 86.

14. "A Simple Tale of American Slavery," Blassingame, *Papers,* 1 : 401.

15. "England Should Lead the Cause of Emancipation: An Address Delivered in Leeds, England, on 23 December 1846," Blassingame, *Papers,* 1 : 482.

16. "Colored People Must Command Respect: An Address Delivered in Rochester, New York, on 13 March 1848," Blassingame, *Papers,* 2 : 112 – 13.

17. See, for example, Douglass's speech "An Account of American Slavery: An Address Delivered in Glasgow, Scotland, on 15 January 1846," Blassingame, *Papers,* 1 : 138, or his speech "Slavery Attacks Humanity: An Address Delivered in Birmingham, England, on 29 June 1846," Blassingame, *Papers,* 1 : 315.

18. "I Have Come to Tell You Something About Slavery: An Address Delivered in Lynn, Massachusetts, in October 1841," Blassingame, *Papers,* 1 : 3.

19. The roots of the sentimental ethos in Scottish Common Sense philosophy may be perceived in David Hume, *A Treatise Of Human Nature,* esp. part 3 of book 3, and Adam Smith, *Theory of Moral Sentiments,* part 1, section 1, chapter 1.

20. Theodore Weld, *American Slavery As It Is: Testimony of a Thousand Witnesses,* (1839; reprint, New York: Arno, 1968), 7.

21. *The Liberator,* 10 January 1845, p. 8. The poem has four stanzas. I am citing the first and fourth.

22. Frederick Douglass, *Narrative of the Life of Frederick Douglass, An American Slave, Written by Himself,* ed. Benjamin Quarles (1845; Cambridge, Mass.: Belknap Press of Harvard University Press, 1973), 24.

23. Ibid., 77.

24. Grandy, *Narrative of the Life of Moses Grandy,* 32 – 33.

25. George Tucker, *Valley of the Shenandoah, or, Memoirs of the Graysons,* ed. Donald R. Noble Jr., 2 vols. (Chapel Hill: University of North Carolina Press, 1970), 1:82.

26. Douglass, *Narrative,* 76.

27. Ibid., 77.

28. Ibid., 77–78.

29. Ibid., 78.

30. Frederick Douglass, *My Bondage and My Freedom,* ed. Philip S. Foner (1855; New York: Dover, 1969), 179.

31. Douglass, *Life and Times,* 443.

32. Douglass, *Narrative,* 28.

33. Ibid., 29–30.

34. See Jenny Franchot, "The Punishment of Esther: Frederick Douglass and the Construction of the Feminine," in *Frederick Douglass: New Literary and Historical Essays,* ed. Eric J. Sundquist (Cambridge: Cambridge University Press, 1993), 141–65. In Franchot's view, the whipping of Esther becomes a primal scene that leaves intriguing racial, psychological, and sexual issues to resolve.

35. Douglass, *Bondage,* 85–89.

36. Grandy, *Narrative of the Life of Moses Grandy,* 18.

37. Myra C. Glenn, "Wife Beating: The Darker Side of Victorian Domesticity," *Canadian Review of American Studies* 15 (spring 1984): 18.

38. Ibid., 28.

39. Douglass, *Bondage,* 37.

40. Ibid., 36.

41. Douglass, *Narrative,* 25.

42. Douglass, *Bondage,* 52. It is William S. McFeely who identifies the likeness as that of an Egyptian pharaoh. See *Frederick Douglass* (New York: W. W. Norton, 1991), 6.

43. Douglass, *Bondage,* 56.

44. Ibid., 58.

45. Ibid., 58.

46. Ibid., 57.

47. Ibid., 57.

48. Franklin and Washington were two of the great heroes of the age. Weems' first biography of Franklin, *The Immortal Mentor; or, Man's unerring guide to a healthy, wealthy, and happy life,* was published in 1796; another followed in 1815. This latter biography went through eleven editions by 1845. Weems' *The Life of Washington,* expanded between the first edition of 1800 and the 1808 edition, was even more popular; fifty-nine editions were published before 1850. Weems had a reputation for inventing colorful incidents to add interest while helping him to make his rhetorical points. The cherry tree incident in the

life of Washington is probably the most famous example of this poetic license. Franklin's *Autobiography* provides another example of exemplary autobiography. An edition was published in 1818 by Franklin's grandson; Jared Sparks issued the *Autobiography* as part of a ten-volume collection of Franklin's works between 1836 and 1840. For more information, see, for example, Marcus Cunliffe's introduction to *The Life of Washington* (Cambridge, Mass.: Harvard University Press, 1962) and Dixon Wecter's *The Hero in America* (New York: Charles Scribner's Sons, 1941), especially chapters 4 and 6.

49. Douglass, *Bondage,* vi.

50. Ibid., vii.

51. Ibid., vii.

52. Ibid., xvii.

53. See William S. McFeely's discussion of the childhood companionship of Douglass and Daniel Lloyd, *Frederick Douglass,* 21 ff, which suggests such a shift, and David Leverenz's discussion of the differing renditions of the Covey fight in Douglass's first two autobiographies, "Frederick Douglass's Self-Refashionings," *Criticism* 29 (summer 1987): 341–70.

54. Douglass, *Bondage,* 40 – 41.

55. Ibid., 41.

Engendered in the South

Blood and Irony in Douglass and Jacobs

ANNE GOODWYN JONES

I N 1845, THE YEAR OF FREDERICK DOUGLASS'S FIRST VISIT TO
Britain, another fugitive slave made a journey to England as
well, though her visit evoked no fanfare then or now.

Nor was there likely to be. Whereas Douglass arrived in Liverpool in
the glow of fame—his *Narrative of the Life of Frederick Douglass* had sold
4,500 copies in the United States by fall 1845 (it had been published in
June) and gone into three international editions—Jacobs' trip was hardly
an antebellum book tour.[1] Her own slave narrative, *Incidents in the Life of
a Slave Girl, Written By Herself,* would not appear in print until 1861.[2]
Instead of a public figure, Harriet Jacobs was a domestic worker. She left
her own children in America sometime after late March (Douglass was
to leave the United States in August) to sail for Liverpool as the nursemaid to three-year-old Imogen Willis, whose mother had just died. Imogen's father, Nathaniel Parker Willis, a New York magazine writer and
brother of the writer Sara Payson Willis Parton (known to her readers as
Fanny Fern), completed the party. Jacobs spent ten months in England
on this trip, staying in London and in Steventon as the family visited
relatives who survived Imogen's mother. She returned in the winter of
1845–46; Douglass stayed for a year longer, returning in the spring of
1847.[3]

It is fascinating to imagine that Harriet Jacobs' path crossed Frederick

Douglass's—their stays in Britain coincided for at least four months in late 1845—but there seems to be no evidence so far to support such a fantasy; in fact, Douglass spent most of that time in Ireland.[4] Four years later, though, Jacobs was working in the same movement, the same town, and even the same building as Frederick Douglass, in the antislavery reading room above the offices of Douglass's abolitionist newspaper the *North Star* in Rochester, New York. She referred to Douglass almost casually by now. She wrote to Amy Post in 1849, for example, that "the Office go on as usual had a few here to meeting on Sunday . . . I suppose we shall have Frederick and the Miss Griffiths here on Sunday to draw a full house. Rochester is looking very pretty the trees are in full Bloom and the earth seems covered with a green mantle . . . The Miss Griffiths has been here this afternoon Frederick went with them to the falls they seemed much pleased with the reading room."[5] But her slave narrative was not to appear for a dozen more years, in 1861, whereas Douglass's *Narrative of the Life of Frederick Douglass, an American Slave,* had appeared before he set sail for Liverpool in 1845. And when Harriet embarked on a second journey to England in 1858 to find a British publisher for her book, her efforts failed. (In 1862 W. Tweedie was to publish it in London under the title *The Deeper Wrong: Incidents in the Life of a Slave Girl, Written by Herself.*[6])

The coincidence of their 1845 visits to England and the tellingly different characters of those visits suggest predictable gender contrasts between the two fugitive slaves. Though both were managed and paid by whites, for example,[7] Douglass had become a heroic figure in the public predominantly male world, while Jacobs, despite an equally dramatic escape from slavery and five years seniority to Douglass, remained in the female world of domesticity. Indeed, their ways of telling their stories of the visit to England differ in predictably gendered ways. Douglass emphasizes the importance to him of the world of political connections. In *The Life and Times of Frederick Douglass* (1881, revised 1893), the last of the three versions of his autobiography, he wrote, "My visit to England did much for me every way. Not the least among the many advantages derived from it was the opportunity it afforded me of becoming acquainted with educated people and of seeing and hearing many of the most distinguished men of that country."[8] Such acquaintances made new links in a continuing narrative of linear progress, the story of a life that was moving from success to success as a public figure. By contrast, Jacobs began her story of her travel to England by telling her readers of her lodgings and supper. She then moved to the privacy of the bedroom she shares with little Imogen in order to emphasize what for her was the major effect of being in England, a feeling that emerged when she was alone. "Ensconced in a pleasant room, with my dear little charge, I laid my head on my pillow, for the first time, with the delightful consciousness of pure, unadulterated freedom."[9] Such an incident, enclosed, interior, almost timeless, is not tied to a narrative of public accomplishment; on the contrary, its very accomplishment is, in a sense, privacy itself. In the 1849 letter to Amy Post quoted above, Jacobs veers suddenly from a sentence about the forthcoming "full house" for a public meeting to a lyrical evocation of Rochester in the spring. Though it is not exactly a green thought in a green shade, a sort of outdoors version of her feelings in bed in Britain—Jacobs may well have been thinking of the effects of the setting on the conferees—it is not a thought or a transition that Douglass would be likely to make, at least in writing. He would have stayed focussed, I think, on the narrative of the public event, at which, of course, he would be the star.

The forking path of gendered binary oppositions clearly lies ahead— after public/private, workplace/home, and culture/nature come autonomous/interdependent, political/personal, rational/emotional, and so on. Although taking such a path is clearly useful, as is evident in the work of such critics as Richard Yarborough, David Leverenz, Stephanie Smith, Jenny Franchot, Valerie Smith, Anne Warner, Jean Fagan Yellin, Frances Foster, and Eric Sundquist,[10] this essay will choose the path less taken, raising questions about the historical and regional specificity of the gendered oppositions suggested above on which gender analysis has tended to rely.

These sets of gender oppositions are to an important extent effects of the culture and history of the American North and are useful only in a limited sense for understanding the complicated polycultural lives and works of Douglass and Jacobs. The gap between the rhetoric of Douglass's and Jacobs' writing and their lives is greater than has been supposed. This gap can be understood as the effect of significant differences between the gender systems of the North and the South. In one the two fugitive slaves and writers were raised, and in the other they lived as adults. It was to the latter–the gender system of the emerging industrial capitalist urbanizing North–that they addressed the rhetoric of their autobiographical narratives. More profoundly shaped by the South than their writing, however, their lives as adults performed scripts of specifically Southern manhood and womanhood. And manhood and womanhood in the South, for black as well as white, slave as well as free, were deeply implicated with meanings of class.

Ellen Glasgow, the Virginia novelist, early in her career made the remark–an ironic revision of Bismarck's call for German "Blut und eisen," blood and iron–that what Southern literature needed was blood and irony.[11] Certainly Douglass's and Jacobs' narratives and incidents fill Glasgow's prescription. Their writings joined a rhetoric that appealed to Northern gender norms with themes that emerged from Southern gender experience. Thus Douglass's *Narrative* and Jacobs' *Incidents* can be read as progenitors of Southern literary thematics, thematics of blood and irony and much more as well.

Analyses of gender in American studies have tended to assume that the contours of gender that developed in the first half of the nineteenth century in the American North can be successfully generalized elsewhere. For example, despite taking his data exclusively from the Northeast, Anthony Rotundo entitled his recent book *American Manhood* and argues that the key definition of American manhood during the first half of the nineteenth century was what he calls "self-made manhood," the product of a market economy, a burgeoning middle class, and "an economic and political life based on the free play of individual interests." A self-made man took his "identity and social status from his own achievements, not from the accident of his birth," according to Rotundo.[12] By the same token, the notion still prevails in many quarters that during the same period domesticity became the gender norm for American women, domesticity in a home that, no longer the man's place of work, now became the woman's center of power.[13]

Yet such gender assumptions could not work so smoothly for people in the American South, white or black, rich or poor, slave or free. For manhood, the notion of the "free play of individual interests" in a rigidly hierarchical and paternalistic society or of gaining "social status through achievement rather than birth" in a culture based on family lineage had to remain only a gleam in the eye for the Southerner born with the wrong blood or condition of servitude and without a silver spoon in the mouth. Most Southern men would not have had access to Rotundo's "American" manhood. And even those most likely so to do—the men of the master class—argued quite explicitly against such ideas in proslavery speeches, sermons, and essays.[14] Yet genders existed and were quite sternly enforced in the South. To understand Douglass and Jacobs, and in particular to understand how their gender identifications developed and changed during their lives, it is critical to look at the ways in which these two were likely to have been originally engendered in the South. Northern gender ideals became their rhetoric and their hopes; it shaped to a great extent their free and deliberate choices as adults; but Southern gender realities shaped their first and irreducible sense of self, a sense that could never entirely be recognized or erased.[15]

Harriet Jacobs' slave youth and young womanhood in Edenton, North Carolina, and Douglass's from Tuckahoe to Baltimore, were shaped by intimate interracial emotional bonds that slavery created in its invention of what plantation patriarchs tended to call "my family, white and black."[16] Jacobs records a life spent within town households, as a child loved and taught by her white mistress, as a young woman obsessively pursued by her white master, and as a fugitive slave hidden for a time in a white friend's house. She spent seven famous years holed up in her "loophole of retreat" in a garret in her grandmother's home a block from her white master's house and a few doors from her white lover's (and her children's father's) house. Jacobs' grandmother, Molly Horniblow, had been bought and freed by the sister of her former white mistress— a woman who, unlike the slave she freed, was illiterate. She signed the petition for emancipation with an X.[17]

Like Harriet Jacobs, Frederick Douglass lived in cross-racial households that produced complicated intimate relations as well: the Eastern Shore home of Aaron Anthony (possibly Douglass's father), assistant to the wealthy planter Edward Lloyd; the Baltimore household of Hugh and Sophia Auld; and the Eastern Shore household of Thomas and Lucretia Auld, in particular. While he lived next to Lloyd's manorial Wye

House, he was chosen at age 6 as the constant companion for the youngest Lloyd son, Daniel, age 12; they hunted, played, and explored the slave "city" together.[18] Later, living with the Baltimore Aulds, Douglass played with a group of boys both black and white in the streets of Fells Point. No doubt their closeness to free people and to white people only underlined for both Jacobs and Douglass the horrific differences of slavery and racism. Their intimacy with the master class affected the construction of their original and fundamental sense of gender. For both slaves and their masters in the South, the identificatory processes that constructed gender were likely to involve multiple mothers and sometimes multiple fathers, complicated kin networks, cross-racial relationships, and a sense of class propriety. Indeed, class identity may have appeared to be more stable than even race, gender, or condition of servitude as a marker of one's "authentic" self. In the passage quoted earlier from Jacobs' chapter "A Visit to England," Jacobs tells us that "for the first time in my life I was in a place where I was treated according to my deportment, without reference to my complexion (183)." Her deportment signified her classed gender; her color was, she thought, correctly read as irrelevant to her social identity. If for Douglass and Jacobs the distinction between slavery and freedom was more important than the distinction between white and black, as seemed to be the case, class divisions may have meant more to them than either. Because of their class identification, both Douglass and Jacobs may have grown up feeling themselves to be more like than unlike their white privileged families.

Bertram Wyatt-Brown argues in "The Mask of Obedience" that male slave psychology emerged from the similarities between African and Southern systems of honor.[19] Both were systems of social order that depended on public shame and humiliation to organize behavior rather than private conscience and guilt. In his analysis, Wyatt-Brown locates three plausible responses to the shame of enslavement: the dignified moral decision to abase oneself, producing self-respect; the internalizing of shame, producing self-blame; and the denial of shame, producing an amoral, trickster-like shamelessness. The majority of slaves fell into the second. Wyatt-Brown's subject is the period of transition from Africa to America; Douglass and Jacobs both were born into families that took pride in tracing several generations in America. Thus the categories may be less useful for them. And both chose a fourth alternative that Wyatt-Brown does not mention—escape into freedom. Yet they seem to have shared with Wyatt-Brown's first group a psychology that allowed them to resist the questioning of slavery and to make dignified moral decisions. Both Frederick Douglass and Harriet Jacobs were able, to some extent through their writing, to separate a sense of personal identity, dignity, and worth from their identities as slaves by perceiving slave identity as imposed rather than earned or essential and by focussing on its exteriority. They were able to observe with vigilance slavery's efforts to produce an internalized sense of shame and humiliation; their vulnerability to such feelings was contained by their strong sense of self and by their capacity to think and act out of that self rather than simply react to the system of slavery. Both recognized early on that for them the only satisfactory response to the shaming designs of slavery was to escape into freedom; and writing their own personal narratives articulated and clarified the distance between their identities as slaves and their identities as free Americans, man and woman. And both found models and solace for their sense of self in identifications with the white upper class with whom they shared "deportment." Douglass deliberately learned to speak "perfect" white upper-class English (to the amazement of his later listeners), just as Jacobs learned the rules of upper-class politeness to which she finally found a positive response not in the rude North but in the white South's anglophiliac dream: mother England herself.

But when they constructed their lives after escaping to the North, and when they wrote their narratives for Northern audiences, inevitably they drew on gender assumptions they knew their new community shared. Those assumptions differed from Southern assumptions and in a sense split the genders still more severely. Thus, as Leverenz has argued, Douglass refashioned himself in *My Bondage and My Freedom* in language and tone that fit a Northern bourgeois man. His emphasis on isolation, individual "self-made" achievement, literacy, professional success, democracy, and equality show his awareness of the meanings of manhood in his new and permanent region.[20] And Jacobs, knowing she spoke to an audience of Northern women whose primary value was married domesticity, addressed them as follows: "Reader, my story ends with freedom, not in the usual way, with marriage. . . . The dream of my life is not yet realized. I do not sit with my children in a home of my own. I still long for a hearthstone of my own, however humble. . . . But God so orders circumstances as to keep me with my friend Mrs. Bruce [the second Mrs. Willis]."²¹

How did these deliberate, adult gender constructions used in their public writing differ from those that shaped the writers when—as children—they were most vulnerable to social construction? In the South, the meanings of gender had been articulated through class and race and working condition to a much fuller extent than in the more homogeneous North. Gender-appropriate behavior changed with one's class, regardless of race; racially specific gender characteristics were ascribed in ways that easily contradicted the gender determined by class; and traditions of gender from British and African sources made contact, mixed, and produced new crosscultural revisions that were not necessarily coherent with either class or race. A light-colored woman working as a house slave could differ more in her sense of womanhood from a field slave than she did from her own mistress. A white heir's personal slave could be a closer friend to the young master than other white boys could be. The young slave's sense of manhood surely would be inflected by his daily life in the company of white men and boys.

In Jacobs' South, upper-class womanhood was not shaped by the turn to domesticity that was required when Northern men left home to go to work. White privileged men may have left home during parts of days or for days at a time, but they did so on different, less predictable and less systematic "schedules" and for various and different reasons, including sport and play. They remained the patriarch at home; rather than becoming the queens of the kitchen and the sole monarchs of domestic space, their wives submitted to their lords and masters (at least in the rhetoric, which many internalized) and shared the authority over the household with female slaves. As Elizabeth Fox-Genovese has emphasized, the home was still the workplace, certainly on the plantations and, in Jacobs' narrative, in town as well. Northern domesticity, like Northern urbanization, simply did not exist in the South. Instead, upper-class womanhood, black and white, in reality and in ideology was marked by a curious combination of power and powerlessness. Such a woman has the power of literacy and education, the power to speak her mind, to move through the town freely, to make independent judgments, even to support herself—Jacobs' grandmother was the town's classiest baker. Such a woman has the power to own, buy, sell, whip, or free slaves as well, though obviously her race and legal and marital status determined to some extent which powers she held and which would be invoked. Yet such a woman deferred to masculinity as a matter of habit. Louisa McCord, one of the most articulate, argued that the pedestal was not only the smartest but the safest place for women to be in a culture infused with and defined by violence.[22]

And such a privileged woman, white or black, was constrained, albeit differently, in matters sexual. Although the white bride could choose her husband freely within familial and social constraints, it seemed to writers like Jacobs and Mary Chesnut a given that her groom would almost inevitably betray her sexual trust and take a black mistress. Eventually the ideal white lady would be culturally marked by her sexlessness. Moreover, the white woman's apparent privilege of having slave wet nurses and slave care of her children resulted, as Lillian Smith put it most dramatically, in the distortion and failure of her maternal bonds.[23] Black women of Jacobs' class—women who could claim the appellation "lady"—shared with whites certain sexual constraints: if not the "double mother" system, the injunction to purity, as Jacobs' representation of Linda Brent's grandmother shows.

Ultimately, both the black woman's and the white woman's power to control her own actions is contingent on the greater power of the white master, the husband, supported by the law. Fear of the white man's power, and ultimately of his violence, undergirds, as I suggested, even the white intellectual Louisa McCord's otherwise complex argument against giving women the vote. Angelina Grimké, in her "Appeal to Christian Woman of the South," tries to convert her white female implied reader to antislavery by creating a wedge between her submission to her husband and her submission to God, suggesting by implication the Southern identification of Lord (in every sense) and master. And the slave woman, whatever her class identification, was of course in every sense vulnerable to the various powers of the white master.

In Douglass's South, white manhood was shaped not by the competitive capitalist emphasis on individualism but by an honor-driven need to perform one's worthiness in the eyes of other men, at least if we accept Wyatt-Brown's argument. Homosocial bonds not only held, they were constantly in the process of being forged and reforged through sometimes bloody rituals that entailed the construction and display of symbols of masculinity and femininity. Physical prowess, passionate self-expression, and violence affirmed and demonstrated manhood in the South to a degree that shocked Northern observers. White manhood clearly must have meant sexual prowess as well, but texts that comment on women's and blacks' absent or dangerous sexuality are strangely silent on the sexuality of white men. Perhaps that is not only a function of gentlemanly circumspection but also in part to protect—to render circumspect—the practice of reproducing two families, one acknowledged and legal, the other unspoken and illegal. Ultimately, in any case, white manhood meant mastery in a hierarchical system in which equality of the sexes and classes was as unthinkable as equality of the races or of the free and unfree. And it meant mastery of one's own domain, including one's family and slaves, a domain in which one's behavior was limited only by one's honor. The effects on black manhood are evident in Harriet Jacobs' brother John's comments on their father: "To be a man, and not to be a man—a father without authority—a husband and no protector—is the darkest of fates."[24] Manhood as authority for children and protector for women, whatever its etiology from African sources, had come as a visible norm more immediately from Southern planter ideals; even John Jacobs' imagery of light and dark, in a troubling irony, come from white discourse.

The shapes that upper-class gender took in the South can be traced in the writings and in the lives of Frederick Douglass and Harriet Jacobs.

"Linda Brent" (as Harriet Jacobs calls herself in *Incidents*) represents herself as a girl with an articulate voice and the courage to speak her mind from the outset. There is no drama of acquiring a voice, no struggle with silencing represented here, as we might expect. On the contrary, her capacity to address her Northern female audience forthrightly and directly appears to be far more limited than her capacity to address her masters and mistresses. Her Southern courage emerged in part from the example of her strong and articulate grandmother, in part from the confidence instilled in her by her first mistress's affection and lessons in literacy and in part by her class privilege as an adult. Her voice falters — or rather, she represents it as faltering — at the moments she tells her readers about her sexual dilemma and, especially, her sexual decision. Unable to escape through her own brave speech from the insistent sexual presence of Dr. Flint, from his unwanted words and gaze, she chooses to enter into an affair with an unmarried white man, "Mr. Sands," who lives near her grandmother, who will soon be elected to Congress, and who has no claim on her but, as she puts it, kindness. Linda tells us she believed this decision would serve both as revenge on and protection from Dr. Flint. How true Jacobs' representation of her motives was to her experience we may know better when Jean Fagan Yellin completes her biography of Jacobs. There are implausibilities in the account as it stands, however, that suggest that Jacobs' choice may have been one of sexual desire as well; there is no explanation given, for example, for Linda continuing the relationship after it fails to discourage Dr. Flint. Representations of an active sexual desire on Linda Brent's part or of a loving and sexual relationship between Sands and Linda would have been entirely unfathomable to a Northern white female audience. Yet Linda's anxiety over the decision appears in her fear of her grandmother's disappointment and ire. The crisis Linda faces when her determined and intelligent will, whatever its motivations, confronts the cultural limitations on her sexual freedom embodied by her grandmother differs in that respect from the crisis of a slave pursued by a master; Linda's conflict could happen to any Southern woman, white or black, whose desire and will did not coincide with her class constraints or whose "lord and master" exercised his legal rights against her will. However, a husband or father's rights over a white woman's body did not approach the near totality of an owner's rights over that of a chattel slave.

Linda has named her son by Mr. Sands after her escaped brother and her daughter after the sister of her father's white mistress. The namings suggest the complexities of interracial relationships within her form of slavery, representing as they do objects of affection from both groups, slaves and enslavers. The desire to sustain maternal bonds with her children is evocatively presented in *Incidents* through representations of tender and intimate moments that give still more impact to the awareness of slavery's power to sever those bonds. Whatever Southern white women can lose of mothering to slavery and the double mother system it encouraged, it is clear that slave women, despite class privilege, live in constant risk of losing the children themselves. The power of Jacobs' representation of the life of a woman in slavery is underscored by her identification with privileged Southern white women, for the sole difference Jacobs continually returns to is the ever-present, total, and arbitrary power of slavery.

Douglass's intimacy with white people in his early life as the favored friend of Daniel Lloyd, then as a child loved by and loving Thomas Auld, in William McFeely's persuasive interpretation, and then as part of the loving Hugh and Sophia Auld family in Baltimore highlighted the differences that slavery made. These intimate relations must have also meant that his primary identification as a man was not as an idealized Northern bourgeois but as a white Southern master. Unlike Harriet, who had her grandmother to claim as kin and serve as mother, Douglass had no black man to claim as intimate kin or serve as father. The significant males in the plantation and town households in which he spent his early years, the years of learning what gender means, were for the most part white. His love- and hate-filled long-term relationship with Thomas Auld must have been marked by the emotions and the identifications of father and son. And Frederick's relationship to Daniel Lloyd and his family put him in a position both to desire the great house and to recognize his exclusion from it.

With this in mind, certain pieces of the Douglass puzzle may fall into place. How could the great antislavery advocate bring articulate, politically active white women—possibly as lovers—to live in the house with his dark wife, who stayed in the kitchen while the guests were in the living room and who remained illiterate all her life? How could he live later at Cedar Hill with a white wife in a big house apart from the black community? Why was he determined to make himself into a gentleman, his grandson into a violinist, and his daughter into a cultured lady? Despite his deliberate and obvious self-refashioning into a Northern man using the rhetoric of self-made manhood, Douglass's primary gender identifications came out of his Southern past. Even the points at which he explicitly sees himself becoming a man—fighting Covey or traveling through Britain as a young lion—even these points were facets of a specifically Southern manhood whose honor is determined by physical prowess and community approval.

It is misleading, then, to assume that all gender possibilities were the same in nineteenth-century America and that Douglass's and Jacobs' rhetorics of gender—which appealed to the structures of Northern gendering—should be taken as historically accurate and complete descriptions of their gender identifications. If we look carefully and imaginatively at the structures in which they grew up, structures that are really nowhere available to us to see today, we can speculate that becoming a man and becoming a woman were both more complicated than has been thought, and more determined.

If Douglass and Jacobs were more Southern than we might have thought, particularly in their gendered selves, can their texts be read as part of a Southern literary tradition?

Glasgow's desire for blood and irony in Southern literature can be used as a way both to identify Douglass and Jacobs as Southern and to differentiate their texts by gender. Both are deeply concerned with blood, with the literal wounds of slavery and the metaphoric implications of blood as a sign of bodily integrity, but also with bloodlines—genealogy. And both take full advantage of the numerous opportunities for irony that slavery offers in the land of the free. But Douglass's 1845 narrative is almost obsessively drawn to representations of blood—I count dozens—whereas Jacobs' is at pains to show the lacerations of language. How then are these markers of Southern gender distinctions in particular? A short answer is that among Southern white men especially, making another man's blood flow, whether in ritual fights within one's cohort or by lashing slaves, had become a sign of masculine dominance as clearly as controlling the passing and naming of one's own family "blood" was a sign of patriarchal power. Frederick Douglass remarked that "everybody, in the South, wants the privilege of whipping somebody else. . . . The whip is all in all. . . . Slaves, as well as slaveholders, use it with an unsparing hand."[25] To make another man's blood leave his body was a sign of effeminization; to keep it within one's own body, and metaphorically within the family or the race, was a sign of bodily and racial integrity. But for Harriet Jacobs, or Linda Brent in the *Incidents,* blood signifies primarily inheritance, and it is words, not whips,

that wound. Her story of slavery, the "deeper wound" that women experience, is the story of a master's insistent whispers, suggestions, and
sexual demands. Her bodily integrity and unmarked beauty are precisely what is at issue now in the register of sex. Dr. Flint wants her to
agree to allow him to penetrate her sexually; this would be more wound-
ing than rape, for it would mean he had her body and soul. Irony thus
becomes her weapon of choice, while blood is Douglass's; she resists
Dr. Flint with language and fools him with letters, while Douglass fights
Covey with his fists.

If Douglass and Jacobs both bring blood and irony to Southern literature, as Glasgow urged, how else can their life stories be read as part
of the Southern tradition? Did Charles Chesnutt write his short story
"The Wife of His Youth" with Douglass in mind?[26] In that story, set in
the postwar District of Columbia, we meet a successful young African
American man as he is about to hold a party for the club to which he
belongs. This club, called the Blue Vein Society by darker blacks, is exclusive to light-skinned wealthy African Americans of free birth. The
protagonist intends to announce his engagement to one of the members
when a knock on his door admits an ugly, poor, old, and very black
woman who tells him the story of losing her husband, a free colored
man, during the war. She knows he is looking for her still, she says, for
their love was deep and real. She is trudging her way North to find him
again, and she asks if the protagonist has met a man by his name. Of
course it is he, so changed as to be unrecognizable to her. Without ac-
knowledging his identity, then, the protagonist holds the party, and calls
the group to attention to hear the story—names omitted—and to give
their opinions on what such a man should do. Unanimously they say,
claim the wife of his youth. The protagonist reveals himself, introduces
his wife, and all is well, perhaps because the rest of the story is left un-
narrated.

Douglass never legally abandoned the wife of his youth, yet clearly his
situation was far from resolved. Unlike Chesnutt's protagonist, Douglass
found it impossible happily to join the two worlds he inhabited. Instead,
he—like the Southern masters he so despised yet loved—reversed the image of the white master, his white lady, and the slave mistress to create a
black master, his "slave" wife, and his lady mistress. If Douglass was

Chesnutt's subject in "The Wife of His Youth," the message Chesnutt sent had to be a critique. For Chesnutt, race solidarity, the solidarity of family and history, should clearly take precedence over white dreams, however deep in one's identity they may rest. Yet Douglass's identity had been shaped in a setting in which slavery and slavery's class system was the defining difference more than race or gender. Cross-race gender identifications naturally emerged within a given class and within a particular family structure that united people regardless of color in shared and intimate daily experience. By the time Chesnutt wrote, race, not slavery, was the defining difference; race loyalty, not class or gender loyalty, was the political desideratum. The time for Douglass's and Jacobs' sorts of gender identity, their sense of what it meant to be a man and a woman, had passed, and race would become the issue for the future of the region and the nation.

With this in mind, a wider Southern literary lineage can be speculated, one that crosses races to show similarities in class relations. If Frederick Douglass's story leads to Charles Chesnutt's "The Wife of His Youth," his longing for Wye also resembles Faulkner's story of a young boy, Sarty Snopes, entranced by the sight of a huge beautiful white mansion, and his father, who recognizes that "nigger sweat" and "white trash sweat" have built that house.[27] It bears even more resemblances to Faulkner's, *Absalom, Absalom!*[28] The novel tells the story of a man seduced by the image of a big house on the hill, a seduction that is clinched when he is rejected at the door and sent to the back by the black slave inside. Thomas Sutpen marries in Haiti; this wife of his youth bears him a son, Charles Bon. But Thomas sets aside this wife and son when he learns of her black blood: she is no longer incremental to his design to found a patriarchal family to inherit the big house he builds in Yoknapatawpha County. Sutpen's design is thwarted; the last surviving bearer of his blood is, ironically, a very black idiot, Jim Bond, whose speech is only a howl. But Faulkner chose to make the construction of a white Southern patriarchy his character's passionate design, and here the similarities end. Frederick Douglass's passionate design was not to produce a white patriarchy: it was to end slavery and work against racism. Yet the power of his having been engendered in the South played itself out willy-nilly. His own family, like Sutpen's, seems to have collapsed under the weight of his desire. His racially and socially double relationships with women, his need for control and mastery at home, created resistances and dependencies in his wife and children that they were never able to work through. Unlike Sutpen, Douglass chose a design that allowed him to construct both a self and a career that meshed well with emerging Northern norms of masculinity. But he carried his Southern past into that Northern story of success.

Harriet Jacobs, too, arguably played out for the rest of her life a narrative that had been written for her as a woman in the slaveholding South. Though she worked for antislavery causes and wrote, found a publisher for, and at times literally sold her *Incidents,* Jacobs was employed for much of her life as a domestic servant, a nursemaid and nanny for the growing number of Willis children. This was a role that emerged from slavery's division of maternal labor. Later in life she ran a boardinghouse in Cambridge, Massachusetts, a single woman turning domestic skills into a business for herself as her grandmother had done in Edenton.

If Chesnutt and Faulkner can be seen at least speculatively as writing within a thematics set by Douglass, who rewrites Jacobs' story? Her story has been taken up more by white writers than by African American Southern women like Alice Walker or Gloria Naylor. I am thinking of Katherine Anne Porter, for example, whose version of Harriet Jacobs in "The Old Order," Nanny, stays with her mistress after the war but finally transforms herself in a free and independent "aged Bantu woman"[29]; of Willa Cather's *Sapphira and the Slave Girl,* another story of mastery, sexuality, and escape[30]; of Ellen Douglas in her remarkable work about contemporary white mistresses and black maids, *Can't Quit You, Baby.*[31]

Finally, if in reading Douglass and Jacobs we need to be cautious about assuming that Northern gender arrangements determine the identities of people raised in the South, perhaps we need to be equally attentive to the differences between slavery and racism. Jacobs and Douglass, Southern born and raised, slaves then fugitive slaves and finally free, wrote and lived their stories in opposition primarily to slavery; race was secondary, in part because they had learned in the South how gender and class can override the constraints of the color of one's skin. These days, though, to be called "slave" (or to be told "yo' mama was a slave") is an insult not for the reasons Jacobs and Douglass protested slavery, that is, for the humiliations produced on a people subject to the whims of totalitarian authority. Those were humiliations that antislavery workers believed could disappear with the erasure of that authority and system. Today it is an insult that is perhaps harder to resist because one's skin color, like one's sex, cannot be erased through legislation. Working against racism and sexism, as both Douglass and Jacobs were to learn in the free North, would pose different problems and require different strategies. Hence the paucity, perhaps, of a literature of narratives of successful fugitives from race and gender. Other literary forms would be required for other forms of freedom.

NOTES

1. William S. McFeely, *Frederick Douglass* (New York: W. W. Norton, 1991), 116.

2. The standard edition is Harriet A. Jacobs, *Incidents in the Life of a Slave Girl Written By Herself,* ed. Maria Child (Cambridge, Mass.: Harvard University Press, 1987).

3. Ibid., 224, 185, xvi; McFeely, *Frederick Douglass,* 145.

4. McFeely, *Frederick Douglass,* 199–227.

5. Harriet Jacobs to Amy Post [Rochester, May 1849], in Jacobs, *Incidents,* 230.

6. Ibid., 225.

7. In the case of Douglass, they were Maria Weston Chapman, William Lloyd Garrison, and Wendell Phillips, leaders of the American Anti-Slavery Society for whom Douglass worked. McFeely, *Frederick Douglass,* 117.

8. Frederick Douglass, *Autobiographies: Narrative of the Life of Frederick Douglass, an American Slave; My Bondage and My Freedom; Life and Times of Frederick Douglass,* edited and with notes by Henry Louis Gates Jr. (1845, 1855, and 1893, respectively; New York: Library of America, 1994), 679.

9. Jacobs, *Incidents,* 183.

10. For recent work on Douglass, Jacobs, and gender–whether explicitly or by implication–see the following work, arranged in order of publication year and by author within each year: Frances Smith Foster, *Witnessing Slavery: The Development of Ante-bellum Slave Narratives* (Westport, Conn.: Greenwood Press, 1979); "Slave and Mistress: Ideologies of Womanhood under Slavery," chap. 2 in *Reconstructing Womanhood: The Emergence of the Afro-American Woman Novelist,* ed. Hazel V. Carby (New York: Oxford University Press, 1987), 20–39; "Form and Ideology in Three Slave Narratives," chap. 1 in *Self-Discovery and Authority in Afro-American Narrative,* ed. Valerie Smith (Cambridge, Mass.: Harvard

University Press, 1987); Susan Willis, *Specifying: Black Women Writing the American Experience* (Madison: University of Wisconsin Press, 1987); Elizabeth Fox-Genovese, *Within the Plantation Household: Black and White Women of the Old South* (Chapel Hill: University of North Carolina Press, 1988); "Binary Oppositions in Chapter One of *Narrative of the Life of Frederick Douglass an American Slave Written by Himself*" and "Frederick Douglass and the Language of the Self," chaps. 3 and 4, respectively, in *Figures in Black: Words, Signs, and the "Racial" Self,* ed. Henry Louis Gates Jr. (New York: Oxford University Press, 1989), 80–120; David Leverenz, "Frederick Douglass's Self-Refashioning," chap. 4 in *Manhood and the American Renaissance,* ed. David Leverenz (Ithaca: Cornell University Press, 1989), 108–34; Deborah E. McDowell and Arnold Rampersad, eds., *Slavery and the Literary Imagination* (Baltimore: Johns Hopkins University Press, 1989); Jean Fagan Yellin, *Women and Sisters: The Antislavery Feminists in American Culture* (New Haven: Yale University Press, 1989); Jenny Franchot, "The Punishment of Esther: Frederick Douglass and the Construction of the Feminine," 141–65, Wayne Mixon, "The Shadow of Slavery: Frederick Douglass, the Savage South, and the Next Generation," 233–52, and Rafia Zafar, "Franklinian Douglass: The Afro-American as Representative Man," 99–117, all in *Frederick Douglass: New Literary and Historical Essays,* ed. Eric J. Sundquist (Cambridge: Cambridge University Press, 1990); Catherine Clinton and Nina Silber, eds., *Divided Houses: Gender and the Civil War* (New York: Oxford University Press, 1992); Jean Fagan Yellin, "Harriet Jacobs's Family History," *American Literature* 66 (December 1994): 765–67.

11. See, for instance, Frederick P. W. McDowell, *Ellen Glasgow and the Ironic Art of Fiction* (Madison: University of Wisconsin Press, 1963).

12. E. Anthony Rotundo, *American Manhood: Transformations in Masculinity from the Revolution to the Modern Era* (New York: Basic Books, 1993), 3.

13. See Fox-Genovese, *Within the Plantation Household,* on antebellum Southern women, and Drew Gilpin Faust, *Mothers of Invention* (Chapel Hill: University of North Carolina Press, 1996) on Southern women during the Civil War. Although differences among these and other thinkers about Southern womanhood in the nineteenth century center on differing convictions as to the definitions and social meanings of the Southern economy, all point out that womanhood in the South suffered strains if read under the rubric of Northern domesticity.

14. See, for example, the excellent collection and introduction in Drew Gilpin Faust, ed., *The Ideology of Slavery: Proslavery Thought in the Antebellum South, 1830–1860* (Baton Rouge: Louisiana State University Press, 1981).

15. Though I disagree with certain of her fundamental propositions, Elizabeth Fox-Genovese has gone a long way toward developing a theory of gender's meanings for Southern white women that takes account of the blurring between public and private spheres and the hierarchical ideology on the slave plantation. Though less has been written about Southern white manhood, arguably Bertram Wyatt-Brown's notion of honor as

opposed to conscience is about masculinity in all but name, and sometimes by name. See Fox-Genovese, *Within the Plantation Household,* and Bertram Wyatt-Brown, *Southern Honor: Ethics and Behavior in the Old South* (New York: Oxford University Press, 1982).

16. See, for instance, Eugene Genovese, "'Our Family, White and Black': Family and Household in the Southern Slaveholders' World View," in *In Joy and In Sorrow: Women, Family, and Marriage in the Victorian South, 1830–1900,* ed. Carol Bleser (New York: Oxford University Press, 1991), 69–87.

17. Jacobs, *Incidents,* 262 n. 6.

18. Dickson J. Preston's *Young Frederick Douglass: The Maryland Years* (Baltimore: Johns Hopkins University Press, 1980) is especially useful for showing the range and depth of interracial relationships in Douglass's childhood.

19. Bertram Wyatt-Brown, "The Mask of Obedience: Male Slave Psychology in the Old South," in *Haunted Bodies: Gender and Southern Texts,* ed. Anne Goodwyn Jones and Susan V. Donaldson (Charlottesville: University Press of Virginia, 1997), 23–55.

20. Leverenz, *Manhood and the American Renaissance,* 108–34.

21. Jacobs, *Incidents,* 201.

22. See, for example, opposing the vote for women, Louisa McCord's "On the Enfranchisement of Women," in *All Clever Men, Who Make Their Way: Critical Discourse in the Old South,* ed. and intro. Michael O'Brien (Fayetteville: University of Arkansas Press, 1982). See also the recent collection of McCord's writing, *Louisa Susanna Cheves McCord, Political and Social Essays,* ed. Richard C. Lounsbury (Charlottesville: University Press of Virginia, 1995).

23. See Lillian Smith, *Killers of the Dream* (New York: W. W. Norton, 1949, 1961).

24. Jacobs, *Incidents,* 262 n. 3.

25. Quoted in Preston, *Young Frederick Douglass,* 60.

26. Charles Chesnutt, "The Wife of His Youth," in *The Wife of His Youth and other Stories of the Color Line* (Boston: Small, Maynard, 1899).

27. William Faulkner, "Barn Burning," in *The Collected Stories of William Faulkner* (New York: Vintage, 1936), 3–25.

28. William Faulkner, *Absalom, Absalom! The Corrected Text* (New York: Vintage, 1936).

29. Katherine Anne Porter, "The Old Order," in *The Collected Stories of Katherine Anne Porter* (New York: Harvest/Harcourt Brace Jovanovich, 1965).

30. Willa Cather, *Sapphira and the Slave Girl* (New York: Vintage, 1975).

31. Ellen Douglas, *Can't Quit You, Baby* (New York: Penguin, 1988).

PART FOUR

Douglass, Race, and Ethnicity

The Slavery of Romanism

The Casting Out of the Irish in the
Work of Frederick Douglass

RICHARD HARDACK

A S SHELLEY FISHER FISHKIN AND CARLA PEDERSON ARGUE
with regard to his journalism as a whole, Frederick Douglass transforms himself from the personal "I" to the representative "we," not just to become an Emersonian representative man
for his fellow blacks but to establish who is within and outside the abolitionist community.[1] In his invocations of England, Ireland, and Scotland during his lecture tours and in his journalism, Douglass orchestrates
an anti-Catholic diatribe that situates Romanism as a foreign proslavery
element infiltrating America. Douglass's publication *The Douglass Monthly*
in its individual and collective or community voice sets up implicit but
consistent contrasts between Ireland and the rest of Britain – distinctions
partly based on what Douglass perceives as the shortcomings and pre-
dilections of the Catholic Church – and uses a collective "we" to establish the Irish as a collective "they." Given the context of the economic
and cultural relations between African Americans and Irish Americans
and the ways Douglass's rhetoric situates Irish Americans as members
of a separate religion and race, the groups become forced to vie in what
Ralph Ellison might depict as a kind of battle royal of American citizenship – a no-win false opposition that could keep both sides running.[2] In

sympathizing with the plight of the poor Irish abroad while renouncing the political maneuvers and religious affiliations of Irish Americans, Douglass had to play both sides of the issue, asserting that the enemies of his enemies—the "blacks" of Europe—were friend and foe alike.

Irish Catholics, and especially Irish Americans, are not simply ignored or critiqued, they are systematically cast out of Douglass's circle. As the victims of religious rather than political prejudice in Douglass's eyes, Irish Americans cannot enter into fellowship with American blacks. For Douglass, Ireland becomes a potential second or rival America, a colony seeking its independence. Douglass does seek parallels between the political condition of the Irish and black slaves in America when he wants to marshall support from non-British sources, but he otherwise distinguishes fiercely between their two predicaments. Throughout his life, Douglass worried about Irish American prejudice, intemperance, and competition with blacks regarding foreign support, jobs, and voting rights, anxieties partly reflected in and partly caused by his distaste for all varieties of Catholicism and Irish Catholicism in particular. In this light, one should not simply dismiss Frederick Douglass for not being Frantz Fanon but try instead to contextualize his often disturbing partisan representation of the Irish as a historically circumscribed response to political conditions in America and part of his attempt to foster support in England and Scotland. Through the largely consistent rhetoric with which he isolates the Irish, Douglass then demonizes Catholicism rather than British colonialism for personal and political reasons.

Before moving to the larger context of African American–Irish American relations, a brief overview of the role of *The Douglass Monthly* in Douglass's representation of Irish Catholicism is in order. Douglass often uses the *Monthly*'s articles about Great Britain published from 1859 to 1863 to echo directly his own rhetorical positions; like Benjamin Franklin, he is adept at using foreign voices to ventriloquize his own in his paper. Because of this repetition of voices, opinions published in *The Douglass Monthly* serve as a reliable index of Douglass's experience in Britain on his lecture tours to promote and raise money for abolitionism. In his letter to his "British Anti-Slavery Friends," for example, Douglass himself had written in 1860, "the Republican Party, is, as I have often said in conversation with you, only negatively anti-slavery. It is opposed to the *political power* of slavery, rather than to slavery itself." [3] In the October 1861 *Monthly,* the chairman of the Methodist Free Church Assembly in Leeds is quoted as saying, "some people thought that the Northern States were fighting against the South to put down slavery. This was not the case." For Douglass, much the same might be said of the stance of religion in America, whose greatest representative, despite its minority status in the United States, is the Catholic Church, here imagined as a foreign influence: "The two hundred years this curse has set in the sanctuary proves that there is no warfare between slavery and church." [4] Douglass upbraids the American Catholic Church when he claims that "there is no question that in the earlier history of this republic all religious organizations were decidedly opposed to slavery," and then mentions Methodists, Presbyterians, Quakers, Baptists; but when he had commented much earlier on how little the church had done to end slavery, he had pointedly included Roman Catholics on his list.[5]

Douglass's paper furnishes progress reports to both sides of the Atlantic on the cause of liberation, letting British readers know, for example, that "not even a white man with anti-slavery sentiments is safe in the slave States." *The Douglass Monthly* also kept readers up to date on British abolitionism, printing, for example, the minutes of the Glasgow Association for the Abolition of Slavery, a transcript of Reverend Cheever's antislavery speech in Glasgow, and an account of the West Indian Emancipation Celebration, again in Leeds. In Douglass's paper, England, even before itself possessing a substantial black population, becomes a clearinghouse for information, one Western locus for the circulation of information about all aspects of the diaspora.

Consistent with the tone of *The Douglass Monthly,* Douglass generally differentiated among Catholic and Protestant English, Scottish, and Irish abroad but not among the Irish in America. His warm reception among a family in Cork seems predicated on their having been themselves outcasts, "members of the Church of Ireland" rather than Roman Catholics.[6] Though he chides Protestant sects for complacency and complicity—and repeatedly berates Dr. Chalmers' Free Church of Scotland—Douglass advances a specific antislavery hierarchy in which Catholics always occupy the periphery. Douglass prefers to give speeches to Methodists, Wesleyans, and Quakers, but not Catholics. When he notes that "slavery found no support in the Baptist, Methodist, or congregational churches, in England, Ireland, or Scotland," he again emblematically omits the Catholic Church.[7] As William McFeely notes, Douglass renounced his "Catholic Irish fellow citizens" who, despite England's oppression of Ireland, were themselves often prejudiced against and oppressive of blacks. In America, a worsening competition of economic interests was then played out in terms of religious factionalism.

Wary not only of the prejudice of color but of class, caste, and religion, Douglass admonishes that "we want no black Ireland in America. We want no aggrieved class." Much later, in 1883, he asked Americans to remember the black soldiers employed during the Civil War and not to "convert the cheerful and loyal brows of six millions into a black Ireland."[8] A "black Ireland" is then a significant threat to Douglass, not a potential political ally. Douglass at times distances himself from Catholic poverty in Ireland to downplay British colonialism. Slavery becomes a rhetorically contested site – one which Irish and African Americans both lay claim to – and he must ultimately propose that the Irish are responsible for their own fate at the hands of the church rather than at the hands of the British, who may help him combat slavery in America. While eloquently denouncing to certain audiences the extreme poverty he witnesses in Ireland, Douglass disregards that poverty if the cause of reform threatens that of abolition. It is also important to remember that many Irish nationalists themselves think that "the white slaves of Ireland . . . [are] a people in serfdom [who] cannot afford to make new enemies," preventing them risking involvement with abolitionism: as the editor of the *Irish Waterford Freeman* writes in 1845, "when we ourselves are free, let us then engage in any struggle to erase the sin of slavery from every land."[9] Ironically, this sentiment entirely recapitulates Douglass's periodically cynical position and epitomizes the central role his depiction of the Irish plays in his own sense of international politics: "We feel for Hungary and for Ireland, but how can we as a nation exert an influence favorable to freedom in the old world while we are oppressors at home?"[10] In their very agreement about local cause, the Irish and African Americans can thus find themselves in reciprocal, yet wholly isolated, positions.

Douglass can maintain and capitalize on his anti-Catholic convictions and rhetoric because America was not receptive to what it perceived as a foreign religious incursion. In *Roads to Rome: The Antebellum Protestant Encounter with Catholicism,* Jenny Franchot argues that "anti-Catholicism operated as an imaginative category of discourse through which antebellum American writers of popular and elite fictional and historical texts indirectly voiced the tensions and limitations of mainstream Protestant culture." In trying to become a kind of representative man, Douglass thus participated in a complex antagonism against Catholicism and what Franchot identifies as its distinct alliance with Native American culture and ethnicity, its anti-Protestant emphasis on the body, and its connection with a foreign power.[11] That Douglass personally harbored anti-Catholic animus is clear from his descriptions of religious practices throughout his life, and this largely overlooked hostility influences much of his rhetoric regarding immigration and national character. In 1869, for example, Douglass provokes a controversy when an Ohio priest accuses him of castigating Catholics in his audience for the role Pope Gregory XIII played in the assassination of William the Silent, who led a Dutch uprising against the Catholic Spanish in the sixteenth century. Douglass identifies William's anti-Catholic revolt as a precursor to the emphatically Protestant American Revolution.[12] Douglass is alleged to have made "a very ugly insinuation against Catholics when he spoke of the here-existing danger of a dreaded connection between Church and state. . . . Had Mr. Douglass left out of his long and tedious lecture, all the repetitions of 'Pope,' and 'Bishops,' and 'Inquisition,' and 'Catholic persecution,' . . . [in this] senseless tirade, he could have given the really good sense of the lecture in 15 minutes."[13] At least for most of the remaining hour and three quarters, Douglass apparently reviles Catholicism, reflecting his own self-fashioning as a reformationist at all levels.

But Douglass had specific reasons to worry about economic and social competition between African Americans and Irish Americans, and much of the political rancor between black Republicanism and Irish American Democratic affiliation stemmed from each group's sense of possessing irreconcilable interests. If Douglass calculatedly participated in antebellum anti-Catholic baiting as part of a more general American nativism, he does so to further the cause of black Americans, not specifically disempower another group. As Noel Ignatiev points out in his illuminating study *How the Irish Became White,* "Ireland had an old antislavery tradition . . . which had prohibited Irish trade in English slaves"; yet one must join Ignatiev in asking, as Douglass would, "how the Catholic Irish, an oppressed race in Ireland, became part of an oppressing race in America."[14]

At this point, some brief background on the Irish in America is crucial for understanding Douglass's attitude to immigrant politics. In the colonial period, most Catholics settled in Maryland, with priests as well as laymen involved in slaveowning. (In 1785, 15,800 Catholics owned 3,000 black slaves in Maryland: Catholics in the early Republic were more associated with slavery than they would be in later periods.) As H. Shelton Smith notes in his study of Southern religion, though some Catholics lamented the existence of slavery, Catholic doctrine disavowed only abuses in slavery and never the institution of slavery itself, which was held to violate neither natural nor divine law; Catholic spokesmen adamantly dissociated themselves from the abolitionist notion that slavery was inherently sinful.[15] By 1860, 1,600,000 Irish resided in America, accounting for half the country's Catholic population and helping contextualize their virtual identification with Catholicism.[16] Catholics were also increasingly identified as opponents of emancipation; during the Civil War, for example, one of the severest critics of abolitionism was Courteny Jenkins, editor of the Baltimore *Catholic Mirror,* who wrote that "It is fanaticism or hypocrisy to condemn slavery as in itself criminal, or opposed to the laws of God."[17] Before the Civil War, many immigrant Catholics, politically marginalized and wary of radical movements, felt that abolitionism was disloyal to the existing government of the North; many were also deterred by the sense that abolitionism was closely allied to rationalism and to virulently anti-Catholic enlightenment propositions about the equality of men. While Daniel O'Connell was able to stir European Catholics against slavery, he largely failed with Irish Americans, who found Archbishop Hughes of New York and even the reformist Bishop England of Charleston more politically palatable. (The former, while opposed to slavery, was perceived in his arguments with Orestes Brownson to favor the slave trade: he wrote, "sometimes it has appeared to us that abolitionism . . . stands in need of a strait jacket and the humane protection of a lunatic asylum."[18]) The white family most associated with abolitionism, the Beechers, were noted for preaching notoriously anti-Catholic sermons.[19] Still, whether for reasons of poverty or conscience, as Bishop England noted, by the mid-nineteenth century few Catholics owned slaves, and in the Protestant South the Catholic Church itself had little contact with slaves.[20] Against this background in the United States, abolitionism was imagined to have a largely Protestant base of support in Britain; as a result, English colonialism in Ireland was thus often entirely separated from the issue of slavery. This state of affairs left Catholic Irish immigrants as inevitable targets, for they offered few political advantages to what became a largely Northern, Protestant abolitionist cause that was perpetually coveting British support.

While the Irish immigrant allegedly could not see the plight of blacks in America, Douglass is apparently rare among abolitionists in commenting on the stifling poverty he encounters in Ireland, much of which strikes too close to home. But though concretely sympathetic, he is usually careful to distance himself in the abstract. The Irish at home offer uncomfortable reminders of how a people not held in slavery can still be victimized, and at certain points Douglass seems to feel more comfortable among the Protestant Irish than the Catholic. In a letter from Belfast to R. D. Webb, Douglass writes that "the field here is ripe for the harvest; this is the very hotbed of Presbyterianism and free churchism, a blow can be struck here more effectively than in any other part of Ireland. One nail driven in a sure place is better than a dozen driven at random."[21] That is, the Protestants are certain while the Catholics are unreliable and random, uncontrolled signifiers in the battle over slavery. (Douglass also remarks of his success in "getting the Methodist meeting house [in Belfast], in the face of letters prejudicial to [him] both from Cork and Dublin."[22]) Presbyterian and Methodist Ireland are singled out as allies, while others remain conspicuously unmentioned. Douglass inveterately imagines his stronghold to be among the non-Catholic population of Ireland, and he identifies the unsympathetic Irish with the Catholic population that immigrates to America, an identification that repeatedly puts him at odds with those who seek emancipation from Ireland. In this inversion, Douglass identifies with victims at home but oppressors abroad.

Still, Douglass does feel at liberty to promote the overarching cause of human freedom to certain audiences. Though expressing great pleasure at Irish Catholic hospitality in his letters, Douglass primarily conveys

shock at the poverty inflicted upon the Irish; in his letters he less cyni-
cally asserts that "I see much here to remind me of my former condition,
and I confess I should be ashamed to lift up my voice against American
slavery, but that I know the cause of humanity is one the world over." [23]
Douglass also repeatedly commends Daniel O'Connell, who claims that
his "sympathy is not confined to the limits of [his] own green Ireland":
in "Impressions Abroad," Douglass writes that O'Connell, though fervently pursuing Irish independence, "refused bribes and sent back what
he considered the bloodstained offering of [Southern churches], saying he
would 'never purchase the freedom of Ireland with the price of slaves.'" [24]
In admitting that Southern attempts to turn the Irish against emancipation fail with O'Connell, Douglass acknowledges that Irish independence and abolition are not mutually exclusive goals. [25] But for Douglass,
the Irish American cause is never reconciled with abolitionism.

Ironically, Douglass elaborates the continuing sentiment of the British
themselves, who in this context sound all too much like the opponents
in his own struggle. Partly in response to the same pro-labor Chartist
movement Douglass had been involved with, "The English governing
classes in the 1860s regarded the Irish and the non-European 'native'
peoples just as they had, quite openly, regarded their own labouring
classes for many centuries: as thoroughly undisciplined, with a tendency
to resort to bestial behaviour . . . naturally lazy and unwilling to work
unless under compulsion." [26] The Irish had thus explicitly been catego-
rized alongside blacks long before they had emigrated to the new world.
While still maintaining the possibility of common cause, Douglass writes
that poverty has scarred the Irish exactly as it has his race: he offers that
he had

> no wish to wound the feelings of any Irishman, that these people lacked only
> a black skin and woolly hair, to complete their likeness to the plantation Ne-
> gro. The open, uneducated, mouth – the long, gaunt arm – the badly formed
> foot and ankle – the shuffling gait – the retreating forehead and vague expres-
> sion – and their petty quarrels and fights – all reminded me of the plantation
> . . . . The Irishman ignorant and degraded, compares in form and feature,
> with the Negro! [27]

With these comments on personal traits and the racial signs of poverty,
Douglass situates blacks and Irish Americans as competitors within a

new system; if the degraded Irish are "Negroes" at home – almost family in race and religion – they become Catholics in their adopted home. This comparison is double-edged, revoicing the very connections the British make between the Irish and blacks. Douglass's empathy with the social conditions that cause degradation helps account for his need emphatically to distance himself and his cause from that of Irish Americans; once in America, the Irish can only participate in an internecine sibling rivalry with African Americans.

Douglass also remarks that "when England wants to set the heel of her power more firmly in the quivering heart of old Ireland, the Celts are 'an inferior race.' So, too, the negro . . . [becomes] an inferior man," (a stipulation Douglass returns to repeatedly).[28] But in this case, their conditions are rendered parallel, equivalent in political terms without reference to religion or the victim's contribution to his own fate. In his public speeches, however, Douglass more often conveys the opinion that to promote one cause is to detract from another: to seek close parallels with the Irish or Irish liberation would in the end undermine the black freedom movement.

On his trips abroad, Douglass thus envisions a highly mutable coalition of the oppressed. Like O'Connell, Douglass professes that "the cause of humanity is one the world over"; but he must, for example, object in Scotland to Dr. Chalmers' insistence on the specific fellowship of all Presbyterians, which would include slaveholders. Douglass then does not consistently appeal for the creation of a fellowship of other colonized people – whom he at times seems to distrust – but instead only for an end to the fellowship of the oppressors. Douglass more frequently utilizes a local politics whose alliances shift according to immediate goals. Rather than call on the "weak" Irish for help, he appeals primarily to the more powerful Scots, partly because he cannot fully imagine any community of interests not negated by difference of religion. Douglass of course has a special affinity for Sir Walter Scott's *Lady of the Lake,* from which he takes his own surname: this initial symbolic connection to a Protestant Scotland emblematizes a larger allegiance to Scottish politics and Scottish influence in America. In general, Douglass's anglophilia, a trait he notes happily sharing with Emerson, sage of Concord,[29] does not extend to the Catholic sections of Ireland.

Douglass does remark that "one of the most pleasing features of [his] visit [to Ireland] thus far, has been a total absence of all manifestations of prejudice against [him], on account of [his] color."[30] Douglass does presume that the Irish at home are colorblind; yet as soon as they leave Ireland, their Catholicism exigently intervenes. In the October 1859 issue of *The Monthly,* the author of "The Irish Deputation to America" bitterly responds to the requests of Irish evangelicals seeking to rid Ireland of its form of "slavery," the British authorities; such exhortations can only detract from the cause of American abolitionism. The author begins by admitting that, "coming from a country whose soil has ever been uncursed by the presence of a single African slave, or a single African *slave-trader,* the deputation must be supposed to be, with their country and religion against slavery." Yet such sentiments and suppositions turn out to mean little and strategically set up the delegation: the Irish are "under the dominion of a most crushing system" but cannot look to American evangelicals for help, since these same evangelicals have not aided their own oppressed. And the Irish are held responsible for this crushing religious—and not political—system. The tone of the article is strident, as if the black cause were in direct competition or even conflict with that of the Irish: "the [Irish] deputation has made a most lamentable mistake" in seeking help in America, for "how can Satan cast out Satan?" The force oppressing Ireland is thus explicitly transformed from the British political enterprise to "Romish superstition and priestcraft."

The Douglass Paper minces no words in literally demonizing the Catholic Church as a force of evil and in following popular prejudice in equating Irish Catholicism with popery. Douglass often "spoke of the prevalence and power of the Christian Church and religion at Rome and of the strange things that are believed and practiced there in the way of religious rites and ceremonies." Douglass's own pro-Scottish bias further helps contextualize his anti-Catholic bent: while visiting Avignon, for example, Douglass writes, pun in hand, "what a horrible lie the Romish church has palmed off upon the people."[31] We wind up with a circular process. Douglass acknowledges that "we, as a nation have no right to claim exemption from criticism from abroad. . . . By casting out the blacks from the sympathies of this country," America has forced them to seek redress abroad.[32] Blacks have been "cast out" but must in turn cast out both those who have shown prejudice against them and those who would contend too closely for their position. If blacks have a right to seek aid from foreign countries to further the cause of abolition, Douglass is reluctant to grant that right to the Irish seeking support in America.[33] Catholicism becomes the scapegoat for the fact that the Irish bear a position too close to that of blacks for an allegiance to be formed between them. Douglass thus effectively seeks to preempt any Irish American Catholic involvement in the abolitionist movement, often on the pretext of religion rather than political grounds.

Though he considers the Irish to have suffered as much as the American Negro, Douglass makes religion in general and Catholicism in particular the enemy: he claims that "the persecution of [Ireland's] people resulted from religious bigotry and political folly, and not from a difference of race. The fact that religious differences have caused far more persecution and oppression than any physical peculiarities among men, often affords me a melancholy satisfaction."[34] That melancholy satisfaction also generates Douglass's dismissive tone toward Catholics, denying the victimhood of and blaming the victim. For Douglass, it would insult and denigrate blacks to see Americans first respond to the suffering of the Irish, and the "deep complicity of the American evangelical churches with slavery" would in any case prevent our saving Ireland from what is sardonically called "the slavery of Romanism."[35] Douglass and those he publishes make Catholicism, not British domination, the source of an Irish slavery. Yet if the Irish have been the victims of prejudice at home—of oppression partly generated by their acceptance of Catholicism—Irish Americans have on entirely voluntary terms become oppressors in a way consistent with that Catholicism.

Anti-Irish sentiment had different sources for different subject positions, but Douglass could recalibrate the resentment to suit a variety of political ends, some of which would initially seem to be at odds with others. As Jenny Franchot quotes from the nativist Joseph Berg, "I count the poor slave . . . a freeman, when compared with the man who breathes the atmosphere of liberty, and yet voluntarily feters his soul . . . bound hand and foot, to the sovereign will and pleasure of a popish priest." What is startling is that Douglass himself actively partakes of this nativist rhetoric, always arguing that Catholicism represents a voluntary form of

bondage. In tracing ways Catholicism represented a threat of white enslavement and captivity, Franchot pinpoints "a depressing capacity to
rationalize chattel slavery as one (and not the worst) among a series of
enslavements, a reasoning that suggests how images of bondage to papal
captivity could minimize objections to race slavery." Catholicism thus
represented both a consensual form of bondage and a species of imprisonment, inquisition, or potential contamination, ultimately reflecting fears of "Protestant captivity to Rome."[36] Even if Irish Catholicism,
in the period before the Ultramontane policy of Rome, was essentially
distinct from Roman Catholicism, in America it was largely conflated
with Romanism in the latter half of the nineteenth century. In a form of
circular cultural logic, Rome came to represent a bondage more threatening than the actual slavery for which it became a scapegoat as well as
a form of sublimation.

As Noel Ignatiev alerts us, opposition to slavery did not imply approval of abolitionism, which, in the words of the Boston Irish newspaper *The Pilot,* was "thronged with bigoted and persecuting religionists;
with men who . . . desire the extermination of Catholics by fire and
sword."[37] As Ignatiev suggests, the Repeal Movement–the campaign to
dissolve British rule over Ireland–became identified with slavery, with
Robert Taylor, son of a slaveholding president, becoming one of Repeal's prominent spokesmen. William Lloyd Garrison admonished that
the Irish took a sudden interest in preserving the "sacredness of Southern Institutions," and that the diabolical bargain had become that "the
South shall go for Repeal, and the Irish, as a body, shall go for Southern slavery!" Thus was abolitionism equated with an anti-Catholic sen-
sibility, and a wedge driven between the groups in America; as Ignatiev
chronicles, through the late 1840s it became increasingly possible and
common for Irish politicians at home openly to advocate slavery: "instead of the Irish love of liberty warming America, the winds of republican slavery blew back to Ireland."[38]

In America, meanwhile, Catholics were rarely vocal opponents of
slavery in the South. As Randall Miller contends, "whenever possible,
the Church avoided conflicts with local powers. . . . Catholic leaders were
sensitive to the Church's minority status in the Protestant South. . . .
Hostilities between Irish Catholic immigrants and slaves only intensi-

fied th[e] rift separating lower-class black and white Catholics."[39] Ironically, *The Douglass Monthly* chides evangelicalism as much as many Irish Catholics themselves do for seeking the religious conversion of Irishmen abroad—the eradication of their Catholicism—rather than the political salvation of African Americans at home.[40] The flaw that corrupts Irish Americans diverts political reform from Douglass's people. These "amazing and pernicious" attempts of the Irish to solicit political support against England from the South, from those who support American slavery, thus oddly allies them with the very forces they wish to supplant: American evangelicals, meanwhile, with the exception of a few preachers like Reverend Beecher, would "much rather deliver Ireland from Roman bondage, than the slave from Southern slavery."[41]

Douglass's courting of solidarity with England, but not Ireland, also reminds us how important the role of community could be to him: Douglass inveterately returns to that rhetoric—prominently displayed in *The Douglass Monthly*—of caste, of being cast out, and even more so of being out of caste. In his *Narrative,* what Douglass cannot leave behind is the position of the castout, the castaway: "The singing of a man cast away upon a desolate island" might sooner be construed as joyous than that of a slave, and the comparison resonates throughout his work.[42] (The rhetoric of casting out or being cast away retains a religious tone, and Douglass's obloquies against Catholics retain a polemical religious aspect.) From his position as former slave, Douglass always abhors such exclusion yet also continues to imagine that someone must precisely wind up being cast out; he who was once cast away must now accept the responsibility of having to vie for the center. Douglass orates that "The spirit of caste is malignant and dangerous everywhere. . . . There is, worst of all, religious prejudice. . . . Perhaps no class of our fellow-citizen has carried this prejudice against color to a point more extreme and dangerous than have our Catholic Irish fellow-citizens, and yet no people on the face of the earth have been more relentlessly persecuted."[43] Catholicism, or Romanism as Douglass erroneously typifies it, thus represents a double evil: the evil that brings to Ireland "ignorance, cunning, and crimes"—and hence diverts attention abroad and away from the cause of American blacks—and the evil that remains silent about American slavery at home. For Frederick Douglass to have embraced the Irish cause and also tolerate Catholicism would have required an internationalism entirely beyond the reach of African Americans struggling to attain a position within the American nation. One should also remember that Douglass himself was an ordained deacon and "licensed as a local African Methodist Episcopal Zion Church preacher," part of a group that included many of the most prominent abolitionists, including Sojourner Truth and Harriet Tubman.[44] This "freedom church" associated with the Episcopal tradition implicitly espoused a literally liberationist theology, standing in marked contrast to what could at best be termed the neutrality of the Catholic Church.

Though it claimed to accommodate men of all races in its universal church, Catholicism in practice made few objections to the importation of African slaves, showing more concern for Native American populations.[45] As Randall Miller details, "When several Southern cities charged the Catholic Church with abolitionist sympathies because of its opposition to the slave trade [in the early 1840s], Southern Catholic churchmen almost fell over themselves to correct such calumnies."[46] In a representative article in the March 1861 *Douglass Monthly,* "Slavery and the Irish Element," readers are presented with the warnings of Thomas D'Arcy McGee, who writes that "twice within a few years, I have had cause to hang my head in shame, for Irish honors in America. Once, when a brilliant and honest writer . . . publicly advocated the reopening by the South of that traffic accursed of god and man. . . . The second when [Charles O'Connor] . . . laid down the extraordinary proposition, 'political parties should never be divided upon moral questions.'"

Throughout the run of *The Douglass Monthly,* Irish Americans become the enemy within, former slaves now riddled with prejudice and corrupted by the church. Unlike the Scottish at home and abroad, who are criticized but also acknowledged as crucial supporters of the abolitionist cause, Irish American Catholics are reproved in *The Monthly,* depicted as those most loudly advocating "the reopening of the African slave trade" or the continuation of slavery by other means.[47] For rhetorical reasons, Douglass often fails to differentiate among those Irish Americans, though he does often demarcate the differences among Irish Catholics and Protestants and between Irish classes abroad. As Donald Akenson notes in *Small Differences: Irish Catholics and Irish Protestants, 1815–1922: An Inter-*

national Perspective, even many contemporary historians configure all Irish Americans as Catholic and "wall off the Irish Protestants into some non-Irish category."[48] The Catholic Irish emerged as what many writers would call British ethnics in America and came to subsume all other categories of the Irish in popular discourse. Like many Americans, Douglass tends to consider Irish Americans as *de facto* Catholics and to conflate Irish Catholicism with the still often separate ontology of Roman Catholicism. For example, Douglass almost never berates the typically more powerful English Catholics, who paradoxically maintain innocence through their closer connection with the empire.

Well over a million Irish emigrated to the United States during the Great Famine from 1845 to 1852, just as the debate over slavery proceeded with full force. These Irish were imagined as susceptible to the political influence of the church, which remained resistant to taking a political stand against slavery.[49] Irish Americans might otherwise have rebuked abolitionism simply through its affiliation with an often virulently anti-Catholic evangelicalism. As Jenny Franchot remarks, "New England hostility to immigrant Catholicism in the three decades prior to the Civil War facilitated the mounting racial attack on slavery by popularizing a usefully improbable and clearly regional rhetoric of purity and contamination. . . . One could attack the South for the Romanism of its slaveholding practices rather than the white supremacism of such customs."[50] Again, it is ironic that Douglass joins in this campaign against Romanism—in part because the campaign would divert attention from the real issues of slavery and in part because it did not espouse abolitionism—even while others attacked Romanism not for its association with slavery but simply as its own form of slavery. Clearly, Romanism was as subject to as many attacks from opposing quarters, and as subject to political manipulation, as the issue of slavery itself. Tellingly, Douglass uses the same rhetoric to condemn these "contaminations" of slavery that he applies, along with other orators, to Catholicism.[51]

Against this background, the Irish are endemically referred to as an unseemly *element* of America: Douglass is "told that the Irish element in this country is exceedingly strong, and that element will never allow colored men to stand upon an equal political footing with whites."[52] Universalized Irish Catholics are both cast out and "elementalized" throughout Douglass's work. Once cooperation proves impossible, the specter of mixture appears: if, as Noel Ignatiev suggests, the Irish were imagined in the early nineteenth century as inverted blacks, and African Americans as blackened Irish, a rhetoric of elements and mixture becomes more understandable. Irish and African Americans lived in close proximity and often in the same social sphere, brought so close together that tensions were inevitable.[53] As Ignatiev chronicles, the Irish "became white" at the expense of blacks; with terms like "element," Douglass responds with a kind of racial rhetoric to categorize Irish Americans as a competing, but emphatically more foreign, minority group.

In a September 1855 issue of the *Frederick Douglass Paper,* Douglass writes, "if native born colored Americans experienced the same treatment at the hands of the National and state governments, as aliens do, we should not have so much about which to murmur and complain." Here Douglass's anger is directed against the Irish immigrant T. F. Meagher, who was granted exceptional privilege to immigrate and practice law. Douglass writes, "Now, we have not one word to utter about the admission of Mr. Meagher, on the account of his being an Irishman. We call attention to the fact; and ask those who voted against us on the equal suffrage question, to consider it, and contrast it with the fact of our treatment. The colored man, the native born American receives nothing by 'courtesy.'"[54] Once more Douglass resorts to a rhetoric of nativism in trying to characterize blacks as native, as having precedence over foreigners, or later, to some extent in the case of voting rights, over women. The issue of precedence creates a similar rift between the women's suffrage movement and post-emancipation African American reform movements.[55] Douglass repeatedly remarks, recycling the stock images he accumulates for his speeches, that he "saw Pat, fresh from the Emerald Isle, requiring two sober men to keep him on his legs, enter and deposit his vote for the Democratic candidate amid the loud hurrahs of his fellow citizens."[56] Douglass here does criticize the still-Irish citizen before he has been conditioned to fear or dislike blacks; in the process of being made an Irish American, he is unfortunately transformed into a Democrat and a supporter of slavery as an American institution. Douglass continues, again invoking his standard scenario, that if the Negro "knows as much when he is sober as an Irishmen when he is drunk, he should be able to vote on good American principles." [57] Douglass remarks, still using the collective, representative voice of *The Monthly* in treating the Irish, in a sense, race to race.

> We hope that when the question of Equal Suffrage shall again be presented to the consideration of the citizens of this state, they will ponder well upon the impracticability (to use no stronger term) of extending to aliens, rights and privileges, denied to their own fellow-citizens. At the polls, we were defeated on this very question, by the Irish, who rushed, as it were, en masse to the ballot box, and impudently declared that *we should have no equal rights* with them . . . . We throw this remark to those "*foreigners*" who proscribed *us* at the polls. But we are told that we are not citizens! [58]

When he is appointed in 1872 as an elector for the Republican Party during the Grant campaign, Douglass writes that this was a bold move "considering the deep-rooted sentiment of the masses against Negroes, the noise and tumult likely to be raised, especially among our adopted citizens of Irish descent." [59] For Douglass, the newly adopted Irish then systematically come to compete against and gain the upper hand over the blacks, who were forcibly brought to America and have never been recognized as its legitimate children. In consistent terms, Douglass chides the Irish themselves for escaping the bondage of Ireland by usurping the social caste blacks should have next achieved in America. Douglass admits that he "finds it strange that the Irish people are among our bitterest persecutors. In one sense it is strange . . . but in another it is easily accounted for. It is said that a negro always makes the most cruel negro driver. . . . The Irishman has been persecuted for his religion about as rigorously as the black man has been for his color." [60] Douglass then resorts to attacking their religion as the Catholic Irishman implicitly attacks his color. In the end, the two groups still compete in having a history of being persecuted, yet in Douglass's eyes the Irish are no longer oppressed in America; once freed, they attempt to assume mastery over blacks.

If the Irish show Douglass no manifestation of color prejudice when he visits their country, the same can rarely be said of the Irish who emigrate to America:

The Irish who, at home, readily sympathize with the oppressed everywhere, are instantly taught when they step upon our soil to hate and despise the Negro. They are taught to believe that he eats the bread that belongs to them. . . . Every hour sees us elbowed out of some employment to make room for some newly-arrived emigrant from the Emerald Isle, whose hunger and color entitle him to special favor . . . while a ceaseless enmity in the Irish is excited against us . . .[61]

Throughout 1849, Douglass repeatedly notes that

there is one class of transatlantic men who come to this country, to which I wish to call special attention. It is the Irish. Now I am far from finding fault with the Irish for coming to this country . . . but I met with an Irishman a few weeks ago [who] conversed with me on the subject of slavery. . . . And that man, newly imported to this country, gravely told me that . . . the colored people in this country could never rise here, and ought to go back to Africa. What I have to say to Ireland is,—send no more such children here.[62]

Once like blacks, the Irish have now displaced them. Douglass then seeks precise parallels for mistreatment between Irish and blacks, but not future political strategies of allegiance: "If this description [of brutality] can be given of Ireland, how much more true is it when applied to the sons and daughters of Africa, in the United States?"[63] Douglass here tries to reclaim a black position from Catholicism. In 1851, Douglass tells a crowd in Rochester, New York, that previously it was "not the Catholic's skin but the Catholic's faith that subjected him to persecution. Legislators were offended at his faith. . . . *Precisely* where England was a hundred years ago in legislating for the Irish, just there the American people are now in legislating for the free colored people of the United States."[64] In other words, Catholics have been freed, and Douglass can't grant them any more rights here or abroad at black expense. Again, Douglass claims in 1853 that "if this [saying about a bloody history] were true in relation to the Irish people it was still *more true* in relation to the colored people of the United States."[65] As part of his method of reclaiming a moral imperative, Douglass repeatedly argues that what is true of Ireland is "more true" of America. One of Douglass's favorite stock anecdotes involves Daniel O'Connell's remark that Ireland's history "can be traced like a wounded man through a crowd, by the blood," and that black history in the United States more than follows suit: for Douglass, O'Connell's remark is "incomparably more truthful . . . respecting the negro." Douglass also notes that his friend once called him the "Black O'Connell of America." [66]

But Douglass is startlingly Emersonian on this issue, contradicting himself to create the effect he requires. In 1850 he observes that "It is often said, by the opponents of the Anti-slavery cause, that the condition of the people of Ireland is more deplorable than that of the American slaves. *Far* be it from me to underrate the sufferings of the Irish people. . . . Yet I must say there is *no analogy* between the two cases. The Irishman is poor, but he is not a slave." [67] In such instances, Douglass must undo all his previous assertions to emphasize the difference, the lack of common cause, between the two peoples. Douglass thus frequently laments that where the black man has no access to state jobs, "an ignorant Irishman, however, but just come to this country . . . is, the moment he lands on our shores, thought fit to be entrusted with the mail bags." [68] He later notes that though he deplores them, "the condition of the Irish tenant is merciful, tender, and just as compared to the American freedman." [69] Douglass systematically imagines that anti-Irish prejudice, religious rather than political, has been resolved abroad, while rhetorically sublimating issues of direct political and economic competition between Irish Americans and African Americans in America. He must now be sure to downplay, for instance, the very poverty he had emphatically denounced while in Ireland.

One would like to imagine that Douglass's final resolution on the issue of common cause was to double back to unite the two groups on political grounds, though he would never accommodate Catholicism: "The Irish people, warm hearted, generous, and sympathizing with the oppressed everywhere when they stand upon their own green island, are instantly taught upon arriving in this Christian country to hate and despise the colored people. . . . The cruel lie is told the Irish that our adversity is essential to their prosperity. Sir, the Irish will find out one day . . . that in assuming our avocation he has also assumed our degradation." [70] The hope for unification then rests on common degradation: here Douglass equates Irish Americans and African Americans by noting that the logic of slavery relies on the contemporary desire of the "Anglo-Saxon [to] boast [of] his superiority to the negro and to the Irishman."[71] The Irish and blacks could now finally be allied along the lines of class rather than race. In 1871, after emancipation had been achieved, Douglass does write that England is no longer a leader in social progress; he avers that it horribly mistreats "its own rebellious subjects in Ireland as well as in the colonies," and laments the persecution of Irish Catholics as "worthy of the darkest days of fanaticism." Once the Civil War is over, Douglass is more often able to criticize the British colonial enterprise at home. But even here, Douglass continues to comment on the Irish presence in America, for instance again noting that "in our country the Irish form a troublesome element of the population."[72] While Ireland was no longer an external threat, Irish Americans remained an internal source of conflict.

Douglass's complicated anxiety over economic competition with the Irish, his personal antipathy for the tenets of Catholicism, and his embrace of a nativist individualism that imagines Catholicism as a foreign value system all contribute to the development of an anti-Catholic, anti–Irish American discourse in his work. Though Douglass succumbs on many occasions to his own prejudices and to seeking political advantage against another still relatively disenfranchised group, he also consistently upholds the overarching principle that any short-term gains attained through disunity would only enslave the seeming victor. At some level, Douglass remains keenly aware that the traits he projects onto Irish American Catholics, real or imagined, are generated by a history all too closely mirroring that of his own people.

NOTES

1. See Shelley Fisher Fishkin and Carla Peterson, "'We Hold These Truths to be Self-Evident': The Rhetoric of Frederick Douglass's Journalism," in *Frederick Douglass: New Literary and Historical Essays,* ed. Eric J. Sundquist (New York: Cambridge University Press, 1990), 189–204.

2. Contrary to the claims of some critics—for example, George Bornstein in his article "Afro-Celtic Connections: From Frederick Douglass to the Commitments"—African American and Irish and Irish American self-representations have not been entirely reciprocal. African Americans and Irish Americans were often similarly represented in cultural discourse in early America. In Tabitha Gilman Tenney's 1801 novel *Female Quixotism,* for

example, black and Irish stereotypes are prominent and in many ways overlap: early anti-Catholic and anti-Irish prejudice and racism are mutually supporting, even as the association becomes a point of tension. For a primarily literary and positive overview of black-Irish relations, see Bornstein in *Literary Influence and African-American Writers,* ed. Tracy Mishkin (New York: Garland, 1996), 171–88.

3. Philip S. Foner, ed., *The Life and Writings of Frederick Douglass,* 5 vols. (New York: International Publishers, 1950–55), 2:482.

4. John W. Blassingame, ed., *The Frederick Douglass Papers. Series One: Speeches, Debates, and Interviews,* 5 vols. (New Haven: Yale University Press, 1979–), 2:353.

5. Ibid., 4:364; 2:51. See also Frederick Douglass, *Life and Times of Frederick Douglass* (1893; London, 1962), 505.

6. See William McFeely, *Frederick Douglass* (New York: W. W. Norton, 1991), 119.

7. Blassingame, *Papers,* 2:83.

8. Ibid., 5:68.

9. Ibid., 1:77 n.

10. "Important Truth," in Foner, *Life and Writings,* 1:228. Issues of European emancipation were also crucial to Douglass, as well as other African American writers. In *Clotel,* for example, William Wells Brown conveys many of the same objections as Douglass, noting that Americans "have an abundance of sympathy for 'poor Ireland': they can furnish a ship of war to convey the Hungarian refugees." Brown contrasts how, as Christopher Mulvey notes, Americans could celebrate "European liberationists such as John Mitchell of Ireland and Louis Kossuth of Hungary and on the other hand [allow the] persecution of fugitive liberationists such as himself and Frederick Douglass." As Mulvey reminds us, "Almost from the first day of his arrival in the United States, [the Irish] Mitchell declared himself a strenuous opponent of abolition." See Mulvey, "The Fugitive Self and the New World of the North: William Wells Brown's Discovery of America," in *The Black Columbiad: Defining Moments in African American Literature and Culture,* ed. Werner Sollors and Maria Diedrich (Cambridge, Mass.: Harvard University Press, 1994), 99–111. In contrast with his anti-Catholic tendencies, Frederick Douglass by comparison rarely displays anxiety about serfdom or religion in Hungary.

11. Jenny Franchot, *Roads to Rome: The Antebellum Protestant Encounter with Catholicism* (Berkeley: University of California Press, 1994), xvii, 87–8, 363–64.

12. Blassingame, *Papers,* 4:186. For further discussion of pervasive anti-Catholicism, see Eric Lundquist, *To Wake the Nations: Race in the Making of American Literature* (Cambridge, Mass.: Harvard University Press, 1993), 137, 146–48.

13. Ibid., 4:615 16.

14. See Ignatiev, *How the Irish Became White* (New York: Routledge, 1995), 7, 1. While the force of his argument is on Douglass's perceptions of Ireland, rather than the historical context of Irish class attitudes or Irish–African American relations per se, Ignatiev's

book provides an invaluable supplementary framework for understanding the abolitionist's position on national and international justice. For more general background on Irish immigration to the United States, see P. J. Drudy, ed., *The Irish in America: Emigration, Assimilation and Impact* (Cambridge: Cambridge University Press, 1985). Also see David R. Roediger, *The Wages of Whiteness: Race and the Making of the American Working Class* (London: Verso, 1991).

15. H. Shelton Smith, *In His Image But . . . Racism in Southern Religion, 1780–1910* (Durham, N.C.: Duke University Press, 1972), 7.

16. Ibid., 98.

17. Ibid., 200.

18. Reverend Benjamin Blied, *Catholics and the Civil War* (privately published, Milwaukee, 1945), 32. Douglass usually blatantly identifies Catholicism for its proslavery bias: "O. A. Brownson had then recently become a Catholic, and taking advantage of his new Catholic audience in Brownson's *Quarterly Review,* had charged O'Connell with attacking American institutions [i.e. slavery]." (*Life and Times,* 238.) Though he does differentiate among foreign Catholics—most notably in always praising Daniel O'Connell for his antislavery stance as a universal champion of freedom—Douglass tends to assume American Catholics support slavery until proven otherwise.

19. Blied, *Catholics and the Civil War,* 20–21. Harriet Beecher Stowe's "evangelical critique of the Catholic household of the St. Clare family in *Uncle Tom's Cabin,* [which] indicts slavery for its spiritual tyranny over the soul more than for its racial tyranny over the body" would parallel only parts of Douglass's renunciation. While Douglass would repudiate Catholicism for its spiritual slavery, he would never downplay the physical realities of slavery nor place abstract spiritual liberation above specific and literal emancipation. See Franchot, *Roads to Rome,* 103. Stowe's views regarding colonization and black "repatriation" to Africa and her evolving view of Catholicism also clearly differentiate her from Douglass (whom Martin Delaney nevertheless chided for being Stowe's "attorney"): according to Ann Douglass, for example, Stowe "genuinely welcomed the potential Catholicism of the Anglican Church in an immigrant and urban culture." See Ann Douglass, *The Feminization of American Culture* (New York: Avon, 1977), 299. On Delaney, Douglass, and Stowe, see Richard Yarborough, "Strategies of Black Characterization in *Uncle Tom's Cabin* and the Early Afro-American Novel," in Mishkin, *Literary Influence and African-American Writers,* 49.

20. See John T. Gillard, *The Catholic Church and the American Negro* (Baltimore: St. Joseph's Society Press, 1929), 25.

21. "To R. D. Webb," in Foner, *Life and Writings,* 1 : 13.

22. Ibid., 1 : 14.

23. "To William Lloyd Garrison," Blassingame, *Papers,* 1 : 141.

24. See Douglass, *Life and Times,* 238. As James Haughton writes—paralleling Doug-

lass's position in urging him to intervene among their countrymen now in America—the considerable Irish influence in American politics had "most unfortunately . . . been given heretofore in favor of slavery." See Ignatiev, *How the Irish Became White,* 9.

25. In fact, the strong potential for collaboration existed. According to Eric Lott, it is clear that O'Connell and William Lloyd Garrison frequently corresponded in the 1840s, "attempting for a time an 'internationalist' labor abolitionism . . . though it ultimately failed in its project." A tavern in Philadelphia sported a placard with a bust of O'Connell and a snippet from Byron's *Childe Harold* "that may have permitted a variety of political investments: 'Hereditary bondsmen! who would be free, / Themselves must strike the blow.' " Lott further notes that Frederick Douglass appended this couplet to the end of the Covey chapter [18] of *My Bondage and My Freedom.* See Eric Lott, "White Kids and No Kids at All: Languages of Race in Antebellum U.S. Working-Class Culture," in *Rethinking Class: Literary Studies and Social Formations,* ed. Wai Chee Dimock and Michael T. Gilmore (New York: Columbia University Press, 1994), 175–211 (quotations on pp. 190–91).

26. Bernard Semmell, *The Governor Eyre Controversy* (London: MacGibbon and Kee, 1962), quoted in Peter Fryer, *Staying Power: The History of Black People in Britain* (London: Pluto Press, 1984), 170.

27. "Negro Claims Ethnologically Considered," in Foner, *Life and Writings,* 2:305.

28. Blassingame, *Papers,* 4:67.

29. See Waldo E. Martin, *The Mind of Frederick Douglass* (Chapel Hill: University of North Carolina Press, 1984), 199. Here Douglass the representative man would also find the Scottish enlightenment emphasis on individuality and property an appealing (and in some ways equivalent) alternative to the Jacksonian individualism to which he could not have full access at home. Douglass becomes Emersonian in several specific respects, not just in his ability to manipulate rhetoric. Douglass can be "atemporal" in his writing, using his speeches throughout his life much as Emerson used his journals, as almost random ur-sources of material, thereby creating a historical pastiche; charting a specific linear development in his thought about any topic, such as Catholicism, can thus be difficult.

30. *The Liberator,* 10 October 1845, in Foner, *Life and Writings,* 1:120.

31. Blassingame, *Papers,* 1:38.

32. Ibid., 2:332.

33. Douglass late in life even writes that "poor, ragged, hungry, starving and as oppressed Ireland is, she is strong enough to be a standing menace to the power and glory of England," simultaneously admitting and denying that a colonized Ireland might need external assistance to free itself. See Douglass, *Life and Times,* 547.

34. Blassingame, *Papers,* 2:291.

35. *The Douglass Monthly,* October 1859, 146.

36. See Franchot, *Roads to Rome,* 171, 103.

37. See Ignatiev, *How the Irish Became White,* 13, 16. Once again, even in Garrison's

rhetoric, "the Irish" are unified as a monolithic block, much as African Americans are reified into one essentialist category.

38. Ibid., 31.

39. See Miller, "The Failed Mission: The Catholic Church and Black Catholics in the Old South," in *Catholics in the Old South: Essays on Church and Culture,* ed. Randall Miller and Jon Wakelyn (Macon, Ga.: Mercer University Press, 1983), 156–67.

40. *The Douglass Monthly,* October 1859, 146. Douglass manages to abjure Catholicism while simultaneously denouncing religious prejudice. If we understand that–in a representative Northern city in the latter half of the nineteenth century–"while the Irish [in America] initially suffered economically from anti-Catholic bias . . . the second and third generations were able to achieve economic mobility," we can sense why Douglass would be careful not to let sympathy for Irish Catholics abroad lead to empathy with Irish Americans: "even with the passing of several generations, black workers" did not achieve anything like the economic parity with immigrants and were "usually trapped in the lowest occupational strata." See C. Eric Lincoln and Lawrence H. Mamiya, *The Black Church in the African American Experience* (Durham, N.C.: Duke University Press, 1990), 238.

41. *The Douglass Monthly,* October 1959, 146. The paper singles out John Mitchell as especially reprehensible in his attempt to use American evangelicalism as a front to support his political aims in Ireland. It is worth noting that Mitchell went on to edit a proslavery paper during the Civil War. See Ignatiev, *How the Irish Became White,* 31.

42. Frederick Douglass, *Narrative of the Life of Frederick Douglass, An American Slave, Written by Himself* (1845; New York: New American Library, 1968), 31–32.

43. Douglass, *Life and Times,* 546.

44. See Lincoln and Mamiya, *The Black Church in the African American Experience,* 58, 247.

45. Blassingame, *Papers,* 1 : 302.

46. See Miller, "A Church in Cultural Captivity: Some Speculations on Catholic Identity in the Old South," in Miller and Wakelyn, *Catholics in the Old South,* 15. Aside from any mercenary reasons Catholics did not want to alienate themselves from other Christians in the South by vocally opposing slavery, it is unlikely that the Church would have offered an effective means of combatting its ills: as Gary McDonough reminds us, "The Catholic Church, as an organizational structure, was primarily urban while much of the South remained rural," along with the vast majority of the black population. See McDonough, *Black and Catholic in Savannah, Georgia* (Knoxville: University of Tennessee Press, 1993), 145. It is not surprising to learn, then, that in 1929 only 200,000 of almost 12 million African Americans identified themselves as Catholic. In addition, the overarching attachment of Catholics to an orthodox, Church-sanctioned and official view of the Bible, which condones slavery, might not as readily allow an "antinomian," local, antislavery interpretation of Biblical doctrine to stand. For Catholic census figures, see John Gillard,

The Catholic Church and the American Negro (1929; reprint, New York: Johnson Reprint, 1968), 47.

47. *The Douglass Monthly,* March 1861, 428.

48. See Akenson, *Small Difference: Irish Catholics and Irish Protestants, 1815–1922: An International Perspective* (Montreal: McGill-Queen's University Press, 1988), 100.

49. See Franchot, *Roads to Rome,* 100. As Noel Ignatiev suggests, one reason the heterogeneous Irish population–differentiated by class, religion and language–became the monolithic "Irish" involved the change in emigration patterns during the Great Famine. In the wake of this wave of poorer immigrants, older immigrants were reclassified into Scotch-Irish, with the result that the Irish in America now became Catholic, and a "racial (but not ethnic) line invented in Ireland was recreated as an ethnic (but not racial) line in America." See Ignatiev, *How the Irish Became White,* 39.

50. Franchot, *Roads to Rome,* 103.

51. For a discussion of Douglass's use of a religious rhetoric of pollution in his transformation to free man, see Richard Hardack, "Water Pollution and Motion Sickness: Rites of Passage in Nineteenth-Century Slave and Travel Narratives," *ESO: A Journal of the American Renaissance* 41.1 (1995): 1–40.

52. Blassingame, *Papers,* 3:581.

53. Ignatiev, *How the Irish Became White,* 41–2.

54. *The Frederick Douglass Paper,* September 1855.

55. Elizabeth Cady Stanton, one of the leading nineteenth-century advocates of women's rights and suffrage, also took an actively anticlerical stance throughout her career, a stance illuminating to contrast with Frederick Douglass's. Crucially, she repeatedly used anti-Irish rhetoric, which could also be employed against any group "competing" for women's suffrage–most immediately, blacks. See her "Speech to the Anniversary of the American Anti-Slavery Society [1860]," in *The Elizabeth Cady Stanton-Susan B. Anthony Reader: Correspondence, Writings, Speeches,* ed. Ellen DuBois (Boston: Northeastern University Press, 1981), 83.

56. Blassingame, *Papers,* 3:579.

57. Ibid., 4:66.

58. "Colored Americans, and Aliens–T. F. Meagher," in Blassingame, *Papers,* 365–66.

59. Douglass, *Life and Times,* 416.

60. Blassingame, *Papers,* 3:581. Noel Ignatiev characterizes the inversion by which Irish immigration hindered the cause of emancipation: "The truth is not, as some historians would have it, that slavery made it possible to extend to the Irish the privileges of citizenship, by providing another group for them to stand on, but the reverse, that the assimilation of the Irish into the white race made it possible to maintain slavery." Ignatiev, *How the Irish Became White,* 69.

61. Douglass, *Life and Times,* 299. Douglass cites Irish resistance to the draft in 1863 as final evidence of their racial prejudice, their refusal to fight an abolitionist war: "This was especially true of New York, where there was a large Irish population. The attempt to enforce the draft in that city was met by mobs, riot, and bloodshed . . . the Irish began to hang, stab, and murder the negroes in New York." See ibid., 355; and Blassingame, *Papers,* 5:438.

62. Douglass, *Life and Times,* 2:165.

63. Ibid., 2:27.

64. Ibid., 2:293.

65. Ibid., 2:426.

66. For example, ibid., 3:581; 4:130; 3:275. This process of one-upmanship can have a semicomic tone to it, as when people "compete" regarding how incomprehensibly poverty-stricken their families were when they were growing up.

67. Ibid., 2:258.

68. Ibid., 2:168. Competition for work, deliberately exacerbated by the planting and manufacturing classes, explains some of the basic antagonism between blacks and Irish Americans. See in particular, Dennis Clark, "The South's Irish Catholics: A Case of Cultural Confinement," in Miller and Wakelyn, *Catholics in the Old South,* 195–209.

69. Douglass, *Life and Times,* 5:367.

70. Ibid., 5:433.

71. Ibid., 5:488.

72. "The Position of the British Government Toward Liberty," in Foner, *Life and Writings,* 4:267–69.

Competing Representations

Douglass, the Ethiopian Serenaders, and

Ethnic Exhibition in London

SARAH MEER

F REDERICK DOUGLASS'S TOUR OF IRELAND, SCOTLAND, AND
England in 1845–47 was a crucial event in his own political
development and a significant one in the transatlantic history of antislavery activity. Douglass also used the trip to write about
racial prejudice in America, noting in public and private letters the relative absence of racial discrimination in the British Isles. In one letter
written from Belfast in 1846, for instance, Douglass describes his feeling
of liberation in Britain: "The truth is, the people here know nothing of
the republican negro hate prevalent in our glorious land, they measure
and esteem me in accord to their moral and intellectual worth, and not
according to the color of their skin. Whatever may be said of the aristoc-
racies here, there is none based on the color of a man's skin." [1]

Douglass's statements may well have been disingenuous and designed
to score points against the slaveowning society back home. However different racial prejudice may have seemed in the two countries, Britain in
the 1840s was learning from America some of the very attitudes Douglass despised. Douglass's lectures formed only part of a range of representations of race and slavery in America transported across the Atlantic
in the same period, and his accounts of British friendliness to the black

man and antipathy to slavery can be modulated by considering some of
the other representations. For at exactly the time of his campaign, large
British and Irish audiences were welcoming an American racial parody
far removed from Douglass's commitment to the antislavery cause. The
theatrical ferment over a blackface troupe called the Ethiopian Serenaders reveals a British audience avid for very different representations
from Douglass's and suggests that derisive American portrayals of black
people were quickly and easily absorbed into British imperial fantasies.

Audrey Fisch has suggested that black antislavery speakers provided
a form of "spectacle" for British audiences, who were drawn to them
partly as a kind of entertainment.[2] If the explicitly entertaining racial
spectacles that were popular with audiences exactly contemporary with
Douglass's took any stance on slavery at all, it was ambiguous and equiv-
ocal. At the very moment of Douglass's achievements in Britain, popular
entertainments were offering simplistic or exploitative pictures of black
people and evading the issue of slavery altogether. British accounts of
stage "Ethiopians" conflated them with the African Americans they pur-
ported to represent and with the depiction of other foreign peoples.

Long before Douglass's visit, the allure of the exotic had regularly
manifested itself in other London shows. In the 1820s London had seen
exhibitions at the Egyptian Hall of transplanted "Laplanders" and "Es-
kimos," together with "real" animals, costumes, and artifacts from their
native regions and pictorial representations of them. In 1843 George
Catlin had shown paintings of American scenes at the Egyptian Hall
alongside Native American costumes, weapons, and a wigwam, together
with nine specially imported Ojibway people.[3] Early in 1846 Astley's
Theatre was advertising an "oriental spectacle," *The Rajah of Magpore,
or the Sacred Elephant of the Pagoda,* "in which all the glorious pageantry
of the wondrous East [was] represented with the utmost splendour and
magnificence." This show boasted a pair each of live elephants and cam-
els, whose performances outshone those of other actors in the reviews,[4]
and it was succeeded at the theater by *The Cataract of the Ganges* in 1847.[5]

During 1846–47 the *Illustrated London News* produced detailed sketches
of the "African Curiosities," "botanical, zoological and ethnological"
brought home from an expedition to the West Coast of Africa,[6] and illustrations of events in the "Kaffir war" with the Zulus and the

war with the Sikhs in the Punjab. These included portraits of indigenous characters such as "Damo the Kaffir Doctor and Rainmaker."[7] An extension of the interests demonstrated by shows and exhibitions, these articles were arguably another form of imperial spectacle. A portrait of Douglass, also published in the *Illustrated London News* in 1846, makes a fine contrast with these turbaned or seminaked Indians and Africans, for Douglass is shown appearing at the World Temperance Convention, an immaculately suited nineteenth-century gentleman.[8]

The Ethiopian Serenaders joined these British versions of exotic entertainment in purveying an irreverent and often contemptuous sense of foreign peoples and customs. Although designed to be explicitly amusing and remaining ambiguous about their potentially informative role, the blackface performances of the Serenaders hinted that they were an accurate representation of the American black, and at least one contemporary observer made the connection with British ethnographic exhibitions of the time. In this they may perhaps be compared with Douglass's tour. As one British supporter wrote to the American Anti-Slavery Society in Boston, Frederick Douglass was "a living example of the capabilities of the slave." Douglass too represented African Americans abroad, but unlike the Serenaders he was pleading for his own people. According to his supporters he was very successful, too: one testified that "wherever he goes he arouses sympathy in [the antislavery] cause and love for himself," and attributed this to his "outward graces, intellectual power and culture, and eloquence."[9] The Ethiopian Serenaders provided in contrast theatrical examples that laughed at the pronunciation of American blacks rather than celebrating eloquence and rated their musical ability far above their intelligence.

Caricatures of blacks had featured in American popular amusements since at least the 1820s as variety acts for the theater and more informal entertainments. White actors performed comic songs or sketches in black makeup and with exaggerated "black" accents, a genre usually known as "Ethiopian Delineation." By the early 1840s troupes of blackface entertainers were developing what later became the formal conventions of the minstrel show.[10] The British had encountered the "Ethiopian" mode early on, after the actor Charles Mathews toured New York in the 1820s and visited the black theater at African Grove. Mathews'

Figure 1. "Damo the Kaffir Doctor and Rainmaker," in "The Kaffir War," *Illustrated London News,* October 17, 1846, 243–44.

Figure 2. "World Temperance Convention," *Illustrated London News,* August 15, 1846 (close-up captioned "Frederick Douglass, of Maryland"), 109.

report of this event was replayed in Britain many times in his sketch, *A Trip to America,* and pirated versions were printed in London in 1821 and 1824. In the sketch the black Hamlet at African Grove delivers the famous soliloquy in a garbled version and with what is meant to be a black accent: "To be or not to be, dat is him question, whether him nobler in de mind to suffer or lift up him arms against a sea of hubble bubble and by opossum end 'em." Triggered by the apparent reference, the black audience in the story then demands a rendition of the song "Opossum up a Gum-Tree," with which the actor obliges.[11]

This story, seemingly describing ignorant black American attempts at Shakespeare, is actually classic Ethiopian Delineation.[12] The markers of "black" speech, "de" and "dat," and the drifting off of the text into nonsense echo a standard blackface format in which the stage black would deliver a pretentious disquisition undercut by his "black" accent, malapropisms, and meaningless digressions. In his stage productions too, Mathews changed the lyrics of "Opossum up a Gum Tree," so that, according to Eileen Southern, "it was no longer a slave song but rather an Ethiopian song."[13] This "Ethiopian" version of black performance came to mediate the real thing for British audiences, for when the black actor Ira Aldridge arrived in London he was assumed to be the original of the tale, which British audiences replicated by demanding in their turn that he sing the opossum song. Appearing sometimes at the same theater as Mathews, in the same season, Aldridge absorbed the blackface piece and made it part of his repertoire.[14] Aldridge was still appearing in British theaters when Douglass and the Serenaders visited, advertised in May 1847 playing Othello in Newcastle-under-Lyme.[15]

Thomas Dartmouth Rice, an early Delineator, brought a song and dance act called "Jim Crow" to London in 1836, playing at the Surrey and Adelphi theaters and causing a popular sensation. The dance was said to have come from a lame Southern slave and featured "jumping Jim Crow" wild leg movements.[16] A whole troupe, the Virginia Minstrels, had also toured successfully in Britain in 1843–44. By the 1840s British accounts of America often included a brush with black American culture. Dickens's *American Notes* of 1842 tells of a black dancer in an insalubrious part of New York cutting breathtaking figures: "Single shuffle, double shuffle, cut and cross-cut; snapping his fingers, rolling his eyes, turning in his knees, presenting the backs of his legs in front, spinning about on his toes and heels like nothing but the man's fingers on the tambourine; dancing with two left legs, two right legs, two wooden legs, two wire legs, two spring legs—all sorts of legs and no legs—what is this to him?"[17] Dickens's dancer finishes with a great leap and a call for a drink, and the writer describes his voice as like the "chuckle of a million counterfeit Jim Crows,"[18] referring to the blackface act that London audiences had loved a decade before. In alluding to the "Jim Crow" character, Dickens was translating his encounter with a black American dancer into the idiom of blackface, assuming his British readers to be closer to the impersonation than to its object, and repeating Mathews's transmogrification of black performance into blackface.

Long before the Ethiopian Serenaders, then, British audiences were familiar with Ethiopian Delineation, and British travelers had brought back tales from America that blurred their fascinated representations of black culture with blackface. One review of the Serenaders made precisely this connection, complaining of "the mummeries, and the ridiculous negro melodies which have so often been the staple topics of our transatlantic travel writers."[19]

Like their forerunners, the Serenaders were all white men—Germon, Stanwood, Harrington, White, and Pell—who blackened their faces with burnt cork to perform a variety act consisting of "songs, glees, choruses, comic sayings," and "burlesque lectures."[20] The Serenaders' appearance must have been striking, however, for unlike their predecessors, who wore the rags supposed to befit a plantation slave, they wore elegant evening dress with white waistcoats and wristbands, like the classical conductor and composer Louis Antoine Julien, whose music they imitated. With their faces "painted jet black, with ruddy lips, and large mouths," and the black and white costume, the Serenaders' appearance presented a stylized, if crude, picture of racial difference.[21]

London audiences packed their shows, both when they opened at the Hanover Square Rooms in January 1846 and at the St. James's, to which they transferred in February. The Serenaders' show seems to have been similar to others in America at the time. A portrait in the *Illustrated London News* and others in *Punch* suggest that they performed in the usual semicircle with the banjo, bones, and end-men arrangement, and that

Figure 3. "The Ethiopian Serenaders," *Illustrated London News,* January 24, 1846, 61.

though they wore dress suits rather than rags, they were fully blacked up and threw their bodies around with the abandon that characterized blackface. Their British and Irish audiences may have been more up-market than American ones, though: whereas in the States such shows were patronized by extremely rowdy working men, the Ethiopians' new fans seem to have been quite genteel.[22] J. S. Bratton has remarked on the different audiences drawn by blackface shows in England and America: "The dissenting lower middle classes, the ministers, shop keepers and respectable ladies who were in some ways the most deprived and depressed cultural group in the land, found it possible to go to minstrel shows."[23]

Several scholars have noticed this affinity between respectable British audiences and blackface and the notably more reserved style of performance that subsequently developed in Britain.[24] Some of this may be attributed to the Serenaders, with their sentimental and restrained style, having become a model for British acts. Their respectability can be gauged by the fact that the *Illustrated London News* published its reviews alongside those for classical music, that the Ethiopians' music was published in *The Pianista* that also produced Jenny Lind's, and that the St. James's Theater charged between two and four shillings to see them.[25] The celebrated conductor Julien even borrowed several items from their repertoire for his "American Polka," playing "Lucy Neale," the "Boatman's Dance," and even the "Railroad Overture."[26] Several reviews commented favorably on the shows' freedom from "coarseness and vulgarity," which in Ireland had apparently already "banished nigger dancing and singing from the stage to the taverns and singing houses."[27]

The program seems to have varied on different nights, but their finale, the "Railroad Overture," a musical imitation of a steam train, seems to have been a constant favorite. Their other songs included sentimental ballads, including one about a slave, "Lucy Neale," and the comic or boisterous songs that were already popular in blackface performances: "Old Dan Tucker," "The Dandy Broadway Swell," "Such a Getting Up Stairs," and "Buffalo Gals." Several specifically implied a reference to black Americans, such as "Come Darkies Sing," "Coloured Fancy Ball," "Cudjo's Wild Hunt," and "The Fine Old Coloured Gentleman," and depicted them dressing up and celebrating or, in a Southern context, hunting, often racoons.[28] Like many blackface depictions of blacks, these songs suggested dandies or carefree types who reveled in leisure and never seemed to work.

The *Illustrated London News* called them "capital actors" with "good voices" that "harmonize charmingly," while their "Railroad Overture" "causes an explosion of laughter." In January the *Theatrical Journal* marveled at the "most eloquent music" they elicited from "a banjo and some bullock's bones," and throughout February recorded their "increased success," the "full and fashionable audience" that the railroad number "fairly worked . . . up to high pressure." That same month the *Morning Herald* declared the group's "vocalism [to be] of a very superior description," and their "drolleries" to be "supreme instances of comic tact and fantastic readiness." Even the *Daily News,* despite its antislavery scruples, was "most agreeably surprised to find that, although there is much of a risible nature in the singing, gesticulations, and accompaniments of these pseudo negroes, there is, likewise, a fund of melody and a real and stable excellence, as well of voice instrumentation and harmony, in the majority of songs which they sing."[29] Attracting good audiences throughout April, the Serenaders published one of their numbers as sheet music in May, but may have moved on to tour the provinces over the summer.[30]

Certainly by October they were in Ireland, where the *Freedman's Jour-*

nal heralded their appearance in Dublin with some excitement: "The English press teems with testimonies to their talent, and the patronage of the English nobility, of which they have obtained no small share, stamps them as *artistes* of no common order."[31] During the rest of that month the paper recorded "crowded," "fashionable and numerous" audiences, culminating in the patronage, on 5 November, of "[H]is Excellency the Lord Lieutenant and the Ladies Ponsonby." The *Journal* observed with satisfaction that "His Excellency was observed to applaud warmly."[32] With a few promotional devices this Irish run continued successfully for another three weeks: despite the announcement on the 2nd of the Serenaders' "last week" in Dublin, and, after a reengagement, "most positively the last week" on the 11th, and even a "second reengagement" on the 16th, the performance of the 21st really did prove to be the final one.[33]

In January the troupe was back in London, where they performed four times weekly at the St. James's until 5 July, when they departed for the Continent. As in Dublin the Serenaders tantalized audiences with a number of "last performances" advertised before they left, and souvenir portraits of performers were presented to the occupants of the private boxes and stalls on benefit nights.[34] By the time they left, after over four hundred performances, the Serenaders had become an institution. Complaining in their advertisements of "numerous vulgar imitations which have recently been attempted in the metropolis,"[35] the Serenaders had nevertheless themselves shared the St. James's Assembly Rooms with a sister group, the "Female American Serenaders," whose act included "the principal Songs and Airs with which the Public have been familiarised by the celebrated Ethiopian Serenaders, and also several Native Melodies, and other compositions entirely new to European associations."[36] Despite their name, these actually seem to have hailed from Manchester.[37] Bands of "male and female 'Ethiopians'" were also appearing at the Hanover Square Rooms.[38] Music sellers also traded on the strength of their success: a book of "Ethiopian songs . . . as sung by the Serenaders" was published in *The Pianista* in March, one of "Ethiopian Melodies . . . performed by the Serenaders, and other Nigger Melodists" and another of "New Negro Melodies for the Accordion" in May.[39]

The "Ethiopian" fad was the object of some British humorous attention too: *Punch* alluded to the Serenaders several times, complaining that "music is now literally assuming the character of the Black Art. . . . Song seems to have lately migrated to Ethiopia, if we may judge from the popularity which has been acquired by the serenaders of that nation. Nigger melodies are now all the rage;" and mocking the stage dialect of blackface: "even sentiment–whose accents were always broken, rejoices, or rather mourns, in broken English." [40] *Punch* did not mention Douglass during his visit, but devoted thirteen pieces to the Serenaders in less than a year, seven of them illustrated, fascinated both by their popularity and by the blackface deception. Enjoying the theatricality of the travesty, it made knowing references to the rising price of soot, lamp-blacking, and burnt cork attending the Serenaders. [41] Articles in 1847 described a "Glut of Ethiopians," a "shower of blacks," predicted the adoption of "Ethiopian Fashions" off the stage as well as on, and finally declared that the "Ethiopian Mania is, at last, upon the wane" as the "original band" of American visitors played out their final performances. [42]

The Ethiopian Serenaders and their many home-grown imitators played a significant part in the popular entertainment of Britain and Ireland even as Douglass addressed the question of slavery with other audiences abroad. What effect the Serenaders' show had on British perceptions of race and slavery in America is not clear, however. The correspondent for the *Daily News,* who had attended with worries that this kind of "exhibition" meant a "making light of the miseries of the slave population of the United States of America," came away with an optimistic report: "Their exhibition is not only innocuous, as regards the poor helpless beings they represent, but calculated from its force, truthfulness, and mixture of the ludicrous with sentiment, to raise feelings which may at no distant period produce results that every friend of negro emancipation would hail with satisfaction." [43]

This testament to the Serenaders' compatibility with a belief in "negro emancipation" would suggest an antagonism to racial inequality, and yet the blackface representations of the "negro" as either ludicrous or sentimental also indicate the reductive character of the portrayal. The writer for the *Daily News* celebrated the "feeling of deep commiseration for the unhappy misused beings" that it believed must inevitably be inspired by the show, which depicted them "under all the wrongs which they endure," yet able to "laugh and sing gaily after their labours for the day are over." [44] A skeptical reader, especially one in a position to contrast this picture with the bloodcurdling ones of whips and chains called up in antislavery speeches at the time, might not see these scenes as so "innocuous." These laughing and singing slaves could just as easily provide ammunition for those who asserted that their "labours for the day" were not taxing and that they had nothing to complain of.

Douglas Riach, noting that several blackface shows visited Ireland at its period of most vigorous antislavery activity, has expressed surprise that Irish abolitionists rarely commented on the minstrel shows that visited, especially since "the popular Irish image of the Negro must have been in part determined by these performances." Although R. D. Webb, Douglass's Dublin publisher, printed a version of the blackface song "Dandy Jim of Caroline" with antislavery lyrics, Riach believes that the abolitionists failed to condemn the blackface "image of the negro." [45] Douglas Lorimer has coupled the banjos and bones of minstrelsy with the Bibles of antislavery reform as the determining factors in Victorian images of blacks. [46] The *Daily News* article perfectly blends Lorimer's two images and provides a circumstance perhaps even more surprising than an abolitionist silence on blackface: an antislavery endorsement of it.

Douglass's British tour did interconnect to a very slight degree with the Serenaders' musical one. For the ex-slave had crossed the Atlantic in company with a singing troupe of siblings from New Hampshire: the Hutchinson Family Singers. The children of farmers, the three young brothers and a sister had been a great success in New York since 1843, harmonizing "sad ditties." [47] This white troupe sold themselves, in contrast to the Serenaders, as themselves, a fresh-faced Yankee family. With strong beliefs in favor of slave emancipation, as well as equal suffrage and temperance, the Hutchinsons campaigned as well as sang, and their first British concerts, in Manchester and Liverpool in September 1845, earned some criticism for their antislavery efforts in particular. One review accused them of "pandering to the tastes of ranting Abolitionists." [48] Nevertheless the Hutchinsons rejoined Douglass in Dublin, where they appeared on stage together, Douglass speaking and distributing literature and the Hutchinsons concluding with song. [49]

Back in the States the Hutchinsons had suffered some mockery from the Ethiopian Serenaders, who in 1844 had developed a parody of the Hutchinsons' New England nostalgia number "The Old Granite State." The Ethiopians' version was called "The Old Virginny State," as if a blackface version would necessarily come from the slaveholding South.[50] In London in February and March 1846, the two entertainments competed for audiences, with the Hutchinsons playing at the Hanover Square Rooms, the venue at which the Serenaders had played the previous month and which would produce its own troupe of "Ethiopians" the following year. Advertisements and even reviews of the two groups were printed next to each other in several papers, and the *Morning Herald* even observed that the Hutchinsons "sit in a line, like the Ethiopian Serenaders, [though] they have no other feature in common with those famous masters of bone and banjo."[51] While "the tide of fashion [was] now turned towards the St. James's Theatre . . . to listen to the diverting strains of the 'Darkies,'" the antislavery Hutchinsons sang to "crowded" Hanover Square rooms and "were encored in nearly every piece."[52] Douglass may not have encountered the Ethiopian Serenaders in person, but his friends and co-abolitionists took on the London musical stage at precisely the same time, and while the *Daily News* found the Serenaders compatible with an antislavery stance, the troupe's only real connection with such a politics had been to ridicule the Hutchinsons.

Aside from their position on slavery, there is also the question of the Serenaders' blacking up and the impressions of American blacks their performances may have suggested to British audiences. The degree of specific racial parody implied and assumed in blackface performance has been difficult to assess even in its American home. Eric Lott's comprehensive study rejects both the early interpretations that celebrated the authenticity of the form, and the later ones that have seen it only as "racial domination." Instead he locates "contradictions" in blackface, both a fascination with black culture and a fear of blacks. Despite its varied and slippery significations, however, he argues that blackface demonstrated an "economic logic . . . continuous . . . with slavery."[53]

Several critics have considered audiences' perceptions of "realism" as being different in Britain. J. S. Bratton has stressed the different needs of American and British audiences: "The average Englishman had no need of an art form which would help him deal with complex problems of identity and confrontation with a black population."[54] Instead, she argues that blackface in Britain worked more as a theatrical licensing device, as a signal of its own variety of entertainment. George Rehin's study of British street entertainers who adopted blackface confirms Bratton's impression, noting that both critics and admirers of blackface buskers were rarely concerned with the "quality of impersonation."[55] Michael Pickering has concurred only in part, however, seeing later British minstrelsy as a genre with less and less connection with any sense of African American culture, but also arguing that blackface imparted a complacent sense of racial superiority, and "was undoubtedly integrated into the Victorian culture of imperialism, not in a relation of cause and effect but as a powerful agent of reinforcement."[56]

These views reflect the diversity provided in blackface over the course of the century: music, comedy and variety acts, American touring shows, home-grown theater acts, and street performers and buskers. As Bratton points out, American shows were more likely to be examined for authenticity than their later British counterparts.[57] Perhaps the conclusion to be drawn is that audiences made a variety of responses to what, during the century, developed into a varied range of blackface performance.

The question of authenticity and of the culture of real and even enslaved Americans seems to have been more important for the American troupes who toured in the 1840s. The Virginia Minstrels had advertised themselves in Britain as an insight into slave life in America. The troupe's program in Dublin promised "sports and pastimes of the Virginia Colored Race, through the medium of Songs, Refrains, and Ditties as sung by the Southern slaves," describing the act in almost ethnographic terms, while a notice in *The Times* ignored Ira Aldridge and earlier black lecturers for the American Anti-Slavery Society, declaring the Minstrels "the only representatives of the negro that have appeared in this country." That paper's reviewer described their show, somewhat disparagingly, as consisting of "some of the aboriginal airs of Africa, modernised if not humanized in the slave states of the Union."[58]

Three years later the Serenaders were also judged on the strength of their impersonation of black Americans. When they opened in London the *Theatrical Journal* described the Serenaders' show as "imitating the niggers" and indicated that the object was to achieve verisimilitude rather than denigration, "not to ridicule their *patois,* but to catch their mode of executing their half English melodies." [59] The *Illustrated London News,* reviewing the same concert, also testified to the Serenaders' "avowed purpose of affording an accurate notion of Negro character and melody" and praised the impersonation, stating that "the deception created is so great that wagers have been offered that they are really 'darkies.'" The *Illustrated London News* was unable to decide "as to the authenticity of the African airs," but clearly indicated the departure of this minstrel music from its recognized counterparts, declaring the "compositions of the European masters" arranged in "a grotesque manner." [60]

In London as in New York, the Ethiopians were laying claims to authentic derivation from black culture, and where in America these claims were ironized and undercut by the form's stylized and performative nature, in Britain they seem to have sowed some confusion. The *Illustrated London News* suggested that some unsophisticated audience members were deceived by blackface, but the various reviewers produce a muddled account of the "Ethiopian" product: it is "nigger," "Negro," "Darky," "African," and even "half English." The objects of the Serenaders' imitations are described in terms of their race—they are the "niggers" or "Negroes," or else by a misplaced geographical reference—their music is "African." The presumed subject of blackface slides between several positions in these reviews: it is seen as an American product, as a specifically racial one, and even as an aspect of transplanted African culture. These accounts of the Serenaders concur in finding some exotic essence represented in their act but cannot agree about its identity.

In one of its humorous commentaries on the Serenaders' success in London, *Punch* took up this slippery and imprecise exoticism, making it central to its parody of the Ethiopians' performance. *Punch* affected to believe that the Serenaders were indigenous inhabitants of some real "Ethiopia," ignoring blackface's claims to represent the "American negro," and joking instead about its commercial and theatrical nature. In "What Is Ethiopia?" the writer affected to describe a "modern Ethiopia," not that described in ancient times, he joked, but a place where "as the Ethiopians of antiquity raised a temple to JUPITER AMMON," so "the modern Ethiopians adopt MAMMON AND GAMMON as their idols." [61]

Thus signifying the money-making potential of blackface hams, the writer described their performances in geographical and ethnological terms, reinforcing the staginess of the allusion by pretending to share the experience of an exotic landscape: "Modern Ethiopia is bounded in the front by a row of stage-lamps, which do duty of the equinoctial line, and separate the swarthy children of the night from the rest of the community. As far as the eye can see Ethiopia is bounded at the back by an extensive flat–made of canvas–and the intervening landscape is filled up by gentlemen's seats in the form of chairs of mahogany. The ground is thickly wooded–with planks–and rises by a gentle slope towards the flat scenery in the rear." [62] The Serenaders are next analyzed in ethnographic terms, and the "costume" of "this strange race of people" is listed along with their "manners and customs." Here again the writer uses the language of travel narratives or the ethnological pieces in the *Illustrated London News* to describe theatrical apparatus and suggest the artifice of the stage: "The natural products of our dramatic Ethiopia are black lead, bones, and banjos, with the first of which articles the natives dye their hands and faces; but it is a singular circumstance that the darkness of skin reaches no higher than the wrist, and goes no lower than the throat of this wonderful human family." [63] Blurring the Serenaders' depictions of race with a vaguely foreign context and linking blackface with the discourses of ethnography, geography and travel, *Punch* seemed to erase the American referents of their act in order to emphasize that it was staged.

For *Punch*'s readers in the 1840s, however, the "real Ethiopians" skit may have had a resonance that precisely blended the elements of exhibition and performance with the exposition of the faraway and exotic. Late in 1845 two "Bosjemen" children from the Cape of Good Hope were produced to illustrate a paper read before the Ethnological Society and in 1846, like George Catlin's Ojibways, were placed on display at the Egyptian Hall and made to exhibit tribal dress and native dancing. They were also made to dress up as an English soldier and wife and displayed with several kinds of monkey. In 1847 they were replaced by a larger group. [64] Dickens attacked their exhibition under the ironic title "The Noble Savage," describing one man "in his festering bundle of hides, with his filth and his antipathy to water, and his straddled legs, and his odious eyes shaded by his brutal hand, and his cry of 'Qu-u-u-u-aaa' (Bosjeman for something desperately insulting I have no doubt)." His reaction, he claimed, was to "abhor, detest, abominate and abjure him."[65] Dickens was overstating his difference from the sentimentalists who exclaimed patronizingly over these "savages," but his exaggerated reaction highlights the gulfs of knowledge and culture yawning between the Bosjemen and those who paid to see them. The kindest response these exhibited Africans could expect was condescension.

The Serenaders' blackface imitations thus coincided with the exhibition of "real" black people for information, entertainment, and profit. They also came only a few years after some Native Americans had been presented in London in exactly the same form as *Punch* employed to mock the Serenaders. *Punch*'s juxtaposition of these two kinds of exhibition of the exotic was not too far-fetched, since the appearances of the Bosjemen were noted in the *Dramatic Mirror,* which also advertised and reviewed "Ethiopian" acts.[66]

In "What Is Ethiopia?" *Punch* likened the Serenaders to the exhibitions at the Egyptian Hall, but in another contemporary piece it borrowed from blackface imagery for an imperial subject. In "Colonial Annuals" *Punch* notes the announcement of an annual for New Zealand in *The Times,* and, mocking the pretensions of such a venture, proposes the publishers of the New Zealand Annual follow it up with a native "Book of Beauty." It then offers a specimen encomium to an indigenous beauty.

The piece is illustrated with three pictures. One of the "beauties," a black figure in female evening dress, has facial scarification that is perhaps meant to look Maori, but the other two have the enlarged eyes, nose, and lips characteristic of minstrel types and seem to owe more to the conventions of blackface America. The male figure appears in evening dress very like *Punch*'s representations of the Serenaders, while the female wears a towering turban exactly like that iconized in an earlier *Punch* fantasy of "Ethiopian Fashions." Even the name of the poem's subject, "The Squaw Quareeshee," is a composite of a Native American title and the feminine of the West Indian stereotype slave name "Quashie."[67]

Here blackface has been included among a range of ethnic markers, some derived from the new imperial project in New Zealand, one derived from an older one in the Caribbean, and one from another set of

WHAT IS ETHIOPIA?

THE tremendous influx of Ethiopians which has occurred within the last year in this country, has rendered it desirable that we should know something of the country to which we are indebted for these sable visitors. STRAND places the Ethiopians near the Atlantic Sea; and we sometimes wish that STRAND had placed them all at the bottom of it, and thus have prevented them from becoming so great a nuisance as they have lately proved themselves.

The Ethiopians of antiquity raised a temple to JUPITER AMMON, but the modern Ethiopians adopt MAMMON and GAMMON as their idols. The origin of the Ethiopian race is lost in obscurity, but it is evident that we must look in the dark ages for the object of our search; and it is equally certain that we shall remain in the dark if we pursue our investigations in the quarter alluded to. Our business is more with the modern than the ancient Ethiopians, and with the geography of the country of the former we are only too familiar.

Modern Ethiopia is bounded in the front by a row of stage-lamps, which do duty for the equinoctial line, and separate the swarthy children of the night from the rest of the community. As far as the eye can see Ethiopia is bounded at the back by an extensive flat—made of canvass—and the intervening landscape is filled up with gentlemen's seats in the form of chairs of mahogany.

ETHIOPIAN SCENERY.

The ground is thickly wooded—with planks—and rises by a gentle slope towards the flat scenery in the rear.

The costume of the inhabitants of this curious locality is by no means varied or picturesque, but is supposed to be well adapted to the manners and customs of this strange race of people. The dress they wear is exceedingly plain, and exhibits a desire to have everything in black and white, which is carried to a wonderful extent; but the black appears to predominate. The natural products of our dramatic Ethiopia are black lead, bones, and banjos, with the first of which articles the natives dye their hands and faces; but it is a singular circumstance that the darkness of skin reaches no higher than the wrist,

COSTUME OF ETHIOPIA.

and goes no lower than the throat of this wonderful human family. Their pursuits are chiefly musical, and they extract melody from bones in a most astounding manner.

It is a wonderful trait in the Ethiopian character, that the people renounce their country and their colour the moment they quit the landscape we have

already described, and become citizens of the every-day world in a true cosmopolitan spirit, directly after they have left the haunts and homes of their dramatic existence.

It is a distinguishing mark of the Ethiopians, which separates them entirely from the blackamoor race, that whereas the latter cannot be washed white, the former are easily susceptible of this process. The increase of the tribe has lately been a serious injury; but there is no doubt that they will disappear in due course, with the spread of enlightenment.

GROSS INSULT TO MR. PUNCH.

SOME soulless, graceless, tasteless being has put the subjoined advertisement into a morning journal:—

LOST, late on Friday, a PUNCH'S POCKET BOOK. ONE SOVEREIGN will be given for it and its contents.

For Punch's Pocket Book and its contents! The idea of offering such a paltry sum as one sovereign! For a treasure which—but that same modesty has put the small figure of two and six upon it—is absolutely priceless! For a work whose value the preponderance of demand over supply has raised to—we are afraid to say what! Any spirited gentleman who had lost his Punch's Pocket Book would offer at least A HUNDRED GUINEAS for its recovery, and even then be rather sanguine in hoping he might get it.

"Thus bad begins, but worse remains behind." Mark the conclusion of this vile announcement:—

"It" (our Pocket Book) "is of no value to any but the owner, payment of the small bill of exchange being stopped. Apply, &c."

PUNCH'S POCKET BOOK of no value to any but the owner, and only valuable to him on account of the bill in it! That all that he prizes among its contents! Let this unworthy owner of Punch's Pocket Book know that half the world is scrambling for a sight of it, the number of copies printed being only just sufficient to accommodate the other half. The mere loan of it would be a greater favour than the cashing of any bill of exchange. Punch hereby retorts the contempt which he has been treated with, and begs to tell this individual, in the words of the Eton Grammar,

"Ego illum flocci pendo qui me pili æstimat:"
"I regard him at a rush who esteems me at a hair:"

a quotation which he has felt himself obliged to translate for the benefit of a person so very illiterate as to see nothing in his Pocket Book but a paltry bill.

Dreadful Continental Failures.

IT has been objected against the new House of Lords, that it has too much of an "ecclesiastical" appearance; and certainly the seats have exactly the look of cathedral pews. This is borne out by a remark SIBTHORPE made when he went over the building. He was asked by MR. BARRY if he could see any room for improvement? "Plenty of room," he said "if, 'non tanti pia,' there were not so many pews." LORD BROUGHAM made a similar observation. After comparing the seats to "church sittings," he exclaimed, "But the place took so long building, that I suppose the seats were only put by degrees, or as we say in France, 'pew à pew.'" ("Our London Correspondent" is welcome to either of these jokes for his provincial papers.)

CAPPING THE HAT.

AN order will shortly be issued from the Horse Guards, out of compliment to a noble Prince, who is in training for the Commander-in-Chief, that for the future all the percussion caps for the new muskets of the Army are to be modelled after the design of the ALBERT Hat.

TAKING ORDERS.

A CLERGYMAN, who is just on the point of marrying a second time, has made his intended promise, before she enters into the matrimonial state, that she will never exceed thirty-nine articles of dress.

Figure 4. "What Is Ethiopia?" *Punch* 12 (1847): 167. Reproduced by permission of the Syndics of Cambridge University Library.

COLONIAL ANNUALS.

THE publication of the first Colonial Annual has just been advertised in the *Times*, under the title of the *New Zealand* something or other, and we have no doubt the work will be followed up by a whole tribe of Caffre-land Keepsakes, Sarawak Books of Beauty, and Sandwich Islands Forget-Me-Nots.

If Sarawak is entitled to a Rajah, it undoubtedly deserves an Annual; and we hope that the enterprising MR. BROOKE will brook no delay in illuminating the Sarawakians with some light literature, in the style of our English Annuals.

The New Zealand publishers will, we hope, meet with sufficient encouragement to justify them in following up their already announced speculation with a Book of Beauty, embracing the native objects of loveliness that abound in their neighbourhood. We can picture to ourselves, and of course, therefore, can picture to our subscribers, some of the portraits that would adorn the Annual we have suggested. The contributions in prose and poetry would correspond with the style of the embellishments, and a galaxy of beauty, both real and ideal, would be constituted, by the aid of a little judicious editing. There would probably be a careful selection of the *élite* of the different styles of New Zealand Beauty, with descriptions of appropriate poesy; from which it will be sufficient to furnish the public with a single specimen :—

TO THE

SQUAW QUAREESHEE.

My bulbul, dingy is thy skin,
  But yet to me thou seemest
    bright;
Like the dark coal, that holds
    within
  Its shade the elements of light.

Figure 5. "Colonial Annuals," *Punch* 12 (1847): 170.
Reproduced by permission of the Syndics of Cambridge
University Library.

ETHIOPIAN FASHIONS.

been in the morning. There is every reason to expect, that, in the course of the ensuing season, we shall have "a grand Ethiopian *ballet*," in which TAGLIONI will appear as *Lucy Neal*, while the renowned VENAFRA, the O. SMITH of the Opera, will be called upon to "get out of the way," as the representative of "*Old Dan Tucker*."

We have on previous occasions called attention to the Ethiopian mania, but have not yet succeeded in checking it. Ethiopians are to be found in every quarter of the town and every corner of the kingdom; for a pennyworth of bones and a banjo, a ha'porth of soot, and an ounce of suet, will set up a party of four, without further outlay.

Some of these Ethiopians, after surreptitiously holding themselves out as blacks, and colouring their fingers and their faces, cannot be expected to come out with clean hands, though when they practise the imposition of calling themselves the Original Ethiopians, they are little better, notwithstanding all their manual nigritude, than light-fingered gentry. It must be admitted that the public has not dealt out its patronage with a niggard hand to these niggered melodists. We shall not be surprised if the rage for Ethiopian blackness extends to the occupants of the boxes as well as to the performers on the stage, and we shall expect to see Ethiopian headdresses, and Ethiopian masks for the upper part of the face, becoming popular as the

COSTUME DU SOIR.

He haw! He haw!

COLONEL SIBTHORPE tells us that it takes three years to make a good dragoon. We wonder how many it takes to make a good member of Parliament; but we forget that the perfection of the latter depends not so much upon the number of years as the length of them.

THE ABSENT ONE.

THE Ethiopian mania has had a wonderful effect upon the blacking market, and WARREN's jet has gone up half a sixteenth in the market;

IF it be true that absence makes you all the fonder of a person, how desperately in love the electors of Westminster must be with MR.

Figure 6. "Ethiopian Fashions," *Punch* 12 (1847): 138. Reproduced by permission of the Syndics of Cambridge University Library.

American racial types. Some of this may be due to *Punch*'s deliberate play with several conventions, but blackface itself could easily accommodate a variety of ethnic and national differences. The "Female American Serenaders," for instance, advertised themselves with a peculiar collection of foreign sounding names: "Mesdames Cora, Jumba, Woski, Miami, Yarico, Womba, and Rosa."[68]

The *Punch* jokes blended Ethiopian Delineation into the representation of a number of foreign types and imperial subjects. In so doing they shifted blackface a little out of its specifically American context and associated it with a range of comic foreigners and subject peoples. Connecting blackface, and therefore black Americans, with black Antipodeans, *Punch*'s treatment of the Serenaders expanded the possibilities for racial ridicule. Despite the "innocuous" verdict of the *Daily News*, *Punch*'s elaborations on "Ethiopian" acts showed how easily the acts could be parted from any suggestion of a black person's dignity or need for "emancipation." The Serenaders' British tour could well have combined with British traditions of exhibiting racial difference to make an unsavory mixture of titillation and contempt.

There are blackface echoes of this kind in Henry Mayhew's description of some other street musicians in the 1850s. Mayhew describes two "tom-tom" players, originally Arabs, who have come to London via Bombay and the 77th Bengal Native Infantry. He marks one as being like a prince from the *Arabian Nights,* and also as an "Othello," while his partner, he says, is "what a Yankee would call a 'rank nigger,' who rolls about in his chair like a serenader playing the 'bones.'"[69]

Groping for a telling description of these alien Londoners Mayhew thus draws on blackface alongside Shakespeare and the *Arabian Nights,* mixing his other ethnicities as indiscriminately as *Punch* in 1847. As an ironic impersonation that both claimed authenticity and joked about its paint-deep superficiality, Ethiopian Delineation was ideally placed to deal with the fascination and disturbance that aliens like the tom-tom players provoked and to contribute to the vocabulary available for dealing with the new encounters and migrations that the empire was beginning to enable. As a primarily comic and sentimental mode, however, it was much less likely to promote the dignity and worth of American blacks or to address slavery critically.

One of Mayhew's informants in *London Labour and the London Poor* estimated that there were fifty blackface entertainers on London's streets in the 1850s, all of whom were styled "Ethiopians."[70] The Serenaders had made their mark in Britain, and it is still reflected in the language: the *Oxford English Dictionary* contains an entry for "Ethiopian serenader" as a general term for "a 'nigger' minstrel, a musical performer with face blackened to imitate a negro."[71]

When Douglass returned to America in April 1847, the captain of the steamer *Cambria* denied him the first-class berth he had paid for and banished him from the saloon. Douglass's letter to *The Times* attacking this "proscription on account of my color"[72] secured a peculiar endorsement in the pages of *Punch.* A paragraph entitled "Black and White Distinctions" referred unmistakably to the indignity suffered by Douglass, but linked it with the magazine's most favored target:

Four of the four thousand Ethiopian Serenaders at present in England applied for berths on board the *Cambria,* to return to their native Ethiopia, but
were refused on account of their colour. It was only when they had taken the
soot off their faces, and had washed their hands of the foul disgrace of being
genuine blacks, that they were allowed to associate with the American passengers. We wonder [that] the Yankees, in their hatred of everything black,
do not, when they represent *Othello,* make him a white General.[73]

Punch took up the public condemnation of discrimination on the *Cambria* provoked by Douglass's letter but could not resist another jibe at the
ubiquity of blackface entertainers ("four of the four thousand"). Drawing attention to the common origins of Douglass's ill treatment and the
Ethiopians' act, *Punch*'s jokes about the artificiality of blackface are for
once designed to make a serious point, one with which Douglass could
have agreed. On the American ship *Cambria,* the stage blacks had a social position that real blacks would not be allowed. Blackness there could
be feted only if it washed off.

Like Douglass's letters home, *Punch* directed its rhetoric against American racism, but the mention of the Serenaders belies the assumption of
a superior national attitude. For many British audiences had loved this
American representation and taken black makeup for black reality too
easily to identify fully with Douglass. *Punch* was implicitly joining the
outcry against Douglass's treatment on the *Cambria,* but it did so by
imagining the Ethiopians in Douglass's place, replacing the black orator
with the racial travesty. Even in retailing this episode from Douglass's
own life, *Punch* rapidly supplanted his image with that of the Ethiopian
Serenaders.

The coincidence of the Ethiopian Serenaders' tour with Douglass's
and their subsequent effect on British culture may seem only to undermine the significance of the abolitionist's visit. As Richard Blackett suggests in this volume, Douglass himself came to feel that blackface had
had a discouraging effect on antislavery feeling in Britain. Certainly the
Serenaders' tour raises questions about both the significance of Douglass's antislavery audiences and the relation of those audiences to less
sympathetic aspects of British opinion. In some ways the Serenaders'
success suggests how poignantly limited Douglass's impact in Britain as

antislavery orator and exemplary black may have been. Yet the "Ethiopian" phenomenon also indicates precisely how Douglass, in the persuasiveness of his argument and in the example of his intelligent and self-educated person, was providing a crucial counterrepresentation to the blackface entertainments already patronized by British audiences in the 1840s. As Douglass's upstanding figure in the *Illustrated London News* portrait suggests, the Ethiopian Serenaders were never allowed to represent American blacks alone in Britain, for they had to contend with Douglass's "living example."

NOTES

1. Frederick Douglass to R. D. Webb, 1 January 1846 (Boston Public Library, Microfilm, RBD 370).

2. Audrey A. Fisch, "'Negrophilism' and British Nationalism: The Spectacle of the Black Abolitionist Movement," *Victorian Review* 19 (summer 1993): 20–47.

3. Richard Altick, *The Shows of London* (Cambridge, Mass.: Harvard University Press, 1978), 274–75, 276–79.

4. "Astleys," *Theatrical Journal,* 14 February 1846, p. 51: "Great sagacity was evinced in the performances of both the elephants, and especially of the larger one, who seems, indeed, almost gifted with the faculty of reason."

5. "Astleys," *Dramatic Mirror,* 4 October 1847, p. 162.

6. "African Curiosities," *Illustrated London News,* 28 November 1846, p. 341.

7. "The Kaffir War," *Illustrated London News,* 17 October 1846, pp. 243–44; "The Capture of the Fort at Kote Kangra," *Illustrated London News,* 22 August 1846, p. 117.

8. "World Temperance Convention," *Illustrated London News,* 15 August 1846, p. 109.

9. S. Hilditch to Maria Weston Chapman, 31 October 1846; Mary A. Estlin to Chapman, 1 September 1846, Weston Papers, Boston Public Library.

10. See Robert Toll, *Blacking Up: The Minstrel Show in Nineteenth Century America* (New York: Oxford University Press, 1974), 27; Alan W. C. Green, "'Jim Crow' 'Zip Coon': the Northern Origins of Negro Minstrelsy," *Massachusetts Review* 11 (spring 1970): 385–97.

11. [Charles Mathews], *Mr. Mathews at Home* (London, 1824), quoted in Herbert Marshall and Mildred Stock, *Ira Aldridge, The Negro Tragedian* (London: Rockliff, 1958), 40. See also the 1821 version printed by J. Duncombe, reproduced in Richard L. Klepac, *Mr. Mathews at Home* (London: Society for Theatre Research, 1979), 98–117.

12. Eric Lott notes that this, together with Mathews's written imitation of a black Methodist, anticipates blackface acts of twenty years later. Lott, *Love and Theft: Blackface Minstrelsy and the American Working Class* (New York: Oxford University Press, 1993), 45.

13. Eileen Southern, *The Music of Black Americans: A History,* 2d ed. (New York: W. W. Norton, 1983), 120–21.

14. Marshall and Stock, *Ira Aldridge,* 43–44.

15. "Provincial Theatres," *Dramatic Mirror and Review of Music and the Fine Arts,* 10 May 1847, p. 40.

16. For an account of the origins of the act from one of Rice's contemporaries, see C. L., "An Old Actor's Memories," *New York Times,* 5 June 1881, p. 10.

17. Charles Dickens, *American Notes* (1842; London, Granville, 1985), 82.

18. Ibid., 83.

19. "Ethiopian Sere–St James's Theatre," *Daily News,* 18 March 1846, p. 4.

20. Harry Reynolds, *Minstrel Memories: The Story of Burnt Cork Minstrelsy in Great Britain from 1836 to 1927* (London: Alston Rivers, 1928), 88.

21. "The Ethiopian Sere," *Illustrated London News,* 24 January 1846, p. 61.

22. On blackface and class in America see Toll, *Blacking Up;* Lott, *Love and Theft;* Alexander Sexton, "Blackface Minstrelsy," in *The Rise and Fall of the White Republic: Class, Politics and Mass Culture in Nineteenth Century America* (London: Verso, 1990), 165–82; and David Roediger, *The Wages of Whiteness: Race and the Making of the American Working Class* (London: Verso, 1991), 95–131.

23. J. S. Bratton, "English Ethiopians: British Audiences and Black-face Acts, 1835–65," *Yearbook of English Studies* 2 (1981): 128.

24. See for instance, Michael Pickering, "White Skin, Black Masks: 'Nigger' Minstrelsy in Victorian England," in *Music Hall Performance and Style,* ed. J. S. Bratton (Milton Keynes: Open University Press, 1986), 70–91 (esp. 76); Barry Anthony, "Early Nigger Minstrel Acts in Britain," *Music Hall* 12 (April 1980): 118–23 (esp. 121–22).

25. Advertisements, *Illustrated London News,* 22 January 1846, p. 14; 24 January 1846, p. 61; Ethiopians' *Pianista* advertised 6 February 1847, p. 190; Lind's *Pianista* advertised 29 May 1847, p. 350.

26. "Julien's Concerts," Playbill, Theatre Royal, Covent Garden, 27 November 1846, British Library, Playbills 1836–46.

27. "Music Hall," *Freeman's Journal,* 28 October 1846, p. 2. See also ibid., 26 October 1846, p. 3, and "The Ethiopian Sere," *Illustrated London News,* 14 February 1846, p. 114.

28. These titles are taken from advertisements cataloged under "Music Hall" from the *Freeman's Journal,* 26 October 1846; 2, 9, 11 November 1846, all p. 1.

29. "The Ethiopian Sere," *Illustrated London News,* 24 January 1846, p. 61; "Chit-Chat," *Theatrical Journal; A Weekly Review of Public Amusements, Metropolitan, Provincial and Continental,* London, 31 January 1846, pp. 39–40 (esp. 40); "Chit-Chat," 7 February 1846, p. 47; "Chit-Chat," 21 February 1846, p. 63; "St. James's Theatre," *Morning Herald Supplement,* 11 February 1846, p. 11; "Ethiopian Sere–St James's Theatre," *Daily News,* 18 March 1846, p. 4.

30. "New Music," *Illustrated London News,* 2 May 1846, p. 290.

31. "Music Hall," *The Freeman's Journal,* 26 October 1846, p. 3.

32. Ibid., 28 October 1846, p. 2; 30 October 1846, p. 3; 5 November 1846, p. 3.

33. Advertisements, *The Freeman's Journal,* 2, 9, 11, 16, 21 November 1846, all p. 1.

34. See advertisements in the *Illustrated London News* for 2, 9, 16, 23, 30 January; 6, 13, 20, 27 February; 13, 20 March; 3, 10, 17, 24 April; 1, 8, 15, 22, 29 May; 5, 12 June 1847.

35. Advertisement, *Illustrated London News,* 15 May 1847, p. 318.

36. "Female American Sere," Playbill, St. James's Theatre, 1847 British Library, catalogued under St. James's, Large Playbill.

37. Advertisement, *Illustrated London News,* 17 April 1847, p. 254.

38. "Ethiopians at the Hanover-Square Rooms," and "Ethiopian Sere at Crockford's, St. James's," *Dramatic Mirror and Review of Music and the Fine Arts,* 26 April 1847, p. 22.

39. See advertisements in the *Illustrated London News* for 6 February 1847, p. 95; 1 May 1847, p. 286; 8 May 1847, p. 303.

40. "Music in Ebony," *Punch* 11 (1846): 263.

41. "The Last of the Ethiopians," *Punch* 12 (1847): 249.

42. "Glut of Ethiopians," *Punch* 12 (1847): 122; "Britannia and the Blacks," *Punch* 12 (1847): 176; "Ethiopian Fashions," *Punch,* 12 (1847): 138; "The Last of the Ethiopians," *Punch* 12 (1847): 249.

43. "Ethiopian Sere – St James's Theatre," *Daily News,* 18 March 1846, p. 4.

44. Ibid.

45. Douglas Riach, "Blacks and Blackface on the Irish Stage, 1830–60," *Journal of American Studies,* 7 (December 1973), 231–41 (esp. 231).

46. Douglas Lorimer, "Bibles, Banjoes and Bones: Images of the Negro in the Popular Culture of Victorian England," in *In Search of the Visible Past: History Lectures at Wilfred Laurier University, 1973–4,* ed. Barry M. Gough (Waterloo, Ontario: Wilfred Laurier University Press, 1975), 31–50.

47. George C. Odell, *Annals of the New York Stage,* 15 vols. (New York: Columbia University Press, 1927–49), 4:684.

48. Quoted in Philip D. Jordan, *Singin' Yankees* (Minneapolis: University of Minnesota Press, 1946), 123.

49. Ibid., 121–24.

50. Odell, *Annals of the New York Stage,* 5:56.

51. "Hanover Square Rooms," *Morning Herald Supplement,* 11 February 1846, p. 11; also see advertisements in *Morning Herald,* 23 February 1846, p. 1; 7 March 1846 p. 1; and "Concerts of the Week," *Illustrated London News,* 28 February 1846, p. 139; 4 April 1846, p. 226.

52. "Concerts of the Week," *Illustrated London News,* 28 February 1846, p. 139.

53. Lott, *Love and Theft,* 7, 234.

54. J. S. Bratton, "English Ethiopians," 128.

55. George F. Rehin, "Blackface Street Minstrels in Victorian London and Its Resorts: Popular Culture and Its Racial Connotations as Revealed in Polite Opinion," *Journal of Popular Culture* 15 (summer 1981): 31.

56. Pickering, "White Skin, Black Masks," 76; Michael Pickering, "Mock Blacks and Racial Mockery: The 'Nigger' Minstrel and British Imperialism," in *Acts of Supremacy: the British Empire and the Stage, 1790–1930,* ed. J. S. Bratton (Manchester: Manchester University Press, 1991), 212.

57. Bratton, "English Ethiopians," 131.

58. "Virginia Minstrels," Dublin, 1844, quoted in Toll, *Blacking Up,* 34; "Theatre Royal, Adelphi," advertisement, *The Times,* 26 June 1843, p. 4; "Adelphi Theatre," ibid.

59. "Chit-Chat," *Theatrical Journal,* 31 January 1846, p. 39.

60. "The Ethiopian Sere," *Illustrated London News,* 24 January 1846, p. 61.

61. "What Is Ethiopia?" *Punch* 12 (1847): 167.

62. Ibid.

63. Ibid.

64. Altick, *The Shows of London,* 280.

65. Charles Dickens, "The Noble Savage," *Household Words,* 11 June 1853, p. 337.

66. "Entertainments of the Week," *Dramatic Mirror,* 26 April 1847, p. 77.

67. "Colonial Annuals," *Punch* 12 (1847): 170; "Ethiopian Fashions," ibid., 138.

68. "Female American Serenaders," Playbill, St. James's Theatre, 1847, British Library, cataloged under St. James's, Large Playbill. Some of these names derive from earlier entertainments with a "racial" theme—Woski and Yarico for instance come from George Colman's "Inkle and Yarico; An Opera in Three Acts," [1787] in *Plays by George Colman the Younger and Thomas Morton,* ed. Barry Sutcliffe (Cambridge: Cambridge University Press, 1983), 65–112.

69. Henry Mayhew, *London Labour and the London Poor,* 4 vols. (1861–2; reprint, London: Frank Cass, 1967), 3:185.

70. Ibid., 3:191.

71. *Oxford English Dictionary,* 2d ed., 20 vols. (Oxford: Oxford University Press, 1989) 5:422.

72. Frederick Douglass, *My Bondage and My Freedom* (1855; Urbana: University of Illinois Press, 1987), 238.

73. "Black and White Distinctions," *Punch* 12 (1847): 161.

PART FIVE

Douglass and Transatlantic Reform

Frederick Douglass and the Chartists

RICHARD BRADBURY

I N THE RECENT DEVELOPMENT OF WHAT WE MIGHT CALL "Atlantic studies," Paul Gilroy's *The Black Atlantic* and Peter Linebaugh's essays have conceived of the Atlantic not as the empty space between two cultural and historical locations but as the site of exchanges that have connected and enriched the continents at the margins of this watery place.[1] Connecting the abolitionist desire to end chattel slavery and the Chartist desire to extend political rights to working-class people under wage slavery by examining their links across the Atlantic illuminates a continuum between these two great liberatory mass movements of the nineteenth century.

The most obvious and beguiling connection between Frederick Douglass and the Chartists lies in the names of two newspapers, the *Northern Star* (the Chartist paper) and the *North Star* (the paper begun by Douglass after his return to the United States). This connection is strengthened when we remember Peter Fryer's assertion that during this first visit Douglass "teamed up with the Chartist leader Henry Vincent and specifically called himself a Chartist."[2] However, the similarity of the newspapers' names can also be somewhat misleading. Douglass had other motives for calling his paper the *North Star*—the name represented in compelling fashion a guide to liberation for African Americans fleeing the Southern slave states to freedom. The paper was a star in the north, a pole star by which to orient the journey out of bondage. And the *Northern Star* spoke for a faction of Chartists with whom Douglass had few allegiances. Although he may have "teamed up" with Henry Vincent and William Lovett, there is no evidence that he met with other Chartists such as Feargus O'Connor or William Cuffay. In a letter to William Lloyd Garrison in May 1846, Douglass wrote, "I was invited to speak at a meeting of the Complete Suffrage Association, called thus in contradistinction from the Chartist party, and differing from that party, in that it repudiates the use of physical force as a means of attaining its object."[3] Douglass not only associated with Chartists—for only the most sectarian would deny that Joseph Sturge, founder of the Complete Suffrage Union, was a Chartist—but he also understood the debates within the movement well enough to choose his allegiances carefully.

Douglass's dealings with the Chartists mirror the more general relationship between these two mass movements. The internal dynamics of mass movements are not easily summarized by a single assertion: on the one hand, abolitionists and Chartists could summarize their political relationship in the phrase "our cause being one and the same";[4] on the other hand, Chartists reportedly organized disruptions of abolitionist meetings precisely because abolitionists ignored the connection between chattel slavery abroad and wage slavery at home. To examine Douglass's relationship with the Chartists in detail, we must first discuss the structures and general policies of the two mass movements.

Neither abolitionism nor Chartism was a tight political organization with a monolithic set of political positions and practices. Both were very broad churches within which debates about tactics, strategy, and principles led to compromises, disagreements, and fractures. Abolitionism divided between those who believed in the power of moral suasion and those who sought to employ the persuasiveness of physical force; between those who sought to use existing institutions and those who stood outside "politics"; and between those who saw the abolition of chattel slavery as the be-all and end-all of their work and those who saw abolition as part of a wider campaign for social justice. The biographies of many abolitionists can be seen as navigating (and vacillating) between these poles. Chartism was similarly divided between the advocates of moral force and the proponents of physical force; between those who sought to extend existing structures and those who attempted to set them aside as inevitable restrictions; and between those who saw mass mobilizations as a tactic and those who saw them as a principle. Again, the biographies of many Chartists demonstrate that these are not easy divisions.[5]

This heterogeneity is the product of and reflects the more general climate of movements for social reform in the mid-nineteenth century. The development of British and American capitalism created what might be called a critique of the nature of social development in the two countries. F. O. Matthiessen wrote of the situation in the United States that "the forties probably gave rise to more movements of reform than any other decade in our history; they marked the last struggle of the liberal spirit of the eighteenth century in conflict with the rising forces of exploitation."[6] Although that "liberal spirit" took different forms in the two countries—for example, the utopian movement as a critique of prevailing conditions was much stronger in the United States than in Britain—both shared a number of broadly similar concerns. The growth of the temperance movement on both sides of the Atlantic can be seen as a response to the spiralling levels of alcohol dependency, which can in turn be traced to the spread of the kind of conditions Engels described in *The Condition of the Working Class in England* (1844). These similarities can be seen in the echoes between Engels' descriptions of Manchester and Rebecca Harding Davis's images of life in the unnamed town clearly modelled on her hometown of Wheeling, West Virginia, in *Life in the Iron Mills* (1861). The "reform spirit"[7] took many forms, and as a general expression employed to cover a range of specific responses it can be seen as a description of different reactions to the phenomena of development.

Describing his time in Britain and Ireland, Douglass wrote in *Life and Times* that "the object of my labours in Great Britain was the concentration of the moral and religious sentiment of its people against American slavery. To this end I visited and lectured in nearly all the large towns and cities in the United Kingdom, and enjoyed many favorable opportunities for observation and information."[8] Even if promoting abolition was the avowed intention of Douglass's transatlantic voyage, that object was complicated by his encounters with the various factions of the social reform movements in Britain and Ireland at the time.

Abolitionism and Chartism have two elements in common with each other and with other reform movements. The first and most obvious is

that both were mass movements for civil and human rights that helped
to reshape two powerful nineteenth-century bourgeois democracies. If
history is made by people, albeit not in circumstances of their own
choosing, those who make history are usually compelled to change by
the prospect of the loss of their power and privilege.[9] The importance
of mass action in these movements must be emphasized. Chartism, for-
mally initiated in 1837, grew out of the anger and despair at the consequences for ordinary people of the industrialization of the preceding fifty
years. Throughout the subsequent surges and resurges of the movement, new generations of leaders came forward and stood alongside
those who had been tempered by previous struggles. These leaders re-
lied upon, and indeed assumed their positions of leadership as a result
of, their connections to the mass movement. While the connection to the
mass movement was not so immediately intimate for the leading abolitionists, a similar dynamic applied. One of the best illustrations of this is
in Truman Nelson's novel of the activities of Theodore Parker, *The Sin of
the Prophet,* in which Parker is seen as both inspired and tortured by his
relationship to the mass movement around him.[10] At the novel's climax
Parker is racked by the contradictions he feels between his abstract commitment to moral persuasion and his experience of the power of a mass
movement.

Yet the two movements had fundamental differences. For the Chartists, self-emancipation was always a driving element in their thinking
even when that drive was directed towards presenting petitions to Parliament demanding the vote. Indeed, at a very early stage the movement
was shaken by a debate on tactics to be adopted once the presentation
of the Charter to Parliament had been rejected. This was the beginning
of the division between supporters of moral force and physical force
in Chartism, which was to characterize the political debate within the
movement thereafter. Abolitionism, though, while still recognizing the
power of mass mobilizations, came very much later and more slowly
to this debate. Self-emancipation was not one of its essential building
blocks, even when the debate about force sharpened in the 1850s. These
differences do not invalidate the utility of investigating the connections
between the two movements; but conclusions from this investigation
must be drawn carefully. Frederick Douglass, for example, from 1845 to

1860 and beyond, can be seen as vacillating between supporting moral force and physical force; his work as a whole can be seen as an expression of the contradictions and tensions of the reformer seeking to reform existing structures while attempting to remain within the conservative logic of those structures.

Because these movements were not unanimous and univocal, they were shaped and limited by their conceptions of civil and human rights.[11] To be sure, abolitionism as a whole agreed on the need to abolish chattel slavery but was equally divided on other immediate questions: the participation of women in the movement rocked whatever unity there was, and the splits and divisions that appeared so quickly after the end of the Civil War and chattel slavery indicate the presence of contending forces under the large umbrella. Similarly, Chartism was united by the call for the extension of the vote but split by tactical and strategic debates that seemed to harden into schisms over principle. Questions apparently peripheral to an issue often became more important than the issue itself. For example, if freedom and equality amount to an abstract legal definition, then the legal abolition of slavery or the legal granting of the vote concludes the matter. If, on the other hand, freedom and equality must mean something concrete in people's lives beyond legal definitions, matters such as civil and social freedom, access to education, and the impact of poverty become more important. That this was the case is in large part due to the ways in which the movements were shaped and also limited by their conceptions of civil and human rights. Much of this was rendered both concrete and immediate by the transfer of principle into tactics, by the division in both movements between physical force and moral suasion as two poles. In both cases, the role of the former has been downplayed or abused.

Yet if there were two clear wings in these movements it is also true that many members of the movements vacillated between the two positions, pulled by events in the world beyond the movement and also by the effectiveness of campaigners for opposing positions. This effect appears in Douglass's speeches and letters during his time in Britain as a series of shifting emphases and changing positions. On first arriving in Britain he wrote to R. D. Webb on 10 November 1845 from Limerick that "my mission to this land is purely an anti-slavery one, and although there are other good causes which need to be advocated, I think my duty calls me strictly to the question of Slavery." [12] Yet the following 26 February, in a letter to Garrison from Montrose, he said that while abolitionism had been

> established for the overthrow of the accursed slave system, it is not insensible to other evils that afflict and blast the happiness of mankind. So also, though I am more closely connected and identified with one class of outraged, oppressed and enslaved people, I cannot allow myself to be insensible to the wrongs and sufferings of any part of the great family of man. . . . I am not going through this land with my eyes shut, ears stopped, or heart steeled. . . . He who really and truly feels for the American slave, cannot steel his heart to the woes of others; and he who thinks himself an abolitionist, yet cannot enter into the wrongs of others, has yet to find a true foundation for his anti-slavery faith. [13]

While Douglass may have been writing with a very clear sense of his audience in both of these letters, they cannot be regarded as entirely private correspondence. They are also, in a very real sense, public statements. His change in thinking was not a trajectory from one position to another, but rather a marker of the rise and fall of influences on his thinking, speaking, and writing.

As a result of the transatlantic trade in ideas, Chartism and abolitionism were engaged in debates within themselves and between each other about principles, strategy, and tactics. That Douglass was one of the focal points of these debates can be best demonstrated by considering the occasions on which he had direct connection with and made reference to the Chartist movement, and secondarily, by noting his connections to other reform movements, such as temperance and Irish nationalism. These interconnections should serve as a warning not to limit our understanding by imposing what might be called disciplinary boundaries on any of these movements. One of the themes will be the interconnections between the different activities of the same indiviual. If we too quickly label William Lovett or Henry Vincent as simply Chartists, we miss their other activities and the web of connections that begins to spin when we identify the links they made between different aspects of social reform in their lives. As Robin Kelley has so eloquently argued in his recent book *Race Rebels,* the resistance of the oppressed often takes on an everyday complexity that steps beyond neat definitions of the political imposed too quickly from a historical or abstract standpoint.[14]

The parallels between Chartism and abolitionism may be enhanced by seeing them in the context of a wave of questioning and upheaval that swept the newly developing capitalist economies of the first half of the nineteenth century. In his recent biography of Daniel O'Connell, Oliver Macdonagh acknowledges that O'Connell was "already in 1830, and would remain until his death, a hero of heroes to the American Negroes and many abolitionists."[15] He makes, however, no reference to Douglass. John Blassingame, meanwhile, in his collection of Douglass's speeches from 1841 to 1846, makes no reference to Douglass's presence at a Repeal meeting on 29 September 1845. Yet when we read Douglass's account of the meeting we can see very clearly the impact on him of hearing O'Connell speak:

> Mr. O'Connell was in his happiest mood while delivering this speech. The fire of freedom was burning in his mighty heart. He had but to open his mouth, to put us in possession of "thoughts that breathe, and words that burn." I have heard many speakers within the last four years – speakers of the first order; but I confess, I have never heard one, by whom I was more completely captivated than by Mr. O'Connell.[16]

At the same time, the words that burned demonstrate the committed internationalism of this leading nationalist:

> I have been assailed for attacking the American institution, as it is called, – Negro slavery. I am not ashamed of that attack. I do not shrink from it. I am the advocate of civil and religious liberty, all over the globe, and wherever tyranny exists, I am the foe of the tyrant; wherever oppression shows itself, I am the foe of the oppressor; wherever slavery rears its head, I am the enemy of the system, or the institution, call it by whatever name you will. I am the friend of liberty in every clime, class and color. My sympathy with distress is not confined within the narrow bounds of my own green island. No – it extends itself to every corner of the earth. My heart walks abroad, and wherever the miserable are to be succored, or the slave to be set free, there my spirit is at home, and I delight to dwell.[17]

If Frederick Douglass stated clearly in his writing that abolition was his primary object in touring Britain, he also demonstrated in practice that this was not his only purpose. He spoke on a wide variety of platforms to a wide variety of audiences, and it would be naive to assume that his message was always received as it was intended. When Douglass spoke in Exeter on 28 August 1846, several of the local papers covered the event. The reports, which agree on the text of the speech delivered, vary considerably in their account of the local dignitaries present. *Trewman's Exeter Flying Post* – a paper with clear Quaker sympathies – lists seven people but excludes Francis Bishop, a Unitarian minister, who, according to the *Western Luminary,* was present. This is important because Bishop, a close friend of William Lloyd Garrison (alongside whom Douglass spoke that evening), was the prime motivator of the visit and the author of the motion passed that night affiliating those present to the Anti-Slavery League – of which the *Flying Post* makes no mention. Intriguingly, all the reports also refer to a second meeting at which Douglass alone spoke the following evening, but none give any account of this gathering. By looking at these differing versions of the same event, we can begin to see how different sections of an audience construct different events from the same moment.[18] We know that Douglass spoke that night and we have a clear sense of what he said, but how those words have been understood and employed by his audience is very much at issue both then and now.

In attempting to see the complexities of the situation, there is no intention to dispose of generalization but rather to argue for complex generalization. Indeed, I wish to identify areas of common concern between these campaigners, issues to which they brought different conceptions of social reform. The inability to generalize to a wider, particularly internationalist, context has been the downfall of many movements for change. An inquiry that is rooted in the generalities of the internationalist imagination thus provides the basis for clearer historical understanding and interpretation.[19]

The historical record of the Chartists and the abolitionists shows a tradition of drawing parallels and connections to struggles around the world in order to strengthen their own causes at home. George Julian Harney's description of the multinational crowd dancing through Covent Garden at the news of the fall of Louis Phillipe is joyous in its roll call of unity in celebration at the downfall of a "foreign" tyrant:

The effect was electrical. Frenchmen, Germans, Poles, Magyars, sprang to their feet, embraced, shouted, and gesticulated in the wildest enthusiasm. Snatches of oratory were delivered in excited tones, and flags were caught from the walls, to be waved exultantly, amidst cries of "Hoch! Eljen! Vive la Republique!" Then the doors were opened, and the whole assemblage . . . with linked arms and colours flying, marched to the meeting place of the Westminster Chartists in Dean Street, Soho. There another enthusiastic fraternisation took place.[20]

Historical agents—living and breathing human beings—have a tradition that persistently refuses to be limited by national boundaries. As David Herreshoff has demonstrated, the ideas of socialist change were carried across the Atlantic by German intellectuals and workers fleeing from the post-1848 reaction.[21] The role of the Foreign Language Federations in the development of class struggle politics in the United States in the early twentieth century is well documented. The place of Afro-Caribbean and Indian subcontinental workers in the rise of militant trade unionism in Britain in the 1960s and '70s is starting to be better documented but is still largely ignored at a practical level. Individually, the part played by migrant and dissident intellectuals in the development of ideas and activities in several locations remains poorly researched due to the intellectual limits set by national boundaries: C. L. R. James and Claude McKay are but two examples. And Frederick Douglass's voyage across the Atlantic in 1845 not only took him away from immediate danger, it carried him to two places similarly rocked by the upheavals caused by the movements for reform to which I have already made reference.

Douglass's sojourn in Britain and Ireland coincided with a period of retreat and regroupment in the Chartist movement between the defeat of the general strikes and insurrections of 1842 and the great upsurge of 1848. As Mark O'Brien argues in *Perish the Privileged Orders,* his recent study of the Chartists, this was also a period in which regroupment and redirection was very much the order of the day. O'Brien points to the rise of temperance and educational Chartism as an ideological marker of how the movement fell away from the possibilities of mass direct confrontations, and he emphasizes in particular the rise of Henry Vincent and William Lovett within Chartism during this period.

The immediate appeal of Lovett to Douglass at this time was that he was firmly in the camp of Moral Force Chartism and his strategic thinking was very close to Douglass's conception of the power of argument. O'Brien characterizes Lovett's thinking as "firmly in the 'Moral Force' camp. He did not believe that workers were yet ready for political power. Only after a period of moral and cultural improvement would the working class achieve the necessary knowledge and responsibility to lay full claim to their political rights."[22] The parallels between this and Douglass's repeated emphasis on the importance of education is striking. In one speech he argued that "slavery is a system that can only be abolished by the light of truth being poured upon it, and infusing upon the mind connected with it, a correct knowledge of those principles of justice and humanity," and continued in another that "we ask no physical aid at your hands; but we ask you to exert the mental moral and religious influence within your reach against American slavery."[23] The connection to Lovett was also a personal one, as Lovett's description in his autobiography of a night's singing demonstrates.

> We, however, employed Frederick Douglas for a short time as our missionary, and his and George Thompson's very eloquent discourses called forth great sympathy on behalf of the poor slave. Lloyd Garrison, also, while he was in London, gave a very eloquent lecture on slavery at the National Hall.
>
> During our friends' visit, I recall to memory a very delightful evening spent with them and other friends, at the house of Mr. J. H. Parry. On that occasion we had not only a very interesting account of the Anti-Slavery movement and its prominent advocates in America, but our friend Douglas, who had a fine voice, sang a number of negro melodies. Mr. Garrison sang several anti-slavery pieces, and our grave friend, H. C. Wright, sang an old Indian war song. Other friends contributed to the amusement of the evening, and among them our friend Vincent sang "The Marseillaise."[24]

That they also disagreed on a range of issues is easy to demonstrate, not least by their very differing attitudes towards the emancipation of women—Lovett opposed the clause in the original charter that demanded universal suffrage while Douglass was an advocate of women's rights—but they were in agreement on the broad shape of the tactics and strategies of social reform: a commitment to an educational program that brought ideas of change to the people from above. Indeed, Lovett had spent some of his time in jail in 1842 and 1843 writing a pamphlet extolling the necessity of education within the Chartist movement.

Henry Vincent was a very different figure. Beginning as a Physical Force Chartist whose speeches during the uprisings of 1839 regularly concluded with the rallying cry "Perish the privileged orders! Death to the aristocracy!" he emerged from imprisonment a convinced advocate of temperance and a primary exponent of the theory that the conditions of chattel slaves in the United States paralleled those of wage slaves in Britain. This idea was common currency among many of the Chartists. Lovett described slavery as "a link in the same great chain of oppression which binds all multitudes in all countries and climes." [25] That connection between abolition and electoral reform was spelled out even more explicitly at a Reform Bill meeting in Exeter in 1832, when it was stated that "slavery was one of the foul blots that a Reformed parliament will hasten to wipe off from the face of the king's dominions." [26] One of the strategies developed by Moral Force Chartism was to build links to those elements of the middle class who had supported the reform bill, a strategy pursued by Vincent and Joseph Sturge in their formation of the Complete Suffrage Union in 1842. In that same year Sturge contributed a preface to a book whose title succinctly describes this political strategy: "Reconciliation between the Middle and Labouring Classes." In areas such as the South West where Moral Force Chartism was the dominant tendency, these links were well developed. Again, rather than having clear delineations, the reform movements contain the same names appearing in different affiliations.

Lovett and Vincent are also important because they were the same two "Chartists" with whom Douglass shared platforms, whose meetings on other topics Douglass attended, and whom Douglass and Garrison joined at the public launch of the Anti-Slavery League on 17 August 1846. Indeed, this meeting took place in the same public house in the Strand, the Crown and Anchor, where nine years earlier a meeting organized by the London Working Men's Association attended by "four thousand democrats" had drafted the first version of the Charter. At the later meeting James Haughton used a significant phrase when he welcomed the formation of the Anti-Slavery League as another member of the "family of reform." Haughton apparently means by this phrase that one can divide those who are committed to the principle of social reform from those who are not, and that those who are committed to reform are further divided between those committed to individual aspects of the broader campaign to the exclusion of other aspects and those committed to individual aspects as part of the broader campaign.

This latter division, between what Aileen Kraditor has usefully called "broad" and "narrow" platforms, constitutes the core of most of the tactical debates in movements for social reform in the 1840s. That debate, which had been raging in the abolitionist movement for at least the previous ten years, concerned whether it was possible to effect a particular reform without questioning larger social structures. Kraditor has detailed the various forms this debate took in her *Means and Ends in American Abolitionism,* and her summary of Garrison's position is clear and concise, as is her account of the consequences:

> The Garrisonians were developing a theory of abolitionist organization that required complete toleration within the society of members with all sorts of views and therefore a very minimal platform on which all abolitionists could stand regardless of their opinions on other issues and their activities outside the organization. . . . A Garrisonian-type movement could thus include the conservatives, but the conservatives' type of movement could not include the "ultraists." [27]

However, as abolitionism advanced and the political ideas of activists developed, a series of clashes occurred over precisely these issues, and a number of splits took place involving conservative groups. It is clear from his general pronouncements and his actions while in Britain and Ireland that Frederick Douglass did not see abolitionism as separated from the broad spectrum of social reform movements. He took the temperance pledge from Father Theobald Mathews in Cork, attending and speaking at temperance meetings throughout his visit. On 30 March 1846 at a temperance meeting in Paisley, he said, "I am a temperance man because I am an anti-slavery man; and I am an anti-slavery man because I love my fellow man." [28] He made the connection even clearer on 21 May 1846 at the annual meeting of the National Temperance Society when he said, "I am a teetotaller, and I am so because I would elevate my race from the degradation into which they have been cast by slavery and other circumstances."[29] Douglass also attended and spoke at Irish Repeal meetings, as already noted. He attended at least one meeting of the London Flogging Abolition Society—a meeting that would surely have had extreme resonance for him. He was present at the founding of the Anti-Slavery League and made reference to it in subsequent speeches. From this we can presume that his audiences would have been aware of the connections of the Anti-Slavery League to the Chartists Lovett and Vincent.

In Douglass's speeches and letters of 1845 to 1847 we read a tension between arguing the case for abolitionism by exposing the real nature of slavery and a growing sense that the abolition of slavery would not be the end of the story of the search for African American human rights, or, in Douglass's terms, "the elevation of the race." Indeed, the repetitions in the speeches indicate that he felt it necessary to disseminate information to an audience beguiled and misled by accounts such as that of Charles Lyell's *Travels in North America,* and at the close of his visit it was this activity for which he was most praised. Rather than positioned merely in a "transatlantic trade in ideas," Douglass is also positioned within the polemic between different trades. For abolitionists were not the only participants to connect across the water. Antiabolitionist ideas were also in circulation, as the following from Charles Lyell's writings makes clear:

> The more I reflected on the condition of the slaves, and endeavoured to think on a practicable plan for hastening the period of their liberation, the more difficult the subject appeared to me, and the more I felt astonished at the confidence displayed by so many anti-slavery speakers and writers on both sides of the Atlantic. The course pursued by these agitators shows that, next to the positively wicked, the class who are usually called "well meaning persons" are the most mischievous in society.[30]

Lyell goes on to blame abolitionists and the "trouble" they caused in the South for the restrictive conditions under which slaves were held and defends chattel slavery against wage slavery in terms very close to those employed by the proslavery apologist George Fitzhugh. In short he accepts, employs, and popularizes the arguments for slavery even while appearing to be in favor of a gradual abolition. What becomes clear is that gradual abolition is abolition at a pace set by the slaveholders. Lyell's book appeared in Britain in the summer of 1845 – the dedication is dated 12 June – and was sufficiently successful that it warranted an attack from Douglass during his visit to Limerick in November of the same year.[31]

This conflict also appears in Douglass's visit to Exeter. On 28 and 29 August at Congdon's Royal Subscription Rooms, he made, according to newspaper reports, a great impression with his eloquence and bearing. Yet the same issue of *Trewman's Exeter Flying Post* that reported Douglass's meetings also reviewed the visit to Exeter on 31 August and 1 and 2 September of the Ethiopian Serenaders, a blackface minstrel touring company, who "hit off the fancies and the character of the nigger to the very life."[32] Douglass's presence had persuaded liberal opinion in Exeter to an antislavery position while leaving the racism necessary to justify slavery rather less challenged.

By the conclusion of his visit Douglass had played a major part in turning the tide of opinion from hostility, apathy, or ignorance toward support for abolition. At the same time, his speeches began to include references to other subjects such as the abuse of alcohol and the importance of temperance as a way to prepare for the education necessary to "elevation" on both sides of the Atlantic. The note of impatience that David Turley has detected in this element of the speeches shows Douglass's wish to discuss other issues while needing to cover the same well-worn ground for other and newer audiences.[33]

What we can see, then, is Douglass being influenced by the environment in which he finds himself in Britain in 1845 – 47. Two examples may suffice. On 19 August 1846 (two days after the formation of the Anti-Slavery League) Douglass attended a meeting of the London Flogging Abolition Society at which Henry Vincent was the speaker. Six days later, at a meeting in Bristol, Douglass spoke of "political slavery in England. He spoke of slavery in the army, slavery in the navy, and looking upon the laboring population, he contemplated them as slaves." However, he then went on to observe that he had "not one word to say in defence of any form of oppression on earth – not a sentence in extenuation of the conduct of any tyrant on earth."[34] His wish was that tyranny and oppression of every kind might have an end. Yet he was there to proclaim boldly that there was no more similarity between slavery as existing in the United States and any institution in Britain than there was between light and darkness." Six days later still, in Bridgwater, he explicitly denied the parallels between chattel slavery and wage slavery.[35]

The tension between these statements indicates the degree to which Douglass was influenced by, but not under the influence of, those around him. While Douglass was certainly adept at tailoring his words to his audience, it does not seem that the audiences were significantly different in their composition. Both meetings were in private rooms rather than large public venues, and if anything, the speeches are in the reverse order to that which one would expect: the Bristol speech was delivered to an audience described by a contemporary report as "a most select assemblage."

Rather, what we can see here is that Vincent's argument about the parallels between chattel slavery and wage slavery had organizational and ideological influence on Douglass. It is no coincidence that the clearest statement of the parallels between the two in Douglass's pronouncements of this period comes immediately after the high point in his relationship with these Chartists—the foundation of the Anti-Slavery League—a period of which Lovett wrote that Douglass was employed "for a short time as our missionary." [36] It is also no coincidence that the day after the public launch of the Anti-Slavery League, Douglass wrote to the Lynn Anti-Slavery Sewing Circle that "I am by no means unmindful of the poor; and you may rely upon me as one who will never desert the cause of the poor, no matter whether black or white." [37] This influence faded quickly, though, as other influences reasserted themselves, and within a week the connection between chattel and wage slavery was being denied. In particular, the visit to Exeter between the Bristol and Bridgwater meetings would presumably have generated other influences, as this meeting was chaired by John Clampitt Sercombe, a leading local businessman and vice-consul for Spain and Prussia, and was attended by several of the city's prominent professionals. Nevertheless Douglass continued to argue publicly for support for the Anti-Slavery League.

Frederick Douglass's visit to Britain, then, coincided with a point in the history of Chartism at which the strategic thinking of those dominant in the movement was closest to Douglass's at that time. The power of argument – the possibilities of moral suasion – were still persuasive. Ironically, this situation changed very sharply for the Chartists within a year of Douglass's departure with the great upsurge of 1848. He was no longer near enough to hear the arguments in favor of physical force that gained ground in the face of the government's contemptuous attitude, arguments that would resonate in abolitionist circles throughout the 1850s.

It is impossible to draw neat lines around social phenomena and separate them from other similar phenomena. Although such divisions may make our studies simpler, they may also remove from our sight the complex interconnections all too familiar to the active human subjects who make history. While William McFeely is right to draw attention to Douglass's surprising lack of connection with William Cuffay, the leading black activist in the Chartist movement in London, this lack of connection might be because Cuffay was very much the representative of the militant working-class organizations that acted as the backbone of militant Chartism in its ascendancy. Shared skin color should not blind us to political differences, and Cuffay was an advocate of physical force.

With other leaders of the movement, such as Vincent and Lovett, Douglass's relationship was closer, if also contradictory and complex. Vincent, Lovett, and Douglass stood in a different class relationship from Cuffay to both Chartism and abolitionism, a relationship that allowed them to make common cause with each other in the broader struggle to make the world a better and more humane place. That commitment, whatever other differences pushed them apart, is clear. It is also a shared commitment that those who still continue to believe in the possibility of a more humane and more civilized world – whatever differences we might have as to how to achieve that goal – might wish to emulate. After all, much business begun by Douglass and the Chartists is still left uncompleted.

NOTES

1. Paul Gilroy, *The Black Atlantic* (London: Verso, 1994); Peter Linebaugh, "All the Atlantic Mountains Shook," *Labour/Le Travailleur* 10 (autumn 1982): 87–121. The impulse

for much of this work can be found in the work of Christopher Hill, especially his essay "Radical Pirates?" in *The Collected Essays of Christopher Hill* (Brighton: Harvester, 1986), vol. 3.

2. Peter Fryer, *Staying Power: The History of Black People in Britain* (London: Pluto Press, 1984), 433.

3. Philip S. Foner, *The Life and Writings of Frederick Douglass,* 5 vols. (New York: International Publishers, 1950–55), 1:167.

4. This is, of course, the title of Betty Fladeland's important article, to which I wish to identify my debt in these general remarks. It appeared in James Walvin, ed., *Slavery and British Society 1776–1846* (London: Macmillan, 1982), 69–99.

5. There are numerous invaluable resources describing the heterogeneity of the two movements. My own preferences would foreground Mark O'Brien's *Perish the Privileged Orders* (London: Bookmarks, 1995) and J. R. Oldfield, *Popular Politics and British Antislavery* (Manchester: Manchester University Press, 1995).

6. F. O. Matthiessen, *American Renaissance* (New York: Oxford University Press, 1941).

7. This phrase is intentionally imprecise as it attempts to express a general feeling, part of which was indeed not a reform spirit but a spirit for revolution.

8. Frederick Douglass, *Life and Times of Frederick Douglass* (1893; reprint, New York: Collier, 1962), 255.

9. Robin Blackburn, *The Overthrow of Colonial Slavery* (London: Verso, 1988), provides a particularly valuable exploration of this theme.

10. Truman Nelson, *The Sin of the Prophet* (New York, 1952). Theodore Parker, a Unitarian minister, was a leading figure in the abolitionist movement in New England whose thinking with regard to the strategies and tactics of the movement developed significantly during the period after the passage of the Fugitive Slave Law in 1850.

11. There is much very useful material on these questions in Richard King, *Civil Rights and the Idea of Freedom* (Oxford: Oxford University Press, 1995).

12. Quoted in Foner, *Life and Writings,* 1:123.

13. Quoted in ibid., 1:138–40.

14. Robin D. G. Kelley, *Race Rebels* (New York: Free Press, 1994).

15. Oliver Macdonagh, *O'Connell: The Life of Daniel O'Connell, 1775–1847* (London: Weidenfeld and Nicolson, 1991), 303.

16. Foner, *Life and Writings,* 1:121.

17. Ibid.

18. I am very grateful to the staff of the Devon and Exeter Institution, especially Su Conniff, for helping me to track down these accounts. They appear in *Trewman's Exeter Flying Post,* 3 September 1846 and *Western Luminary,* 1 September 1846.

19. So that this should not be read as an obituary for the internationalist imagination among working-class people, I would also want to emphasize the continuation of its exis-

tence, demonstrated as recently as 1996 by the solidarity shown by U.S. longshoremen for the striking Liverpool dockers.

20. A. R. Schoyen, *The Chartist Challenge,* quoted in O'Brien, *Perish the Privileged Orders,* 80–81.

21. David Herreshoff, *The Origins of Marxism in the United States* (New York: Monad Press, 1967).

22. O'Brien, *Perish the Privileged Orders,* 68.

23. Quoted in John W. Blassingame, ed., *The Frederick Douglass Papers. Series One; Speeches, Debates, and Interviews,* 5 vols. (New Haven: Yale University Press, 1979–), 1:325, 373.

24. William Lovett, *The Life and Struggles of William Lovett* (London: Bell, 1920), 328–29.

25. William Lovett to William Lloyd Garrison, 1 March 1847, in Clare Taylor, ed., *British and American Abolitionists: An Episode in Transatlantic Understanding* (Edinburgh: Edinburgh University Press, 1974), 308.

26. Quoted in D. Coles, *Chartism and Radical Politics in Devon and Exeter 1790–1848* (unpublished Exeter University M.A. thesis, 1979), 42.

27. Aileen Kraditor, *Means and Ends in American Abolitionism* (New York: Random House, 1969), 54–55.

28. Blassingame, *Papers,* 1:209.

29. Ibid., 1:265.

30. Charles Lyell, *Travels in North America* (London, 1845).

31. It is also interesting, in the light of my earlier remarks about the nature of the Atlantic as a conduit for radical ideas, that in his dedication Lyell writes that his happy memories of his journey are mixed with "my frequent regrets that the broad Atlantic should separate so many congenial souls whom we both of us number among our friends in Europe and America."

32. *Trewman's Exeter Flying Post,* 3 September 1846.

33. See David Turley's essay in this volume.

34. Blassingame, *Papers,* 1:344.

35. Ibid., 1:365.

36. Lovett, *Life and Struggles,* 328.

37. Quoted in Foner, *Life and Writings,* 1:188.

Cracks in the Antislavery Wall

Frederick Douglass's Second Visit to England

(1859–1860) and the Coming of the Civil War

R. J. M. BLACKETT

I T WAS IN 1846, DURING HIS FIRST VISIT TO BRITAIN, THAT Frederick Douglass suggested a blueprint for the building of a transatlantic antislavery wall. Its aim: to hem in American slavery within its existing confines and expose it to the moral glare of international public opinion. Such restrictions and exposure would make American slaveholders the pariahs of the Christian world and, in so doing, cajole them into freeing their slaves. Within this wall of antislavery public opinion, bounded by "Canada on the North, Mexico in the west, and England, Scotland and Ireland on the east," the slaveholder would hear "nothing but denunciation of slavery" and would be "looked down upon as a man-stealing, cradle-robbing, and woman-stripping monster" who would see nothing but "reproof and detestation on every hand."[1] By the time of his return to the United States the following year, Douglass was convinced that his efforts had helped to strengthen the transatlantic movement begun fifteen years earlier. There were signs wherever he went that the British public was still deeply committed to the abolition of slavery. With the exception of the failure to persuade the Free Church of Scotland to return money raised in the South, all the signs pointed to a vibrant and effective transatlantic movement. Never one to miss an opportunity to berate his racially sensitive countrymen, Douglass never tired of reminding Americans that he was welcomed with open arms by all classes in Britain. In monarchical Britain he was a free man, but in republican America he was a mere piece of property.

Twelve years later when Douglass returned to Britain, fleeing possible extradition to Virginia for his alleged involvement in John Brown's attack on Harpers Ferry, he was surprised by the changes that had occurred since his first visit. Wherever he went during his second visit he was challenged by two surprisingly contradictory realities. There were those who continued to explore ways to help the slaves and freedmen, with donations to aid fugitive slaves in Canada, settle freedmen in Africa, and abolish the slave trade to Cuba, while continuing to work for the abolition of American slavery. But there were others who had grown weary of such agitation and philanthropy and demanded to know "what have we to do with American slavery?" Douglass was taken aback by what he called this new doctrine of nonintervention, for the foundation of a successful antislavery movement had been the willingness of men and women of goodwill to work for the elimination of slavery, the "sum of all villainies." As he would repeatedly assert during this tour, the reform of the dram shop had to come "from the regions of sobriety," that of the "house of ill-fame . . . from the regions of probity," and so too must slavery be exposed by countries "uncontaminated by slavery."[2]

Everywhere Douglass went, however, he saw disturbing signs of a loss of interest in American slavery and, simultaneously, the creeping influence of American prejudice on British public opinion. Gone were the days when *The Times* of London would republish, as it did in 1850, an item from an American newspaper reporting the attack on Douglass by a "mob" enraged by the spectacle of a black man walking down the streets of New York with two white women on his arms. Douglass had written to thank *The Times,* and by extension all of Britain, for its sympathy: the "influence exerted upon the more intelligent class of American people by the judicious expression of British sense of justice and humanity is immense, and, I believe, highly beneficial." Such support, he concluded, would help to subvert "the aristocracy of skin."[3] By 1859, however, the British voice of justice seemed muted, if not silenced. Samuel Joseph May, who had visited Britain a few months before Douglass's arrival, was also struck by the growing indifference to slavery in Britain. Most in the country, May reported, think slavery "none of their business." Still later, in the midst of the Civil War, Edward Irving, a fugitive slave who had lived in Britain for some time, insisted that "if Wilberforce could appear amongst them . . . he would reproach them for abandoning the principles of freedom."[4]

Despite evidences of retreat from Britain's antislavery traditions, other visitors to Britain still saw signs of hope. Sarah Parker Remond, who had traveled to England with May, wrote friends in America a few months later, "I begin to feel quite at home in Great Britain. I feel so much more freedom here than at home." William Powell, who moved his family from New York to Liverpool in the early 1850s to escape growing racial restrictions, continued to prosper at the end of the decade, as did William G. Allen, who left America for Britain in 1853 because of violent resistance to his plans to marry a white woman.[5] And thousands turned out to hear Douglass and Remond lecture, a clear indication of continued public interest in the struggle to free the slaves in America.

It is not surprising, however, that British antislavery views had undergone changes since Douglass's first visit. Howard Temperley and others have argued that, at least by the end of the 1850s, organized British antislavery "had pretty much run itself into the ground,"[6] and there is no doubt that the movement's ability to function effectively had been hampered by divisions in its ranks that had their origin almost two decades earlier. The movement was also affected by the toll that time had taken on the ranks of those who had fought for West Indian emancipation and who, in the late 1830s, had dedicated themselves to supporting the struggle for freedom in the United States. Henry Highland Garnet, who had first visited Britain in 1851, was struck by these not unexpected changes on a return visit in 1861. But the lesson Garnet drew from them was simple: the survivors of the old movement had to "transmit to their children their hatred of oppression."[7] Douglas Lorimer argues that by 1860 the "abolitionists were an aging group and antislavery a dying cause," conditions that coincided with changing domestic perceptions of class and the acceptance of the distance between the middle and working classes as natural. Further, the association of "alien races with inferior status and the perception of race relations as a form of class relationship prepared the way" for a transition in British racial attitudes.[8]

While questions about the relevance of American slavery to British interests bothered Douglass, in 1859 there was no noticeable drop in British support for his efforts in America. He continued to attract considerable support from a cadre of British followers. Ever since 1847 he had been the star in the firmament of Anglo-American abolitionism. Not only had friends and supporters raised money to purchase his freedom, they had also made it possible for him to begin publishing his newspaper, the *North Star.* The editor of the *British Banner,* for example, had called on one thousand of his readers to send £1 each to support Douglass's newspaper, arguing that there was not "a living man in the New World capable of bringing more power, either of spoken or of written language, to bear upon the question of three million of men."[9] Douglass's split with his former Garrisonian allies, who many in Britain considered the promoters of infidel beliefs, only enhanced his stature among many. Even opponents acknowledged that, by the mid-1850s, Douglass had emerged as the dominant figure in the transatlantic movement and the recipient of the largest share of financial support from Britain. When in 1856 Douglass's former coworker at Rochester, New York, Julia Griffiths, returned home to England to raise funds to offset debts incurred in publishing his newspaper, she met with considerable success. Within a few months, Griffiths had helped to organize twenty new ladies' antislavery societies and had stimulated the reactivation of a number of defunct ones. One of the latter, the Sheffield Ladies Anti-Slavery Association, was reactivated in February 1857 with two principal objectives: to aid Douglass's newspaper and to aid fugitives escaping through Rochester, Douglass's hometown. Griffiths's successes were, to a significant degree, a reflection of Douglass's continuing popularity in Britain. Within a year of Douglass's return home in 1847, some British Garrisonians were reporting that much of the support that had previously been sent to Boston and Philadelphia, strongholds of American Garrisonianism, was now being diverted to Douglass in Rochester. As Jane Wigham later summed up the situation from Edinburgh, the quarrel between Douglass and his former colleagues was winning Douglass considerable sympathy in that city.[10]

Even though Parker Pillsbury, the American Garrisonian, dismissed these "Douglass disciples" as relatively unimportant, and Samuel May toyed with the idea that Douglass's "female satellites" may have held some impermissible influence over him, there is little evidence that Douglass's stature was in any way diminished by the passing of time. As late as February 1862, a considerable portion of the money raised by the antislavery bazaar in Bristol went to Rochester.[11] But the bitterness generated by the continuous dispute between Douglass and his former allies could not have helped to allay the fears of many British supporters that the movement was continuing to dissipate its energies in internecine squabbles. When word of Douglass's proposed visit in 1859 reached Bristol, Mary Estlin quipped that Douglass would succeed "in promoting his own interests whether by assumed friendship, or avowed hostility to the causes of his friends." She also thought that May would have little success in his efforts to warn friends against Douglass, a man who May insisted "villainously and meanly lied about us in order to gratify his own spite, and turn money into his own coffers." The concerns of British and American Garrisonians were eased only by Elizabeth Wigham's report from Edinburgh that Douglass was neither attacking the American Antislavery Society nor giving it credit.[12]

While the question of "nonintervention," that is, the desire to dismiss slavery as largely irrelevant to British interests, worried Douglass, signs of the spread of racial prejudice troubled him more. But the memory of the freedom he had enjoyed there in 1845 and the continued support he had received since may have blinded Douglass to the nature and extent of British racism in 1859. He may even have been reluctant to relinquish the cachet such support gave him in his fight to end slavery in America. As he later explained, this visit could have turned into permanent exile, for, in 1859, slavery "seemed to be at the very top of its power; the national government, with all its powers and appliances, was in its hands, and it bade fair to wield them for many years to come."[13] That possibility helps explain why Douglass attributed these signs of British racism to American influences. In contrast to the absence of any manifestations of racial discrimination during his first visit, in 1859 "American prejudice might be found on the streets of Liverpool and in nearly all . . . commercial towns." This fact, he maintained, was the work of the many "pro-slavery ministers" who were now welcomed in Britain—something he had fought against in 1846 – and that "pestiferous nuisance, Ethiopian minstrels," who had imported into the country "the slang phrases, the contemptuous sneers all originating in the spirit of slavery." Now blacks were being portrayed as happy slaves and as "thoughtless of any life higher than a merely physical one." [14]

Not surprisingly, Douglass's view of conditions in Britain influenced (as it did in 1845) his efforts to rally public opinion in support of American abolition. He took special care to reinvigorate traditional supporters, concentrating much of his efforts in cities and towns that were active promoters of his work in Rochester. These local supporters, and many of the ladies' societies formed during Griffiths's earlier visit, provided forums for Douglass's efforts to influence public opinion against slavery and to warn the British against the creeping and insidious racism that had its origin in the United States. While his lectures hewed to traditional abolitionists' condemnation of the power and influence of the slaveholding South in American politics, they also introduced an element of hope that there would be change both at the seats of power and in areas not directly affected by slavery. He also called for the rejection of American prejudice and a recommitment to the effort to isolate slaveholders and their supporters. It was Douglass's way of patching the cracks that had appeared in the antislavery wall.

The progress of antislavery views was since 1830 unmistakable, Douglass told a large public meeting in Bradford. There was a decided increase in the number of antislavery societies, reflecting a wider public rejection, particularly in the North, of slavery. Whereas in 1845 there had been only two congressmen and one senator willing to support abolition, those numbers had now increased to 109 and 25 respectively. Although this progress had met with growing intransigence among Southern legislators and with willingness on the part of many Northern politicians to placate slaveholders while castigating abolitionists, abolitionist activity had "succeeded in removing much of the prejudice that had long existed against colour in the Northern States." Such progress, however, was seriously threatened by slavery's deleterious effects on the religious sensibilities of the country. As Douglass had argued so fervently in 1846, the "abettor of slavery was too frequently a professor of religion." [15]

In the face of such opposition, successes in the United States could be maintained only with the support of a caring, benevolent international community. Slavery, Douglass insisted, could only survive in America if it were "not held to be disreputable outside." While the antislavery movement had shown unmistakable progress since 1845, he feared that "the moral sense" of Great Britain, the international bulwark against slavery, was "being corrupted by the influence of the system on the other side of the Atlantic," by the activities of the "friends of slaveholders," who were taking "every opportunity to circulate their pernicious views in this country." Many of the estimated forty thousand Americans who annually visited Britain, and who each brought with them their baggage of prejudices, were received into all walks of British society; "and some of these men, many of them religious men professedly some of them doctors of divinity—traveled over the length and breadth of our land and wherever they went they poured the 'leprous distilment' of their pro-slavery poison into the ears and hearts of the British people." [16]

While there were few active British abolitionists who would question Douglass's insistence on the need for continued international support for abolition, some, like George Thompson, his coworker in the "Send Back the Money" campaign of 1846, differed with him profoundly on the nature and extent of America's progress towards equality. Thompson, as Douglass put it when speaking of his differences with American and British Garrisonians, opposed "the Church, the ministry, the sabbath, and the Government as Institutions in themselves." [17] Douglass could have added, so too were their differences over whether the United States Constitution was proslavery. Prior to 1851, when his view on the Constitution changed, Douglass, like other Garrisonians, had insisted that the Constitution was proslavery and, in the words of Garrison, a "covenant with death and an agreement with hell." When challenged by Thompson to explain how a number of clauses and articles could be anything but an endorsement of slavery, Douglass insisted on a literal interpretation: if the document did not explicitly mention slavery, then it stood to reason that it could not be proslavery. There was no validity to discussions about original intent, Douglass countered, or for that matter arguments about the use to which consecutive governments and the courts had put the Constitution. Only a commonsense reading mattered, not the "secret intentions of the individuals who may have had something to do with writing the paper." Thompson was incredulous at this offhand dismissal of an issue that held such profound implication for the future of the country. He asked an acquaintance,

> do we not know who its fathers, framers and founders *were,* what they *meant,* what they *said,* what they *did,* what price they *paid,* and what equivalent they received when the bargain was struck? What laws have been reared upon the Constitution, and what cruelties have been perpetrated under it, what slave states have been annexed, what decisions given and what is, and ever has been, the Universal sentiment of both the pro-slavery and anti-slavery parties. It is not with *a* Constitution in the *Abstract,* but with *the* Constitution in the *concrete* that we have to do.[18]

Such profound differences did little to enlighten audiences unfamiliar with arcane constitutional issues and could only have reinforced the conviction among many that abolitionists were being a little self-indulgent. But if this debate generated quizzical looks and some disbelief in early 1860, it would come to have considerable significance following the outbreak of the Civil War. If Douglass was right and the Constitution was antislavery, then all it took in a war with slaveholders was for the government at Washington to declare slavery illegal. If on the other hand, the Constitution was proslavery, then the only hope for freedom in the North was its permanent separation from the South. In the context of secession, however, both Douglass and Thompson found themselves in a largely untenable position. If the Constitution was antislavery, how to explain the Union's reluctance to declare itself for abolition? For Thompson, Garrison's endorsement of Union policies, tinged as it was with a strong commitment to maintaining the national integrity of the United States, undermined the very foundations of Garrison's traditional views about the nature of the Constitution. By fall 1861 Thompson reported that he was reexamining the Constitution to determine exactly what powers were vested in the president.

By the outbreak of the war, many in Britain with very solid abolitionist credentials had come to accept the Garrisonian view that secession was the surest way to emancipation. Secession, the editor of the *Morning Star* argued, was an instance of the "pure democratic blood purging away the foul humours which have hitherto generated on its fair fame a festering sore." With free states to the north, slaves would flee the plantations in increasing numbers, while the introduction of free labor in the border states would demonstrate its utility over slave labor and in the long run lead to emancipation. The association with slavery had tainted the country's democratic and Christian principles; secession would reestablish their primacy. "Touch pitch, and you will be defiled; share a community of citizenship with the slaveholder, and you must expect to participate in his infamy." [19] Those who saw nothing of value in the republican form of government were less charitable. While one Halifax editor insisted that the success of the Confederacy would be a calamity, he remained convinced that the war had been brought on by a flaw in the political and social character of the nation. Not surprisingly, he wondered why the United States had not followed the British example where slavery was abolished by "enlightened agitation . . . within the dictates of reason and the boundaries of the Constitution, . . . thanks to the openness of our well-balanced Parliament, to rationality and to the well-defined expression of the national feeling." In comparison, the United States Constitution was "less amenable to humane influences, and to the counteractivities of wise and prudent men." Such failures were attributable to peculiar national traits that included "no repose, no moderation, none of that *otium cum dignitate,* which is itself . . . aristocratic. Their vices, habits, and faults are exaggerations of English faults, habits and vices. Where we trade; they speculate. When we, in bad times curtail; they smash. We walk, planting one foot firmly before we take another step; they 'go ahead' on the slipperiest ground, until they fall." These shortcomings, the editor concluded, have been exacerbated by universal suffrage, which has elevated to office not the best men, but self-seekers. "The American nation has been literally a demo-cracy—a *Government,* that is to say, *by the worst.*" [20]

Such national hubris would seem to defy logic, but by 1860 this perceived flaw in America's national character had become an accepted article of faith by both those who knew the United States well and those who had only a glancing acquaintance. Not many would go as far as the provincial editor who suggested that the best way to end the war would be to provide both sides with a European prince who could bring monarchical stability to the separated countries, but it was generally accepted that, had the United States built its political and social system on time-tested British traditions, war would have been avoided. One editorial reached for the apocalyptic, suggesting that the war would purify the country and so permit "the solid strength, the true Anglo-Saxon character" that lay hidden "under the grossness, the swagger, and the 'bunkum' of its social surface" to emerge.[21] In his defense of the Constitution, Douglass warned that views of this sort would lead logically to wide-ranging and distorted condemnations of all things American. Such criticisms would lead "the people of Great Britain to accept as true some things concerning America which are utterly false, and to reject as false some other things which are entirely true."[22] While his views about some American institutions had changed since 1846, Douglass's continued criticism of American slavery and discrimination during his second visit must have reinforced the views of a British public already steeped in the conviction of its national superiority.

One measure of that superiority was the belief that racism, a unique American phenomenon, did not exist in Britain. Douglass reinforced that conviction by insisting that the new signs of racism he saw in cities such as Liverpool were imports from America, the work of the rising number of proslavery visitors and the popularity of "Ethiopian" minstrelsy. If Douglass's long and very positive association with Britain (his anglophilism, even) influenced his views about the source of racism in Britain, his belief that this development was influenced by expanding transatlantic contacts was not that far off the mark. While it is impossible to determine with any precision the extent to which specific Americans influenced British views of race, the evidence does suggest that Britons who returned home after years in the United States were very active in the public debate on the nature of American society during the war. A. F. Stoddard, a Glasgow businessman and Union supporter, had lived for many years in the United States. S. A. Goddard, a prominent businessman in Birmingham, was born and raised in New England. Peter Sinclair, a Scot, returned to Britain in 1861, possibly as a paid agent of the federal government. On the other hand, men like Joseph Barker, the former Chartist who migrated to the United States and became actively involved with the Garrisonian wing of the abolitionist movement, returned home just before the outbreak of hostilities, where he promoted the cause of Southern independence. Another proponent of the Confederacy, the Rev. Joshua P. Balme, claimed to be an abolitionist betrayed and outlawed by his colleagues in New York. Another Scot, who interestingly signed a letter to his local newspaper "C. S. A.," had lived in the South eight years and knew, he said, that slaves were not abused. Southerners, moreover, venerated religion and respected the law. The anarchy of the North was avoided in the South, where "license without liberty" holds no sway. In the South there was "respect for the different ranks of life, an admiration of the institutions of this country, a feeling of pride of their English ancestry, and a training up to their children to despise what is mean and tricky."[23]

Such views as those of "C. S. A." were not unimportant in the midst of uncertainty (and, for some, economic dislocation) caused by the war. They fed directly into a growing skepticism about the successes of West Indian emancipation and the utility of continued efforts to work for the elevation of backward peoples. In the years since the publication in 1848 of Thomas Carlyle's scurrilous attack on the West Indian freedmen, the conviction had grown that emancipation had been an unmitigated disaster and that, in the natural order of things, those of superior social rank must be in command of the reins of political power. Left to themselves, the backward would slip into further barbarism and savagery. The issue of the capacity of the Negro and of his future would come to dominate much of the public debate during the Civil War and does provide some insight into the nature of British racism. D. B. Richards of the West Country may have put the issues most starkly when he wrote his local newspaper condemning abolitionists, whom he insisted thought only of one evil: Negro slavery. But what, he asked, of subjugation of eight million whites, the devastation of land, the loss of life and the possibility of insurrection by the slaves "accompanied, as in former instances, with the wholesale plunder and destruction of property, the rape of women, the murder of the aged and helpless." A race of "very inferior mental capacity, exceedingly ignorant" would have little chance of success against "the descendants of the most intellectual and energetic race which the world has ever seen."[24]

All of these issues were aired in a series of letters to the local newspaper in Todmorden, a cotton town straddling the border between Lancashire and Yorkshire. R. Bell, a local pro-Union supporter, condemned the town's Southern Club for displaying posters that claimed that the North was fighting only to preserve the Union and had no interest in freeing the slaves. Bell further wondered how Confederate supporters could claim to be opposed to slavery when no one in Jefferson Davis's government had advocated emancipation. In response, "A Factory Operative" challenged Bell to explain why, if the South was "unChristian," had the civilized world not condemned it before. Slaveholders were burdened with "the care and control of four millions of an inferior race, who at any moment may be in open revolt, should the machinations of its enemies succeed." There was no evidence, he argued, that missionaries or colonists have had any positive civilizing effects on the African. If, as he believed, inferior races always gave way to the advance of superior races, then the only way to save the African was to remove him from his homeland and introduce him to civilized society. This is what slavery has accomplished. Americans should take warning from the consequences of West Indian emancipation when public opinion, stirred up by "blustering demagogues," compelled emancipation "at a price ruinously below" the market value of the slaves. Concluding in typical Carlylian fashion, he insisted that freed blacks reveled in "licence and riot . . . would not work, but idly squatted in woods, towns, and on the lands of their late employers."[25]

Such views, repeated as they were in many other parts of the country, had a decided effect on the way African Americans were received in Britain. While there was considerable support for efforts to aid destitute fugitive slaves then in London to settle in Africa, and while some fugitives like Jacob Green found work in Britain, the passions unleashed by the debate over the war led to rising instances of racial discrimination. With a few minor exceptions, nothing of the kind occurred in the antebellum period. William Andrew Jackson, Jefferson Davis's former coachman and a leading figure in the effort to rally public opinion in favor of the Union, lamented the fact that he could go nowhere without "meeting

with some prejudice, and . . . thought that there was quite as much prejudice in England as in America." The treatment of Thomas Arthur created a minor furor that resulted in a petition to Parliament. Arthur, an
African American married to a white woman, was refused admission to
his pew at St. Peter's Church, London. To complicate matters, the pew
door opener had allowed his wife to take her seat. Citing the case of
Arthur, "A Looker On" in Leicester lamented "the effect of caste," especially in places like London where blacks were "somewhat numerous"
and were despised and "fearfully neglected." [26]

But this was contested ground. Many, like a newspaper editor in Bacup,
insisted that notions of the inherent inferiority of Africans were totally
unfounded. "Let the negro once get his foot upon the first step in the
ladder of human progress," he wrote, "and his wooly head will eventually look over the top." The accomplishments of free blacks in the
United States attested to this fact, for even in those very trying circumstances they succeeded. Freedom from unremitting "manual drudgery"
and "the ordinary associations of nigger life in the Slave States" was the
prerequisite to the development of "polite manners." Those who insist
that the Negro is inferior "despise the white labourer as much as
the black, and think slavery the fittest condition for both." [27] Clearly,
Douglass's experiences since his escape were ample testimony to this
potential.

But the question remained: how could free blacks attain their potential
in a society steeped in racial discrimination? Whereas in the past abolitionists had argued, with some success, that discrimination was the direct
consequence of slavery, the advent of the war and the reluctance of the
Union government to commit itself to emancipation brought the issues
of slavery and discrimination into stark relief. For many they were now
two distinct and wholly separate issues. Without the ties to slavery, the
logic of abolitionist arguments had insisted, discrimination would abate,
then disappear entirely. Yet it seemed to grow more virulent in the North
in spite of the attempts by Douglass and others to demonstrate that conditions had improved. J. Sutcliffe of Burnley wondered how the Union
could talk about "freedom for the slave in a country where the negro is
shunned and despised in every sphere, and by every class of society."
The effects of discrimination, Sutcliffe argued, were no different from

those of slavery. Not only was Sutcliffe's argument driven by a desire to obscure obvious fundamental differences between slavery and discrimination, it was also a way for many in Britain–even some with impeccable abolitionist credentials–to call down the pox on both the Union and Confederacy. It also provided antislavery cover for many like Sutcliffe to argue that secession was the best guarantee of emancipation. In an effort to drive home the point, one newspaper reported on an imagined discussion between a Northern and Southern Negro in which conditions were so bad in the Union that the "poor disconsolate Northern negro" ends singing the plaintive line "I wish I was in Dixie, hi ho." The fact that the entire discussion was reported in an imagined Negro dialect betrayed the editor's true intentions.[28]

But if Douglass misjudged the source and trajectory of British racism, what of his views about the role of "Ethiopian" minstrels? Douglass was not alone in his scathing criticism of what had become, by 1860, one of the most popular forms of entertainment. Writing some years later, Sarah Parker Remond condemned those who derived their view of the Negro partly from that "class of vulgar men called 'Ethiopian Minstrels'."[29] Douglass's initial reactions to minstrelsy had been ambivalent at best. What seemed to cause him the greatest distress was minstrelsy's caricature of African Americans. His reactions to a performance by Geritt's Original Ethiopian Serenaders, an African American troupe, were typical. The mere fact that a black troupe had given a performance to a white audience, he contended, was a sign of progress and an assault on racist traditions. But he implored the Serenaders to "cease to exaggerate the exaggerations of our enemies; and represent the colored man rather as he is, than as Ethiopian Minstrels usually represent him to be." In a wide-ranging address on the antislavery movement a few years later, Douglass saw signs of progress in the fact that increasingly the country's poets, authors, and scholars were adding their voices to the swelling chorus of antislavery. So too were some minstrels whose songs "constitute our national music, and without which we have no national music." Some of their songs, such as the popular "Lucy Nell," expressed the "finest feelings of the human nature . . . [and] awaken the sympathies for the slave, in which Antislavery principles take root, grow up, and flourish."[30]

If Douglass had such positive things to say about some aspect of minstrelsy's tradition in 1848 and 1855, why his blanket condemnation of its effects in Britain in 1859? It is very likely that Douglass was stunned by its widespread popularity in Britain. There were buskers who performed at street corners, at fairs, and at the seaside; professional companies who played in theaters and concert halls; and amateur productions who performed in working men's clubs and at village fetes. The group of "Amateur Ethiopians" that was formed in Newcastle to raise money for the building fund of the local Mechanics Institute, and the local Colored Minstrels who raised money for the Coal Club and for the building of a library in the villages of Market Harborough and Husbands Bosworth attest to minstrelsy's popularity.[31] These groups, as J. S. Bratton has shown, drew on local traditions and the needs of their audiences, adapting American materials to English tastes and addressing English issues and concerns. By 1860, she concludes, minstrel troupes were "rampant" throughout the country.[32] Minstrelsy also had wide "cross-class appeal" because, divested as it was of its more risqué material, it was viewed as wholesome family entertainment. Harry Reynolds, one of the most prominent figures in British minstrelsy in the second half of the nineteenth century, remembered the time when a "minstrel show was the only approach to a variety entertainment that many respectable citizens permitted themselves to indulge in," especially those who preferred their "amusement to be free from items that leave a nasty taste in the mouth."[33]

Such popularity, as George Rehin has argued, had little to do with the effects of economic dislocation on the lives of the British working class.[34] In fact, the years prior to the outbreak of the Civil War were ones of relative economic prosperity and political stability. Nor did blacks pose a threat to the livelihood of the working class. Hence the popularity of minstrelsy with its caricatures of blacks could not be explained by a psychological need to belittle and dismiss a potential competitor. In spite of its adaptation to British tastes, however, minstrelsy's central concern was the Negro, an American obsession. Ultimately then, it was the American image of the Negro and life on the plantation that pervaded all aspects of a troupe's performance. There is no doubt that much of this image was filtered through national sensibilities, which in the years of greatest concern about the slave and freedman pitied the plight of the Negro and praised Britain for having the wisdom to free her slaves. But as antislavery sentiment waned, pity for the Negro gave way to ridicule, and caricature became reality.[35]

In the heat of the public debate over the Civil War, minstrelsy's caricatures came increasingly to be interpreted as fair representations of the Negro's character. Even among pro-Union sympathizers there was a tendency to conflate minstrel depictions and antislavery. For example, in a lecture to working men at Rothwell, Yorkshire, Rev. E. Lewis made humorous references to "the general habits and feelings of the Negro, his dread of punishment, dislike of hard work, excitability, tendency to sing, and change solemn tunes into jigs." Less surprising was an unsympathetic report of a lecture by William Andrew Jackson in southern Wales. Jackson allegedly addressed the meeting "in a pompous, inflated manner characteristic of the American negro, and created the impression upon the audience that the caricature of negro life displayed by the Ethiopian troupes traveling in this country are not exaggerations." As if to confirm Douglass's worst fears, a correspondent to the newspaper insisted that such displays as Jackson's proved that slavery had and would always have a beneficial role to play, for the "fetish loving African" could not be brought to Christianity in one or two generations. While slavery was an evil, it was a "permitted evil for a certain time," permitted by the same God who in his infinite wisdom allows other evils to exist.[36]

With its use of heavy dialect and caricature, minstrelsy managed intentionally or otherwise to portray the Negro as silly and always ready to break into song. Douglass's earlier ambivalence about minstrelsy aside, visiting African American abolitionists might have played an unwitting role in perpetuating minstrelsy's depiction of the Negro as compulsively musical. It was not unusual for lecturers to end their meeting with a short musical rendition. In fact, earlier black visitors to Britain had made it a habit to sing a selection of songs at the end of their lectures. It was a tradition carried on during the war years. Jacob Green sang "Negro sacred songs," William Watson, slave labor songs, Henry Box Brown, freedom songs; and Jackson promised to sing an "Ethiopian melody" if a meeting in Banbury adopted pro-Union resolutions. Even the famed

Shakespearean actor Ira Aldridge added the well-known song "Opossum Up a Gum Tree" to his "Classic Entertainment," a mixture of dramatic readings, lectures, and singing.[37]

By the time of Douglass's visit what had been a tradition steeped in a general concern for the welfare of the Negro was already giving way to an interpretation that emphasized the grotesque. In the passions unleashed by the public debate over the Civil War, this popular image of the Negro came to influence peoples' perceptions of slavery, emancipation, and the future of the freedmen. That a large cross section of the public attended these performances and thoroughly enjoyed the entertainment meant that these distortions of the Negro's character reached a wider audience. In this sense, Douglass's warning about the impact of minstrelsy on the country's views of the Negro was well founded, but it was a warning that went largely unheard. Douglass could do little to mend this crack in the antislavery wall.

Nor was he very successful in other areas. By the time of his return to the United States in early 1860, following the death of his youngest child, it seemed to many that much of the steam had gone out of the transatlantic movement. As the abolitionist T. Perronet Thompson observed some time later, the antislavery watchdogs had fallen asleep while the proslavery forces were active.[38] But Douglass's (and Remond's) visit helped to reinvigorate old supporters, to make contact with a generation of abolitionists born after West Indian emancipation, and, fortuitously as it turned out, to lay the groundwork for rekindling wider antislavery sentiment during the Civil War. Douglass's visit, coming as it did on the eve of the outbreak of war, helped to anticipate many of the issues raised during the war.

NOTES

1. *Glasgow Argus,* n.d., in *Liberator,* 15 May 1846.

2. John W. Blassingame, ed., *The Frederick Douglass Papers. Series One: Speeches, Debates, and Interviews,* 5 vols. (New Haven: Yale University Press, 1979–), 3:334, 281, 336.

3. *The Times,* 10, 11 June, 18 July 1850.

4. Donald Yacovone, *Samuel Joseph May and the Dilemmas of the Liberal Persuasion, 1797–*

1871 (Philadelphia: Temple University Press, 1991), 166; *Bolton Chronicle,* 30 January 1864.

5. Sarah Parker Remond to S. J. May, London, 18 October 1860, Anti Slavery Society Papers, Boston Public Library; for a biography of Powell, see Philip S. Foner, *Essays in Afro-American History* (Philadelphia: Temple University Press, 1978), 88–111; for William G. Allen, see R. J. M. Blackett, "William G. Allen: The Forgotten Professor," *Civil War History* 26 (March 1980): 39–54.

6. Howard Temperley, *British Antislavery 1833–1870* (Columbia: University of South Carolina Press, 1972), 247; C. Duncan Rice, *The Scottish Abolitionists 1833–1861* (Baton Rouge: Louisiana State University Press, 1981), 190.

7. *Newcastle Guardian,* 30 November 1861; in a tour of the country to raise money to combat the continuing slave trade to Cuba, Louis Chamerovrow, Secretary of the British Foreign and Antislavery Society, lamented the fact that death and "other causes" had removed many supporters from the scene. Douglas A. Lorimer, *Colour, Class, and the Victorians: English Attitudes to the Negro in the Mid-Nineteenth Century* (Leicester: Leicester University Press, 1978), 117.

8. Lorimer, *Colour, Class, and the Victorians,* 117, 102, 107.

9. *British Banner,* 7 June 1848.

10. Benjamin Quarles, *Frederick Douglass* (Washington D.C.: Associated Publishers, 1948), 87; *Annual Report of the Edinburgh Ladies New Anti Slavery Association, 1858* (Edinburgh, 1858), 11; *Frederick Douglass Paper,* 19 June 1857, 18 March 1859; Richard Webb to M. Chapman, Dublin, 26 September, 14 November 1848; J. Estlin to A. Weston, Bristol, 17 September 1850; E. Pease to Chapman, Darlington, 19 November 1849; J. Wigham to "My Dear Friend," Edinburgh, 9 November 1853, all in Anti Slavery Society Papers.

11. Pillsbury to S. May Jr., Dublin, 4 May 1855; Pillsbury to S. J. May, Nottingham, 14 February 1856; S. J. May to Webb, Boston, 12 January 1858, all in Anti Slavery Society Papers; *Bristol Post,* 14 February, 10 April 1862, 4 February 1863; *Bristol Mercury,* 15 February 1862.

12. M. Estlin to M. Chapman, Bristol, 20 October 1859; ? May to Webb, Leicester, 20 February 1859; Wigham to S. May Jr., Edinburgh, 10 February 1860, all in Anti Slavery Society Papers.

13. Frederick Douglass, *Life and Times of Frederick Douglass* (1893; reprint, New York: Collier, 1962), 321.

14. Blassingame, *Papers,* 3 : 335–36.

15. Blassingame, *Papers,* 3 : 308–309.

16. Blassingame, *Papers,* 3 : 308–12, 320, 335.

17. Douglass to Secretary, Edinburgh New Anti Slavery Association, Rochester, 9 July 1857, Frederick Douglass Papers, Library of Congress.

18. William S. McFeely, *Frederick Douglass* (New York: W. W. Norton, 1991), 205–206; Blassingame, *Papers,* 3:348; Thompson to E. P. Nichols, Manchester, 18 March 1860, Robert English Deposit, John Rylands Library, Manchester University.

19. *Morning Star,* 3, 27, May 1861.

20. *Halifax Guardian,* 4 May, 12 October 1861.

21. *Bristol Times,* 24 August 1861.

22. Blassingame, *Papers,* 3:344.

23. *Glasgow Herald,* 7 December 1861.

24. *Western Daily Press,* 23 January 1863.

25. *Todmorden Times,* 17, 24 October, 21 November, 5, 12 December 1863.

26. *Bury Times,* 9 May 1863; *Ashton and Stalybridge Reporter,* 23 February 1863; *Newcastle Journal,* 4 May 1863; *Leicester Mercury,* 28 February 1863. After a meeting by the fugitive William Watson was broken up by opponents in Blackburn, one local newspaper concluded that the "vulgar and wicked epithets which they used towards the lecturer proved that the hatred of the negro is not confined to either the North or south . . ." *Blackburn Times,* 10 December 1864.

27. *Bacup and Rossendale News,* 5 September 1863.

28. *Burnley Advertiser,* 2 February 1863; *Bury Guardian,* 19 September 1863.

29. *The Freed-Man,* 1 February 1866.

30. Philip S. Foner, ed., *The Life and Writings of Frederick Douglass,* 5 vols. (New York: International Publishers, 1950–1955), 5:141–42; Blassingame, *Papers,* 3:48, 2:345.

31. George Rehin, "Blackface Street Minstrels in Victorian London and Its Resorts: Popular Culture and Its Racial Connotations as Revealed in Polite Opinion," *Journal of Popular Culture* 15 (summer 1981): 20; *Newcastle Chronicle and Northern Counties Advertiser,* 18 April 1863; *Hinckley Journal,* 8 March 1862; *Midland Workman,* 7 December 1861.

32. J. S. Bratton, "English Ethiopians: British Audiences and Black-Face Acts, 1835–1865," *The Yearbook of English Studies* 11 (1981): 128, 136–37, 140. See Douglas C. Riach, "Blacks and Blackface on the Irish Stage, 1830–60," *Journal of American Studies* 7 (December 1973): 231–41 for a discussion of minstrelsy's popularity in Ireland.

33. Michael Pickering, "White Skin, Black Masks: 'Nigger' Minstrelsy in Victorian England," in *Music Hall Performance and Style,* ed. J. S. Bratton (Milton Keynes: Open University Press, 1986), 83; Harry Reynolds, *Minstrel Memories: The Story of Burnt Cork Minstrelsy in Great Britain from 1836 to 1927* (London: Alston Rivers, 1928), 47, 71.

34. George F. Rehin, "Harlequin Jim Crow: Continuity and Convergence in Blackface Clowning," *Journal of Popular Culture* 9 (winter 1975): 689; see Eric Lott, *Love and Theft: Blackface Minstrelsy and the American Working Class* (New York: Oxford University Press, 1993) for a discussion of the causes and consequences of minstrelsy's popularity among the working class in New York.

35. Pickering, "White Skin, Black Masks," 83; Bratton, "English Ethiopians," 132; Lorimer, *Colour, Class, and the Victorians,* 82.

36. *Hinckley Journal,* 11 November 1861; *Merthyr Telegraph,* 7 February 1863.

37. *Halifax Courier,* 2 April 1864; *Blackburn Times,* 10 December 1864; *Leigh Chronicle,* 11 January 1862; *Banbury Guardian,* 24 December 1862; Herbert Marshall and Mildred Stock, *Ira Aldridge, The Negro Tragedian* (New York: Rockliff, 1958), 150   51.

38. *Bradford Advertiser,* 7, 28 February, 4 March 1863.

Contributors

R. J. M. Blackett is Moores Distinguished Professor of History and African American Studies at the University of Houston. He is the author of *Building an Antislavery Wall: Black Americans in the Atlantic Abolitionist Movement, 1830–1860; Beating Against the Barriers: Biographical Essays in Nineteenth Century Afro-American History;* and editor of *Thomas Morris Chester: Black Civil War Correspondent.* He is working on a study of British popular reactions to the American Civil War.

Richard Bradbury is lecturer in American studies at the University of Exeter whose doctoral work was on F. O. Mattheisson. He is currently editing a variety of out-of-print African American texts.

Martin Crawford is reader in American history at Keele University and the author of *The Anglo-American Crisis of the Mid-Nineteenth Century* and editor of *William Howard Russell's Civil War: Private Diary and Letters, 1861–1862.* He is currently completing a study of Ashe County, North Carolina, from the 1850s to the 1870s.

Cynthia Hamilton is head of American studies at the Crewe and Alsager Faculty of Manchester Metropolitan University. She has published a book, *Western and Hard-Boiled Detective Fiction in America,* and several essays on popular American literary genres. Her article "Revisions, Memories and Exorcisms: Toni Morrison and the Slave Narrative" was joint winner of the Arthur Miller Prize for 1997. She is currently working on a book on slavery and sentimental culture.

Richard Hardack is visiting assistant professor of English at Bryn Mawr College. His articles have appeared in *Callaloo, Studies in the American Renaissance, The Arizona Quarterly,* and other journals and collections. He recently finished his first manuscript, "Recovering the Bodies: Pantheism and the Seduction of Tran scendental America," and is at work on a second project, "Coming Between Africa and America: Transcendentalism and Race, From Emerson to Morrison."

Anne Goodwyn Jones is associate professor of English at the University of Florida at Gainesville. Her first book, *Tomorrow is Another Day: The Woman Writer in the South, 1859–1936,* will shortly be joined by *Theory and the Good Old Boys:*

Manhood and the Southern Renaissance. She next plans to complete her study of women in the South, *Faulkner's Daughters.*

William S. McFeely is Abraham Baldwin professor of the humanities, emeritus, at the University of Georgia. He is the author of *Yankee Stepfather: General O. O. Howard and the Freedmen; Grant: A Biography* (awarded the Pulitzer Prize in biography and the Francis Parkman prize); *Frederick Douglass* (awarded the Lincoln Prize and the Christopher Award); and *Sapelo's People; A Long Walk to Freedom.* He is presently writing a book on the death penalty in twentieth-century Georgia.

Sarah Meer is a lecturer in English and American literature at Nottingham Trent University and formerly a research fellow at Selwyn College, Cambridge. She is currently finishing a manuscript entitled "Jim Crow and Mrs. Stowe: Blackface Minstrelsy and the Rewriting of Uncle Tom's Cabin."

Alasdair Pettinger works at the Scottish Music Information Centre. He is the editor of a recently published anthology of travel writings of the black Atlantic, *Always Elsewhere.*

Alan J. Rice is senior lecturer in American studies and cultural theory at the University of Central Lancashire. He has just completed his doctoral dissertation on Toni Morrison and the jazz aesthetic and has published widely on African American literature, including essays in *Yearbook of English Studies, Journal of American Studies,* and *Research in African Literature.* His present work centers on the trope of cannibalism in narratives of the black Atlantic.

David Turley is senior lecturer in history and director of the Centre for American Studies at the University of Kent. He is the author of *The Culture of English Antislavery, 1780–1860* and has recently edited and written a long introduction to *American Religion.* His essays cover such areas as American abolitionists, popular representations of Lincoln, and African American critiques of racism.

Index